MAKING ETHICAL CHOICES,
RESOLVING ETHICAL DILEMMAS

D1528822

MAKING ETHICAL CHOICES, RESOLVING ETHICAL DILEMMAS

Gini Graham Scott, Ph.D., J.D.

PARAGON HOUSE
St. Paul, Minnesota

Published in the United States of America by

Paragon House
2700 University Avenue West
St. Paul, Minnesota 55114

Library of Congress Catalog-in-Publication Data

Scott, Gini Graham
    Making ethical choices, resolving ethical dilemmas / Gini Graham Scott.
        p. cm.
    ISBN 1-55778-754-9 (alk. paper)
    1. Decision-making (Ethics) 2. Ethics. I. Title
BJ1419.S37   1998
170—dc21   98-14547
                                                    CIP

OTHER BOOKS BY GINI GRAHAM SCOTT

Resolving Conflict (New Harbinger 1990)

The Truth About Lying (Smart Publications 1994; distributed by Changemakers)

The Empowered Mind (Prentice Hall 1993; distributed by Changemakers)

Mind Power: Picture Your Way to Success (Prentice Hall 1987)

Mind Your Own Business: The Battle for Personal Privacy (Plenum 1995)

Can We Talk?: The Power and Influence of Talk Shows (Plenum 1996)

You the Jury: A Recovered Memory Case (with Bill Craig and Mark Roseman; Seven Locks 1997)

and over 25 other books on various topics

DEDICATION AND ACKNOWLEDGMENTS

This book is dedicated to the many people whose varying ethical approaches and dilemmas helped inspire this book.

I also want to thank the interviewees who cannot be mentioned by name whose stories about their experiences and views about ethics helped me develop the Ethical Choices Map and write this book.

Special thanks, too, to Sylvia Kendrick, for her assistance early in the project in developing the historical overview and other concepts about ethical thinking described in the beginning of the book. And thanks, as well, to Fred Olsen, for his input on ideas about different approaches to ethical thinking, too.

—Gini Graham Scott

TABLE OF CONTENTS

LIST OF SELECTED TABLES, CHARTS, AND SCALES

PREFACE

*M*aking Ethical Choices, Resolving Ethical Dilemmas reflects a new approach to understanding ethics—one's own and others'—based on what people actually do and say they do, rather than what they have been taught are the right and ethical things to do. It has been developed by speaking to people from various backgrounds and discovering the wide range of ethical approaches people use in making everyday choices and deciding how to handle the ethical conflicts they encounter in their lives.

To some, this approach to ethics may seem controversial or inappropriate, because they believe in following a certain code of conduct which they consider the right or "ethical" way to act. In fact, the noted psychologist Jean Piaget who studied child and social development talks of moral development as a process in which the individual moves from an ego-centric, self-centered world to an adult moral world that embraces a concern for others. And numerous professional organizations have devised their own codes of ethical conduct based on traditional ethical principles centered around ideals of honesty, integrity, trust, keeping promises, taking responsibility for action, consideration for others, and the like.

These traditional ideals of right conduct have a long history, going back to the dawn of human history and the beginning of human religious systems, since these codes help to keep society together. They are based on notions of respect and consideration for others that contribute to mutual trust and social bonding. They have been recognized by all the major religions, and many political philosophers have described these ideals as the basis for a peaceful, harmonious, well-governed society. They are expressed in what has become known as the golden rule: "Do unto others as you would have them do unto you," or the more modern platinum rule: "Do unto others as they would want you to do unto them."

Accordingly, in writing this book, I do not want to deny the value of traditional ethical ideals. I, in fact, believe they are part of the time-tested bedrock of society that contributes to preserving our relationships with others, and they should continue to be guides to moral action.

Yet, the question arises, as the people I spoke to brought up again and again in their stories, how do you behave perfectly morally in an imperfect world? How you hold to ideals of conduct in a real world where other people are not behaving in keeping with traditional ideals? What do you do when you confront a competitive and sometimes cut-throat world where being totally honest would be self-destructive? Do you try to leave that world or try to change it? But what if you don't have the power to do anything or have nowhere else to go? And what if you encounter different sets of values in different settings or with different people? How do you know what to do?

These are hard questions and today there are few easy answers. At one time, when societies were smaller and based on face-to-face relations or a homogenous community with a shared culture, religion, and values, traditional moral teachings were much clearer and easier to follow. There were strong leaders and social controls reinforcing these ideals. But that isn't the case today. People are caught up in a quickly changing world where traditional ethical ideals have been impacted, as well. So they have been seeking ethical standards they can apply that represent a mix of moral teachings, personal ideals, and ways of dealing with the everyday situations, issues, and problems they confront.

Thus, while I think it is important to recognize and honor traditional ideals, it is important to also understand the variety of ways people make ethical choices and resolve ethical dilemmas in everyday situations. Then, we can personally strive for higher ideals and encourage the leadership of our groups, institutions, and society as a whole to set an example. The institutions of society, the media, and others with power and influence need to help guide the way to establish higher cultural norms. Then individuals can better follow these guidelines, with a clearer idea of what to do, what is acceptable, what is right.

This book is designed to contribute to this awareness, so we can better understand ourselves and others. Then, with this understanding we can better choose what to do personally, as members and leaders of groups, and as a society.

—Gini Graham Scott

INTRODUCTION

•

Whenever we make choices about anything, we are making moral or ethical decisions without being aware of it. We choose to do something because we think it's right or wrong, good or bad, fitting or not fitting. These are ethical or moral choices which reflect our values and priorities.

Problems arise when we are not sure which approach to use or when other people in the situation have different ideas about what should be done. Each person can think he or she is "right" because of differing values or standards about how to decide.

Such choices are of special concern now, because today there is a call for people to be more ethical, to have more integrity. We are experiencing a time when we have become more than ever a culture of celebrity, when the media is fueled by crime and scandal, and acts of incivility, such as "road rage," have become common. There is a growing concern about the breakdown of traditional institutions and the decline in educational standards we have experienced over the past few decades, resulting in a desire for renewal and improvement now.

As a result of such problems, a cry for higher ethical or moral standards has gone out, and with it has come a renewed recognition of the importance of supporting the community and the values that contribute to the strength of society. Many feel that the high value we have placed on individualism, freedom, independence, and self-interest has gotten out of hand—self-interest has gone too far. A renewed interest in moral behavior has become part of a growing and communal urge to "save society," although ironically, making self-interested personal choices is making an ethical choice, too. However, as a society we now consider these choices to be "wrong," "bad," or "unfitting" ones to make, and therefore describe them as too selfish, unethical, or immoral.

Thus, there's a real need for us individually, as well as a society, to understand the ethical, moral, or value approaches we use in making choices, so we can recognize when we encounter ethical dilemmas within ourselves and with others, and can better know how to deal with them. This understanding will help us see other view points and ways to work out the problems that arise from differing and conflicting moral perspectives.

THE EXTENT OF MORAL DILEMMAS

Situations triggering ethical dilemmas can occur anywhere, from making personal decisions about jobs and relationships to matters of life and death or war and peace. Although we can face these issues as a society, the focus of MAKING ETHICAL CHOICES: RESOLVING ETHICAL DILEMMAS is on individual everyday dilemmas.

Still, the value choices of our society influence our individual choices. For example, since our society has traditionally emphasized freedom and democracy, as individuals we tend to give personal preferences more weight in the moral equation than if our society, like the Japanese, were more socially or collectively oriented. Likewise, our emphasis on technology and progress contributes to our support of more utilitarian, pragmatic, and "ends justify means" solutions. By contrast, people in another society might place more value on promoting the family or community, even if that means less industrial or technological progress, as in India.

If we are to become more ethical in our own lives and better understand how to resolve our ethical conflicts, we need to first understand what these different ethical options and approaches are, to make more knowledgeable choices.

Most people never learned in school how to make ethical choices. Becoming more aware has many benefits, because making informed choices can contribute to leading more conflict-free, satisfying lives. When we act as we usually do, unaware of the moral choices we make, we often encounter conflicting priorities within ourselves or with others.

Take this simple example of the clash of moral viewpoints. A 17-year-old daughter wants to go out on a date and her father tells her: "Be back at midnight." She agrees, and gets a ride to the party from some friends, who offer to bring her back at 12. However, when the party turns out to be a big success, her friends want to stay, and since she is dependent on her friends for the ride, she gets back at 1 am. Then a big argument ensues. Her father is upset because she broke the rule she had agreed to follow. Her mother is upset because she worries about her daughter being subjected to bad influences and possibly getting pregnant. The daughter is angry at her parents for getting upset, because she feels she did the best she could under the circumstances. There were no problems at the party, and not wanting to disrupt her friends' enjoyment and possibly damage her friendship with them, she didn't demand that they leave and take her home.

Here each person feels perfectly justified in his or her view, but does so because each is responding to the situation from a different ethical or moral viewpoint. The father's response is based on the right and wrong approach, predicated on following a set of traditional principles or rules he firmly believes are correct. The mother takes a pragmatic good and bad approach, in which she considers whether an action will have good or bad results in the future—a more utilitarian view. Finally, the daughter's view derives from the "what's fitting or unfitting?" approach, based on choosing the best thing to do given the circumstances.

What then is the best approach to deal with such a situation? The answer is "It all depends." There's really no one best way. By recognizing the different points of view, one can better understand the concerns of others and how they make ethical choices to try to work out a compromise before or after such a situation occurs.

RESOLVING ONE'S OWN ETHICAL DILEMMAS

By recognizing different views, one can also better recognize and resolve one's own ethical dilemmas when one has to make difficult choices. Knowing the options makes it easier to sort out alternatives, determine personal priorities, and make choices.

Take what happened to Dave, a part-time contractor, who helped people with remodeling and repairs. In many cases, he worked for people who wanted to fix up their homes, but didn't get building permits, because in San Francisco, where he worked, restrictions were (and still are) very tight. The laws were developed to protect the safety of the community, as well as the quality of housing, but as a result, many people feel they can't afford the cost or time to deal with all the city's red tape. Instead, they often take a short cut by building without getting the permits—a pragmatic "results-oriented" approach. They decide that the value of doing the repairs or remodeling without the permit is greater than the cost of getting a permit or the risk of getting caught.

Dave's moral dilemma was whether or not to do such building without permits. After much thought, he decided he would, but only within certain limits and only on interior jobs. He decided, if he informed the customer about any potential safety risks and if the customer agreed to take full responsibility for these risks, he would do the job with no permit. Still, there was a line beyond which he wouldn't go, because he wanted to take into consideration the concerns of others. If the project would negatively affect a neighbor or the community as a whole, he wouldn't do it.

"That's where I drew the line," he explained. "I didn't want to interfere with a neighbor's or someone else's rights. Then, too, an outside addition would be more likely to attract the attention of the city inspectors, and that could become very expensive when the person has to tear it down. I didn't feel comfortable contributing to such problems, so I said no."

Thus, by considering the options knowingly, Dave was able to make a decision with which he felt comfortable, and his clients respected him for it, although some may consider his pragmatic approach unethical.

How do other people make their choices? What are the major types of ethical and moral problems they confront on a day to day basis—at home, in relationships, at work, in public? How can you better make your own choices? The rest of the book deals with these issues.

But first it's important to understand the different moral or ethical approaches, to know which ones are being used, and how certain approaches can lead to conflict. In Part I, Chapters 1 to 3 provide a broad overview of why we need new ethical approaches today, the causes of today's social and ethical breakdown, and an overview of the major ethical approaches people use. The rest of the book deals with how to make ethical choices and resolve ethical dilemmas yourself.

PART I:

UNDERSTANDING ETHICAL APPROACHES

CHAPTER 1

•

WHY WE NEED NEW ETHICAL
APPROACHES TODAY

WHY BOTHER WITH ETHICS?

Why should we even care about ethics today? In the past, ethics have been left to the philosophers, academics, and religious teachers who have given us our code of morality. Over time, in professions such as medicine and law, codes of ethics have been worked out to provide guidelines on what to do in different situations. But otherwise, most of us have gone about our lives without thinking much about ethical issues. We have a general sense of what's right and wrong, good and bad, fitting or not fitting, which is based on what we have learned from our parents, teachers, peers, and the culture in which we have grown up. We also learn about what to do or not do from the role models we see in the media, in films, at work, and in other settings, as we act and interact with others from day to day.

So why worry about making ethical choices? We make them automatically and often unconsciously as we live our lives. Why is it important to think about them now?

The reason is because we have reached a point of ethical breakdown and chaos in our society today. This situation not only threatens the very foundations of society but has left us confused and uncertain about what to do. Society is changing. Institutions are being broken down and transformed. Many cultures and influences are thrown together in this upheaval. And as much as we may be called on to respect this new diversity of cultures around us, this diversity brings with it clashes of values, norms, standards, and ways of looking at the world that helps undermine our certainty about how we should think and act.

Normally, the average person doesn't need to think about ethics, because ideas about how to act are ingrained in us as our conscience or as our knowledge of customary codes of behavior in our community or in our social relationships. Additionally, many of these ideals of behavior are formalized in laws which support our ethical principles, such as laws against stealing, fraud, and misrepresentation.

But when there is a social breakdown, as today, our ideas and ideals of the past are called into question as we encounter conflicts over how to act. Because we have lost our moorings, we grope for moral guidance. That's why we need to think about ethical questions and find new ways to understand and resolve the ethical conflicts we encounter in our families and our relationships with others.

The views of one of the foremost philosophers of our times, Jurgen Habermas, a German theorist noted for his contributions to "critical theory" in the social sciences and humanities, are especially apt. As he has observed, we take our moral character and the morality of our everyday actions for granted until we experience a social breakdown or find our usual way of judging what's right and wrong shattered by events. Otherwise, we make our judgments and choices from a moral framework implanted in us, and we don't question that framework. As a result, no one really cares how we make these choices until there is a breakdown or until we experience conflicts. Then this breakdown creates a need for us to go through a process of conflict resolution to readjust our moral framework for making choices. Since this has happened in our society, we now need to reflect on our most fundamental concerns and values to create a new moral theory to guide personal actions.

In short, according to Habermas and other contemporary ethical thinkers, our loss of moral bearings is due to our recent social breakdown, and we are now fumbling about for some guidance in what to do in our conflicted ethical situations, although generally we feel little need to think about ethical issues at all.

DISCOVERING THE NEED FOR ETHICS IN RESOLVING A PERSONAL ETHICAL DILEMMA

This view of Habermas—that we don't think about ethics until there is a social breakdown—was true for me. I had never thought about ethical issues myself until I encountered my own ethical crisis and didn't know what to do. I had never even thought of any conflicts I experienced in ethical or moral terms, because I took for granted my usual pragmatic, costs-benefits, problem-solving approach in dealing with difficulties, and I wasn't aware this approach was an ethical choice itself. But then I experienced a dilemma that led me to recognize an ethical dimension in making choices and resolving conflicts.

This dilemma occurred when I was working with a psychologist who wanted to write a book. I helped the psychologist (let's call her Beth) prepare an initial draft of a proposal and referred her to my agent. But then things began to go awry in my relationship with Beth. She became very demanding and pushy, questioned my usual fees, tried to get me to work for less, showed little concern for accurate historical facts related to her topic, and wanted to sensationalize her subject, since, she believed, this approach would sell more books, yet still appeal to a professional audience of peers. Though I argued for a more serious and accurate approach to give her credibility, she eventually rejected my suggestions and decided to use most of her original material to express her own voice. The project finally led to a messy bill dispute that resulted in my taking her to court and eventually winning a judgment when she didn't show up. Meanwhile, during the course of the project, at a meeting in which I went to interview Beth for the book, I heard her tell her lawyer during a phone call that she had lost her psychologist's license and was now embroiled in a court suit to get it back.

The conflict might have been an ordinary billing dispute in small claims court. But what added the ethical dimension was the question of what I should do about the agent I had found for Beth, since I had my own relationship with the agent, who expected me to be the ghostwriter. Too, if Beth had lost her license, this would affect the marketability of a book based on her expertise as a psychologist. The quandary for me was whether I should tell the agent about this situation or describe my own negative experiences with the woman. Should I ask my agent not to represent Beth, since I was no longer involved as a writer and was having a financial dispute with her? Or would saying anything be interfering in a relationship between Beth and the agent that had acquired a life of its own, despite my initial connection?

Ultimately, I did not tell the agent anything to let her make her own decision, though later I felt relieved and vindicated when she turned down the book, advising Beth that she needed a professional writer to help her and referring her back to me. Though this was the end of the writing project, it got me thinking about the implications of various ethical considerations, particularly those related to confidentiality and disclosure. Although I had learned discrediting information that was available publicly, did the chance way I learned this knowledge make it inside information I shouldn't reveal? Or was my loyalty to my agent paramount, since Beth's loss of a license to practice psychology could undermine the value of her book?

In time, the situation got me thinking about the many ethical dilemmas we all confront from time to time in our everyday lives— at work and in our relationships with friends, family, and others. How do we decide? How do we *know* how to decide? And can we better decide by becoming more aware of how we make ethical decisions in keeping with our own personal integrity?

I didn't understand at the time why this incident should have had such an effect on me. But later, after hearing about Habermas' view that ethical concerns spring from social and ethical breakdowns, I realized this connection in a very personal way, since the breakdown in my usual professional relationships had triggered my ethical concerns.

THE SIGNS OF BREAKDOWN AND CRISIS TODAY

Today, the signs of breakdown are everywhere, resulting in a loss of moral authority in everyday life. A key consequence is that people have turned to personal interpretations of what is right and wrong, causing a constantly changing code of appropriate standards and behavior as different fads and role models arise and supercede each other in the public eye. No wonder we are confused. In the 80s, greed was good—now it's bad. For a few years, macho, Rambo-style males were valued; now males are encouraged to be more sensitive. For a time, sexual freedom and independent, assertive women were valued; now there is a more conservative trend, and women are seeking more protections from some situations arising from their greater independence, such as problems of sexual harassment and abuse. These situations raise ethical questions, because they bring with them changing values and norms about what's important to society and how people should relate to one another.

Such changes, particularly when made in such rapid succession, help to undermine the moral foundations of how we judge what's good and bad, right and wrong, fitting and unfitting. They take away our sense of having a basically correct perspective or a moral anchor, because the scene around us keeps changing, undermining our sense of stability. It's like being in a modern multimedia show, where sounds and images keep whirling around us. Up to a point, the show can be exciting, stimulating, and challenging in its newness and mixing of images. Beyond that, the information overload can become overwhelming, and we become dizzy, losing our sense of being grounded and centered.

Disorienting, too, are the many social problems which have confronted and overwhelmed our institutions, leading us to lose trust in these institutions and their value in guiding our choices. Such crises of our times are legion. We find that the problem of illegal drugs has undermined the ability of families to raise children, leaving an overburdened police and legal system to cope with only a limited effectiveness. We discover pervasive lying and corruption in government and business, and we debate whether some public figures should be forgiven or cast out as scoundrels, while many of these become celebrity heroes. We complain that our schools have failed in teaching, and we worry about our children's lack of discipline and their own resistance to adult moral authority. We also see our society polarized by serious ethical conflicts, such as the right to life or the right to die.

Such problems are made even more difficult by our desire to protect the individual, since we value personal rights, independence, and freedom so highly. By elevating the value of one's self to a pinnacle, we tend to undermine the moral values which protect the community as a whole.

For example, one of the traditional moral teachings is not to lie, and a key social reason for having this value is that trust, based on kept promises and honesty in relationships, is a prime adhesive in keeping the social order together. By contrast, a lie, when discovered, undermines that trust. When self-interest is viewed as a preeminent value, an individual may readily believe he can lie for a personal benefit—such as protecting himself from being discovered doing something wrong. But the lie to protect the self can harm others, as can its discovery, much like the failure of one small part can bring down a big plane. In turn, as the social institutions that promote community-oriented moral principles decline, individuals will be more apt to look to their own self-interest in deciding what to do, which can contribute to even further decline in the social order.

The case of Susan Smith of Union, South Carolina, who killed her children and lied about it for nine days on national TV before confessing, is a prominent example of the extremes to which people can go when motivated by self-centered thinking.

Unfortunately, some of our modern ideals, which were developed to overcome the old views we now consider narrow-minded, have contributed to this decline in traditional ethical ideals. For example, we now place a high value on diversity, equality, and the relativity of ideas, based on the belief there are no absolutes and that all principles have the same relative worth. Additionally, we want to believe that all cultures and viewpoints are of equal value, based on our ideal of toleration and nondiscrimination. However, the problem with cultural relativity is that it leaves us in a state of confusion and chaos as to how and what to choose. If all is relative, what is the basis for choosing one thing over another? We can see this problem of relativity reflected in all our major systems of thought today, from math to music, art, and literature, and in the theory of chaos and the breakdown of systems in physics. We no longer have any solid core holding things together, so things swirl around for us, both conceptually and in our everyday life. As the poet Yeats once wrote in the 1921 poem "The Second Coming": "All things fall apart. The center cannot hold."

One of the responses to this breakdown has been the recent rise of fundamentalism in various forms, such as born-again Christianity, fundamentalist Islam, and nationalistic revival groups. Though their particular belief systems differ, all provide a reemphasis on having strict codes of values and behaviors, creating a new core or center for their adherents. Unfortunately, though, this revival has led to intense clashes between fundamental and non-fundamental groups holding different viewpoints, contributing to further social upheavals and threatening the democratic tradition of mutual respect and tolerance.

Some other values we hold dear as a society often contribute to undermining moral authority, too. For example, since the spread of industrialism in the late 1800s and the era of the Robber Barons and Industrial Capitalists, success has come to be one of our highest values. But over time, the definition of success has changed to emphasize material gains and the appearance of success over the ability of the successful person to contribute meaningfully to society as a whole.

Essentially, our society has experienced a shift from a character ethic to a personality ethic, according to Stephen Covey, who reviewed the literature of the "human potential" and "how to become a success" movements for the past 50 years, and wrote about this in *The Seven Habits of Highly Effective People*. The literature from the 1920s through the late 1950s, he observes, told people what to do to become a "good" person of high character, one who followed the principles of honor and truth. This is reflected in the writings of the early leaders of the "how to become a success" movement, such as Andrew Carnegie and Napoleon Hill. However, by the 1970s, the emphasis shifted to a concern with how to *be* successful, defined by cultivating the right "image" of success. Personality rather than character became the key, as reflected in the writings of success teachers like Dale Carnegie and John Malloy (who coined the phrase: "dress for success.")

The magnitude of this shift is illustrated in the old belief that affronts to one's character or principles were worth fighting about and dying for. For instance, in his battle with Henry VIII over swearing allegiance to the new Protestant faith, Sir Thomas More was willing to be executed for his Roman Catholicism rather than abandon his faith. And until about 100 years ago, a man who was insulted or dishonored by another might honorably challenge him to a duel, which often resulted in death. At the time, people considered these actions noble choices, though today we would find them impractical, foolish indulgences in the name of honor. That's because in our modern times, people are more apt to seek a pragmatic compromise, where personal gain, advantage, and survival are the measure of what is valued.

In short, we are wallowing in something of an amoral morass today, where people are facing a changing, chaotic, and violent world, in which traditional institutions and codes of morality and ethics have broken down. As a result, we feel uncertain, confused, and unsure of ourselves, and we are increasingly faced with ethical dilemmas we can't solve. When we make a decision, we may not be sure we have done the right thing. Or we may question our own judgment when we consider other ways we might have acted or if we learn that others have dealt with the same problem differently. The basic problem is that in this time of change, old standards and values have been undermined, and we're without guides to help us when we encounter ethical conflicts.

For example, ethical dilemmas can easily occur under the following circumstances:

• When we value individualism, independence, and individual rights too highly, people's actions in their own interest can collide with other people's rights.

• When people with different values clash on how to resolve a situation, that can lead to different views of the appropriate ethical result. And even if people reach a compromise, they can still feel upset by the result, because they feel their values have been trampled by someone else.

• When our laws are out of synch with our ethical principles and ideals, such as notions of decency and fair play, this disparity can trigger everyday dilemmas. Though people may know they are legally free to act a certain way, they may feel guilty, because they don't feel what they have done is right.

• When profit-making considerations and concerns about appearing successful conflict with principles of doing the right, fair, or honest thing, this can lead to hard choices. Instead of doing what is "ethical," one may choose to do what's more profitable, and then one may deny doing this to continue to see oneself or appear to others as an honest, honorable person.

And there are many other common ethical quandaries caused by today's changing and conflicting values.

CHAPTER 2

•

THE ROOTS OF TODAY'S ETHICAL BREAKDOWN

HOW DID WE GET TO WHERE WE ARE TODAY?

How did we get into the state of ethical confusion we are in today? How have we come to downplay ideals of honor, integrity, and character and permit self-interest and the profit motive to run rampant? Are we no longer sure what's right or wrong anymore? Might we fear making the "ethical" or "moral" choice, because others will take advantage of us?

At one time, societies had a much stronger sense about how people should act and had the authority to enforce what was right through community pressure and penalties if a person didn't follow these codes. But today, due to various social breakdowns and violence, we have lost community support for behaving ethically and our sense of direction.

How did this happen? A little history will help us understand how we got to this sad state, and it may help us regain what we have lost.

IN THE BEGINNING...

From the beginnings of human society, social groups have adopted ethical or moral principles about how people should or should not behave in order to preserve and protect the community and to curb individual passions and desires that might hurt the group or others. These principles were expressed as ideals, such as the view that group or tribe members should help gather and share food, should honor the gods believed to bring food and other benefits, and should respect the elders and teachers who passed on the group's collective wisdom and traditions.

In the early days, it was relatively easy to follow such rules, since the groups were small and had one culture, one set of values. People usually conformed to the group's code of behavior, and if they didn't, other members would soon put them back in line through early forms of group punishment—ranging from disapproval and shunning to exclusion and banishment from the group.

As social groups got larger, and organized communities and civilizations emerged, leaders—both rulers and priests—came forward to help teach and enforce these moral codes. At the same time, ideas about proper behavior became formalized into everyday customs, norms, moral codes, and laws about what to do. The Code of Hammurabi, which dates from the 18th Century BC in Mesopotamia, was one of the oldest and most widely known code of laws.

For centuries, people continued to have a fairly clear idea about what to do and recognized the limits of proper behavior. And if they deviated from what their society thought was fitting and right, there were priests, judges, and kings to remind them what to do or punish them for what they had done wrong.

THE FIRST MORAL PHILOSOPHERS

But now let's fast forward to the beginnings of Western Civilization with the rise of the classical civilizations of Greece and Rome and the Judeo-Christian tradition in the Middle East. Here we find some of the earliest questions about the moral order of society and how one could live a moral life.

The first social critics were the ancient Hebrew prophets. Starting around 1000 BC, the Jewish religious leaders began to ask questions about how God acts in the world and what he requires of people. This was a very different approach from that of other peoples at this time who believed in multiple gods, many of them nature gods. Commonly, they viewed these gods as amoral and largely indifferent towards humans, engaging in acts that were often unpredictable, vindictive, and capricious.[1] In response, they sought to placate these gods through offerings and rituals to make life better, and they commonly attributed human qualities, like petty jealousies and romantic passions, to these gods.

By contrast, for the first time, the Jewish people conceived of a single all-powerful God, motivated by a sense of justice. According to Jewish thinking, God had entered into a covenant or agreement with the Hebrew people, expecting them to act in certain ways considered "good" to receive His favor and to avoid "evil" or risk His wrath and punishment.[2] Further, the Jews believed in a meaningful life in which the individual would live well with his fellow humans if he behaved morally.[3]

Such ideals for the moral life were contained in the Jewish Law and encapsulated in the Ten Commandments, which provided the basic ethical injunctions for living a moral life. These ideals, subsequently taken over by Christianity and Islam, provided the moral foundations of most of the world today. As religious scholar Huston Smith describes them, the Ten Commandments provide the "minimum standard by which man's collective life becomes an enduring possibility." They are, in effect, a guide for creating an enduring social order, without which there would be "formlessness" and "chaos."[4] Among them are the familiar admonitions against murder, adultery, stealing, and bearing false witness or lying, described in detail in the book of Deuteronomy in the Old Testament. These fundamental principles are the touchstones for traditional morality, though more and more subject to exceptions and qualifications today.

Starting around 500 BC the Greek and Roman philosophers

---

[1]Huston Smith, *The Religions of Man*, New York: Harper and Row, 1965, p. 258.

[2]Geoffrey Parrinder, *World Religions: From Ancient History to the Present*, New York: Facts on File, 1983, pp. 385-388.

[3]Smith, p. 258.

[4]Smith, pp. 270-271.

also began to raise moral questions. One of the first and most prominent was Socrates, who lived from about 470-399 BC and got the
citizens of Greece thinking with his probing questions about what is
right and how to do the right thing. Another was Plato, a pupil of
Socrates, who lived from about 427-347 BC. He spoke of an ideal
state of perfection and correct human behavior to which we all should
aspire, although we might be mired in an imperfect real world. But,
by knowing this ideal, we could at least strive for perfection by becoming become better, more right-acting people. As he wrote in
The Republic, a well-educated citizenry, guided by their "philosopher kings," could lead the way towards this right action. Later,
such ideas about human imperfection were embraced in the Christian tradition and led to notions about human sin, redemption, and
salvation.

Another influential Greek philosopher was Aristotle, who lived
from 384-322 BC. Besides developing ideas about the relationship
of the mind and body, which prefigured the relatively modern concept of the mind-body split, he suggested that we were all doomed
to be imperfect, since matter is imperfect. As a result, as matter, we
could never fully perceive the ideal which exists only as an abstract
idea within the material world.

Soon, numerous other schools of philosophy emerged with competing ideas about how people should act. Among these were the
Stoics, founded by Zeno, who thrived from about 300 BC to 300
AD. They argued that humans should be free from passion and calmly
accept whatever happens as the unavoidable result of divine will or
reason. Alternatively, the Hedonists, who flourished from about
342-270 BC, believed that pleasure was the highest good and only
those thoughts which were pleasant for the mind to contemplate
were intrinsically good.

Why did the Jewish prophets and Greek and Roman philosophers begin to raise such questions? Because, for the first time, societies were becoming less unified and increasingly varied, so now
internal conflicts developed between groups and people with different ideas about how to act. Such tears in the social fabric, in turn,
inspired the first concerns with creating ethical systems to guide

action. Before then, there was little need for critiques about what was right, good, or proper, because society and its priests and teachers had essentially one unified idea about what to do that had evolved over time—the codes of appropriate, acceptable behavior.

But now, in a more complex society, numerous squabbling groups were emerging, especially in Greece, where a new social and political form of organization had developed called a "democracy," based on citizen participation. In this setting, which encouraged new forms of thinking, the first social critics emerged as philosophers. Besides critiquing the present social structure and proposing new ways to educate and structure society, they developed ideas about the correct way to behave.

Subsequently, many of these competing and confusing schools of thought became incorporated into the early Christian Church, which soon created its own system about how people should behave. Many of the inconsistencies and uncertainties of this early smorgasbord of ethical thought have been passed on to us via Western tradition and have become part of our current confusion.

THE RISE OF THE CHRISTIAN TRADITION AND THE JUDGING OF RIGHT AND WRONG

The early Christian Church emerged out of Judaism, as Jesus, a Jew himself, began his ministry in the Jewish community and drew on some of these philosophical ideas from Greek and Roman sources in the Roman Empire. As his teachings spread, they included still other moral precepts that became part of today's fundamental moral beliefs.

Many of these ideas about morality are contained in the many parables of Jesus described in the Bible, as well as in the Sermon on the Mount. They point out how a moral person should behave. Such principles include thirsting after "righteousness," being "pure in heart," being "peacemakers," and following the traditional commandments for living an ethical life. In these teachings, which have become the foundation of Christianity, some ideals of morality include having proper thoughts, not just engaging in proper actions, since not only evil acts, but evil thoughts, can be the basis for acting immorally. For instance, a person who lusts after a woman has "committed adultery with her already in his heart," and "whosoever is angry with his brother without cause shall be in danger of the judgment," just as is a person who kills someone else.[5]

As Christianity spread from being a small sect within Judaism to being a growing faith embraced in the entire Roman Empire and beyond, the Christians adopted these moral principles as fundamental to the faith. Such principles, in Christianity, as in Judaism, formed the basis for an expanding number of laws and guidelines for action that inform our traditional code of morality, still with us today.

In their early years in the Roman Empire, Christians were just one of many religious sects competing for the hearts and minds of the people. Each of these groups had its own ideas about what people should believe and do. However, Christianity became the most successful, expanding from its humble roots within the Jewish Community in Judea to become the officially adopted religion of the Roman Empire. Then, it grew further to become the dominant all-powerful Catholic Church of the Middle Ages, which created and promulgated a code of ethical behavior for all to follow. This code, developed by influential Church scholars, such as St. Augustine and St. Thomas Aquinas, drew on the philosophy of the earlier Greeks and Romans, combined with ideas from the Old and New Testament.

The result was a blend of Greek, Roman, Jewish, and early Christian teachings, now supported by a feudalistic social and political structure that took over much of the Western world. Feudalism, which reigned supreme in the Middle Ages, supported Church teachings, which gave the political system a new moral authority. These teachings included ideas about how people should treat each other, the proper relationship of women to men (inferior, imperfect, and submissive compared to the superior, more perfect, domi-

---

[5]Matthew 5, 5-28.

nant man), what is sin, and other principles of behavior. Absolute values were promulgated, relative values shunned. This system was supported by a hierarchy of religious leaders from the local priest to the bishop, cardinal, and pope, which paralleled the rigid social hierarchy of the times, ranging from the slave or serf to the higher nobles and king.

This strict religious system supported a moral and ethical code that was equally repressive. People had their place in society and within that place they could behave in certain permissible ways. If they didn't, religious doctrines threatened them with eternal punishment and damnation unless they confessed, mended their ways, and were forgiven. Societal laws threatened immediate corporal punishment, including such dire penalties as the rack and screw, burning, or the dungeon or tower. Even religious leaders followed these strictures to control their own supposedly sinful urges and behaviors, punishing themselves with flagellation or other painful penances if they failed.

Thus, the medieval period was a harsh, structured time that differed from much earlier times when social groups were small and simple, and moral ideals and guidelines flowed naturally out of everyday life. By contrast, society was now much more complex and its leaders much more distanced from everyone else through hierarchies that separated people into classes. People were kept in line by controls and by threats of punishment, here or in the hereafter. Because society had become so much more complex, and now included many social groups, there was a great potential for new ideas to burst forth once the controls weakened.

THE BREAKDOWN OF THE SOCIAL ORDER AND THE SPREAD OF NEW ETHICAL IDEAS

This burst of new ideas occurred in the Renaissance. There was a reaction to the rigid controls of the Catholic Church and to its internal corruption spawned by its dominance and power. Many people began to see that the Church was preaching one doctrine of how to be good and do the right thing to gain salvation, while the priests, nobility, and well-to-do seemed to be living lives that contradicted and even flaunted these teachings by engaging in wanton, promiscuous behavior condemned by the Church.

Gradually, the protests began within the Church by priests like Martin Luther, who wrote up his Ninety-Five theses, which listed ways to reform the Church. He tacked them on the door of a local church in Wittenberg, Germany in 1517, and soon the protest movement, that became the Protestant Reformation, spread, resulting in the emergence of dozens of new sects.

Meanwhile, paralleling this spread of new ideas and new religious groups, the rigid social order began to break down. Feudal disintegration helped to make the spread of new ideas possible. It also helped the social classes become more fluid and mobile.

Groups were now free to create their own ideas of what a moral life should be, and many did, pursuing all sorts of possibilities. Some reacted by creating their own highly structured systems of ethics and beliefs, as if to replace the breakdown of established moral authority with another moral institution to give people guidelines on what to do. For example, this period marked the birth of the Calvinists, Puritans, Lutherans, Presbyterians, Baptists, Mennonites, Amish, Huguenots, and many other new Protestant groups. They all had their own ideas about grace, salvation, redemption, and moral living.

Then, when many of these sects began coming to America in the 1600s, fleeing intolerance in Europe, they incorporated their views of morality and ethical behavior into the mix of principles on which the United States was founded. Ironically, many of their ideas about morality were as rigid as those of the Catholic or Protestant churches from which they were fleeing. But their views provided a system of values and norms which helped regulate behavior in the new communities they founded in the wilderness. In fact, many of these groups were quite intolerant, and colonists who didn't agree were often forced out of the community (such as Roger Williams, the liberal leader who founded the Rhode Island Colony, after being banished from the Puritan community in Massachusetts). Others who were branded as sinners were shamed and ridiculed (some put in stocks, others forced to wear letters proclaiming their sin, such as the red "A" for adultery, described in Nathaniel Hawthorne's *Scarlet Letter*).

When the United States was formed, the principle of the separation of church and state was adopted so that the various religious groups that came to settle here could be free to worship as they wished. Much of the religious thought of that time remains with us to today, although in modern times many people have left those ideas behind, letting ideals of self-interest and profit be their guide. Even so, these older ideas of morality still serve as a kind of foil against which we play out more modern ideas of how to behave.

THE RISE OF THE AGE OF REASON AND THE INFLUENCE OF SCIENCE

The rise of scientific thinking in the European Renaissance planted the seeds for the Age of Reason, which helped to further undermine the moral authority of the traditional authoritarian view of what was right. That's because now, besides new religious groups coming up with their own systems of morality and ethics, many philosophers sought to determine what was ethical by applying science to ethical dilemmas. For example, philosophers like Mills, Hobbes, Hume, Berkeley, and Descartes advanced their own ethical systems, and later the influential German school of philosophers, including Hegel, Kant, and Nietzsche, proposed their own theories.

The problem with all this theorizing is that the scientific models for determining what was ethical didn't always fit with what people actually did. They didn't fit, because ethics are fundamentally systems of values, which often derive from religious beliefs about how the world works or should work. Furthermore, values and beliefs, while influenced by social, political, economic conditions, and technology, are rooted in personal and social judgments and in faith, which are highly subjective.

Yet, whatever their source or fit with actual behavior, many ideas which emerged at this time became quite influential and still influence us today. Some were the teachings of the utilitarian schools of philosophy, which emphasized making decisions based on weighing the benefits of a choice versus its cost. Other ideas reflected a pragmatic approach, based on the idea that it's fine to do whatever you can do, if you have the power and desire to do so—a Machiavellian approach to morality.

Such utilitarian and pragmatic approaches are very much with us today, such as in the New Age notion that we create our own reality, and in the personal relativism that strongly influences modern ethical choices. Unfortunately, this ethical orientation is part of the problem of the times, because the rise of making ethical choices based on utilitarian or pragmatic thinking has resulted in a loss of influence of community controls on individual behavior. And this loosening of controls contributes to today's social breakdown. After all, if everyone can become one's own ethical arbiter, we end up with as many ethical choices as there are individuals, and we lose the moral center that holds communities together.

THE RETREAT OF ETHICAL THOUGHT TO AN IVORY TOWER

In the late 19th century and early 20th century, still another trend developed that helped to remove moral authority from everyday life. This was the retreat of ethical thinking to the ivory tower of academe, far removed from practical applications to everyday life. This happened as the philosophers who thought about ethical systems became academics and began arguing about more arcane matters, such as how do we know what is moral, rather than what is ethical behavior and what is not.

As a result, there was less connection between the teaching of ethics by philosophy professors and ethics taught by families and religious groups in the everyday world. The language and thoughts of ethics, as studied in the universities, no longer matched our traditional understanding of ethics. Meanwhile, as academics became more divorced from the community in their approach to ethics, the separation between church and state was reinforced by Supreme Court decisions, which further contributed to the ethical vacuum in community life. People were often left to their own devices to create their own moral codes of what to do.

THE CONTINUING DECLINE OF ETHICS
SINCE THE 1950S

In the 1950s, the moral authority for principles of ethical behavior was further weakened by a new age of anxiety and disillusionment that was born in the wake of the discovery of the nuclear bomb. For the first time, people began thinking that the world as they knew it might be totally destroyed in the blink of an eye from intended or unintended bombs. This was also a time of declining interest in religion, brought about by the growing pessimism in the country. The phrase "God is dead" became popular, too.

The media and popular culture still persisted in the idea that all was well and that the old family and moral verities were still with us, reflected in popular fare like "Father Knows Best" and "I Love Lucy." Also, stern-faced parental images in educational films reminded sexually aware teens to adhere to the traditional moral "truths."

By contrast, the popularity of rock and roll spread, challenging traditional middle class ideals. And under the surface, there bubbled a cauldron of fears and resentment, encouraged in part by the growing anxiety about nuclear destruction. At the same time, a growing antagonism to what was perceived as a repressive, corrupt, and overly materialistic establishment led to the rise of the counterculture in the mid-60s. This counterculture took two forms. One was an inward-turning group, known as "hippies," that withdrew from mainstream America and celebrated liberation through drugs, music, and free sex. The other was a politically active group mobilized by its resistance to the Vietnam War and other social wrongs, like segregation. All of this turmoil led to a seething tumultuous decade, that was marked by increased civil violence and upheavals, and resulted in a wave of political assassinations that shocked America, like those John F. Kennedy, Robert Kennedy, and Martin Luther King.

All of this social and political turmoil was accompanied by a new cultural and moral awakening that involved challenging tradition to craft a new morality based on an ethos of freedom and individualism. Such ideals were summed up in popular slogans of the day, such as "Do your own thing" and "Turn on, tune in, and drop out." One of the early harbingers of this transformation was the popularity of Elvis Presley in the late 1950s. He was idolized by many teens because he dared to challenge the prevailing moral code of parents, who were increasingly seen as overly rigid, straightlaced and old-fashioned. At the same time, the growing concerns about the dangers of the nuclear bomb in the 1950s contributed to this increased focus on living in the present, because of the fear that after a big blast, not much of a future might be left.

This focus on the present was one more nail in the coffin of traditional ethical teachings, because if one was living in the now, there was no reason to listen to the teachings of the old ethics that encouraged self-sacrifice, thinking of others, and delayed gratification. This "now" thinking emphasized self-interest and immediate pleasures—one more link in the chain of new thought which lessened old ethical values. The old values were often viewed as irrelevant to changing new times, encapsulated by Bob Dylan's 1960s song: "The Times They Are A-Changin'." It was as if we were entering the Orwellian world of 1984. We were encouraged to shuck off the outdated ideas of the past, which included the traditional ethical views about how people should behave, in order to create new more modern forms of behavior.

But were these new forms really better? Or did we just experience ever-growing confusion as these old ideas were rejected and erased? It would seem the latter occurred, which led to the moral and ethical crisis and social breakdown of the 1960s, and continues today.

THE PARADOX OF THE 1960S AND 1970S

The irony of the 1960s is that the social revolution and counterculture that produced the inward-turning hippies and outward-turning political activists was propelled by the ideal of creating a more ethical, moral society. There was a revulsion towards the hypocrisy of the 1950s, as the 1960s generation of mostly babyboomers lashed out at the establishment's sacred cows—the military, industry, big business, and the new plastic environment of our growing high-tech culture. This repugnance was expressed forcefully in the cocktail party scene in "The Graduate," where a business associate of Dustin Hoffman's father advises him to go into "plastics"—for therein lies the "future." Hoffman's scowl of revulsion reflects his generation's rejection of the rapidly emerging synthetic and materialistic world with its big business values.

In retrospect, however, this 1960s revolution contributed to the growing deconstruction of American culture and values. For instead of the dreamy new world of innocence—and a hoped for Eden—imagined by the hippies, flower children, and protesters, we had the beginnings of the drug explosion. Academic gurus like Timothy Leary preached that mind-expanding drugs were good, and while some people experienced bursts of chemically-induced enlightenment, many others were psychologically scarred by drug abuse. At one time, much of this drug exploration was considered trendy and linked to spiritual exploration or viewed as the thing to do at urban business and professional parties, where sniffing lines of cocaine was treated as casually as smoking marijuana in the 1960s. But in the 1980s and 1990s, the drug explosion migrated to the lower classes and the inner city, setting the stage for the major drug problems of today.

Meanwhile, ideas of free sexual expression and casual intimacies not only contributed, as many believe, to the epidemic of AIDS and other sexually-transmitted diseases of today, but they helped to break down the traditional moral foundations of society based on committed sexual relationships and the family. Suddenly, the traditional family and ideals of monogamy in committed relationships became quaintly old-fashioned, as did the values of respecting authority and tradition.

Schools came under attack, starting in the 1960s, for passing on inherited values and established curriculums. People wanted to live in the now; they wanted relevance for what was happening today. As a result, traditional authorities and teachers were perceived as dinosaurs from the past, teaching outdated notions of what was important. The emphasis was on immediacy, on the present, while a growing number of students and other protesters staged teach-ins and marches to protest the war in Viet Nam, demonstrated for free speech, and otherwise struck out against traditional ideas and values. The ideal was personal, individual expression. The period became an age of "do your own thing," which opened the way for the "me-generation" of the 1970s, that gave way to the "personal greed generation" of the 1980s.

Unfortunately, these demands for self-expression and individual rights, in the name of personal development, satisfaction, and enjoyment, helped further the collapse of ethical ideals. The individual was now the arbiter of what was right, and what one felt like doing became the new guide to action. Everything became relative, with the source of wisdom in the individual. But what if individual desires came into conflict? In this age of "me first" ethics, it was easy for the individual with more power to prevail. It was also easy for those in conflict to "take off" or "split" rather than face problems. Notions of personal commitment and family obligations went by the wayside. As a result, this self-oriented approach to relationships contributed to individual isolation and alienation, and to the power-based and manipulative ideas of relating that emerged in the 1980s.

Meanwhile, into this vacuum came all sorts of New Age religions and spiritual philosophies that furthered this turn into the self. These flowered in the 1970s, which became for many a kind of playground for personal and spiritual growth. All sorts of groups and gurus emerged pushing individual exploration—groups like est, Lifespring, Actualizations, and others. The ideal was to look within and get in touch with one's higher self to become a more actualized and developed being. However, while some people did become kinder, gentler, and more thoughtful as a result of these teachings, many others became incredibly selfish and demanding, due to their focus on satisfying the self. They ignored notions of ethics based on community values, as they turned inward and glorified the self.

THE COLLAPSE OF ETHICS IN THE 1980S

In the 1980s, this focus on seeking self-fulfillment shifted into a drive for self-aggrandizement. Now the goal was to gain prosperity, profits, and power. The new ethic was that greed was good, and the goal was to acquire as much money and possessions as one could. Success became its own justification; it didn't matter how you made it—as long as you did. People were now judged by how much they made. As a result, if people didn't make enough money, live in the right places, or have the right clothes or contacts, they might find themselves "out." Old friends might shun them; they might lose out on promotions; they wouldn't make the "A" party list—however success was measured for a particular situation.

Supporting this emphasis on individual success and greed, a whole new profession emerged, based on creating the all important image of success. The underlying character or qualities of personal goodness didn't matter—most crucially the person needed to have the right presentation of self for the success image. Hence, image consultants and "dress for success" gurus like John Molloy helped to revamp the individual's personal appearance and personality, outfitting armies of corporate climbers ready to move up the success ladder.

Public relations specialists played an increasing role in creating images for corporations, entertainers, and political figures, and a new generation of stars and celebrities were born. People, such as Donald Trump, Madonna, Michael Jackson, and others, became masters at image making. They became, in effect, celebrities for their celebrity, and that kept them up in the firmament of stars of the 1980s—many still flying high in the 1990s. Popularity centered on the imagery and symbols of success, and in time, that imagery and symbolism became the door to success. The then- current New Age philosophies supported that imagery, too, with ideals such as "you can create your own reality" and "just visualize and affirm the reality you want, and you can get it."

Needless to say, this new criterion for success based on personality, image, and possessions battered the old values of character, integrity, and contributing to others and society. In fact, in the 1980s, people thought very little about questions of ethics and values. In the everyday business and professional world, any ethical consideration became a utilitarian one of increasing profits, reducing costs, and using power and success imagery to manipulate one's way to achieving personal or company goals.

THE NEW SEARCH FOR ETHICAL FOUNDATIONS IN THE 1990S

Unfortunately, as we now realize, the disintegration of ethical values in the "me-me," profit-oriented, image conscious, and power-fueled decade of the 1980s has led to a major collapse in many of our institutions. The examples of betrayal and downfall of once respected personalities and institutions are legion. They include the insider trading revelations on Wall Street; the many tele-evangelists who preached the glory of gain through God and fleeced their followers; and the banking scandals, in which once-respected banks and saving and loans were found full of corruption, leading to a series of bank failures that rocked the economy. We are now in a period of retreat and recovery, groping for new foundations on which to rebuild anew.

Some of the biggest, most "successful" icons of the 1980s are now part of the litany of doom and gloom, as we have come to recognize the destruction of society that their emphasis on aggrandizing the self has brought. Their names bring instant recognition— Ivan Boesky, Charles Keating, Jim Bakker, and others—all variously charged with crimes, most jailed or punished in some way for a time. And many have gone through bankruptcy or company restructuring to pay off debts. At one time, these were role models and heroes, because their huge financial success expressed our need for a modern Horatio Alger story—a golden tribute to what human ingenuity could achieve.

But like a star exploding from the intensity of too much heat, at the end of the 1980s most of these huge successes vanished like novas or play a much diminished role in the 1990s. They now serve as a reminder that ethics based only on self-interest are doomed to failure, since ethical systems, as handed down through the ages, have always involved balancing the needs of the community with the desires of the individual. We forgot that in the 1960s, and in subsequent years we allowed individual and personal self-interest and gratification to subvert community values, until the contradictions brought the process to a crashing halt in the 1980s.

Now we are in a state of both breakdown and the beginning of recovery. On the one hand, the signs of breakdown are everywhere—drug wars, violence in deteriorating inner cities, the failings of the educational system, economic uncertainty, mountains of debts, downsizing industries, high divorce rates, abandoned and molested children, high pregnancy rates for teenagers, and increasing rates of violence by children and teens. The evidence goes on and on, despite some recent signs of healing, such as a declining crime rate and a growing philanthropy by wealthy individuals like Ted Turner, to social and environmental causes. But the perception of out of control crime and violence remains, fueled in part by the media.

Also, many cultural trends highlight this state of breakdown, such as popular radio and TV personalities, who express insults and sarcasm in the name of good humor and free expression, like Howard Stern and Dennis Rodman. Another example are the musical and artistic groups that express their rage and alienation by being as outrageous as they can. For example, some rap groups sing about death and destruction and call for the killing of women and cops. And some artists have gained fame for mocking established images, such as one man who exhibited a crucifix dunked in a bottle of urine. Another recent development has been serial killer trading cards and web sites devoted to these killers on the Internet.

Nevertheless, despite many indications of breakdown, there are some signs of recovery, and hopefully, this book will be part of the trend to help us heal. For example, in business and in professional groups, a new call for ethics has gone out, and these groups are trying to develop codes that reflect fair practices and honest relationships based on trust. Also, instead of the bottom-line emphasis on sales and profits of the 1980s, many businesses have a new focus on customer service, satisfaction, and creating quality products in the 1990s. Too, many people in the business world have a new concern with reaching out to help others in the community, and they are gaining satisfaction through service, rather than seeking personal gain. Even Mike Milken, jailed for security fraud and derided as a symbol of greed in the 1980s, has joined this shift by teaching his knowledge of business to others. As a result, the spirit of voluntarism has been growing, as people get involved in various church and community groups to help the less fortunate. Colin Powell's summit for community service and mentoring is only one high profile example of this growing trend.

CHAPTER 3

•

THE MAJOR ETHICAL APPROACHES WE USE IN EVERYDAY LIFE

One key to resolving our current uncertainty about what is or isn't ethical behavior is being aware of the different ethical approaches we use. This way we can better understand our choices when we are in a difficult conflict or decision-making situation. Also, we can better understand the viewpoint of someone else with whom we are having a conflict. Then, being more informed, we can better work together to resolve any conflicts. Having a greater understanding can help us make decisions about ourselves, as well. Do we like our usual ethical approach to everyday experiences, or are our approaches limiting us?

For example, if we usually see things in terms of right and wrong, might we be too rigid in dealing with certain situations? If we usually trust our emotions or instincts to tell us how to act, might we make mistakes by misreading the signs or being too impulsive? Do we know why we feel so angry at someone with a different ethical approach? Could we be hostile because we feel that person is "immoral" or "amoral" and hence unethical, when, in fact, he or she is using an alternative ethical approach we aren't aware of or don't understand?

Today, many disputes and misunderstandings occur because people come from different backgrounds and from different ethnic, racial, religious, and cultural groups, with a variety of ways of looking at the world, including preferred styles of making ethical choices. What we consider wrong, bad, or unsuitable behavior may be perfectly acceptable from someone else's perspective.

Thus, even though we may not be aware of it, we choose among different ethical approaches when we make decisions and act in everyday life. Knowing what these are can help us make our own choices and deal with others.

THE SIX MAJOR ETHICAL APPROACHES

Although dozens of ethical systems have been proposed by writers on ethics and ethical thinking can become very abstract and theoretical, we all use a few basic approaches, sometimes in combination with one another. The six major approaches which are the most commonly distinguished by ethical theorists are the following:

1) looking to moral principles—deciding what's right and wrong, by drawing on traditional morality, which provides a code of general principles and rules for action;

2) applying moral strategies—deciding what's good and bad or when the ends justifies the means, through using a pragmatic or utilitarian approach;

3) evaluating the situation—deciding what's fitting or not fitting by following the appropriate rules, or using situational ethics to fit the particular circumstances;

4) following one's intuition—looking to one's inner voice, inner eye, inner knowing, or gut level instincts by using an intuitive approach;

5) following the pleasure or power principle—choosing what has the most personal benefit by responding to self-interest;

6) seeking the greater good—choosing what will help the most people through being concerned about others.

In addition, as will be discussed in Part II, I found two other approaches, not often included in categorizing how we make ethical choices, leading me to develop the Ethical Choices Map. These two other approaches are being an *innovator* in creating new rules and using a *rational analysis* to decide the best thing to do under the circumstances. Here though I will focus on the six most commonly described approaches.

These approaches represent a synthesis of the many different ethical guidelines suggested by ethical thinkers, and they are not meant to be formal categories, as distinctions often overlap. For example, someone might look to his intuition to help decide what's right or wrong, or a person may follow the pleasure principle to choose what has the most personal benefit, because that seems to be the most appropriate and appealing action to take in that situation. Or perhaps a person may seek the greater good as well as what's best for himself in deciding that the end justifies what he wants to do.

However, despite such possible overlap, these categories were chosen as a starting point in exploring ethical decision-making to learn the major reasons ordinary people—not philosophers or academics trained in ethical thinking—give for why they do what they do. I wanted to learn the major guidelines or strategies that people follow when they confront an ethical dilemma and have to make a difficult choice. Whatever source these guidelines come from—traditional religious teachings, family values, accepted standards among peers, principles inculcated by educators, codes of ethics from work—what are the main approaches people use?

The following section describes each of these six approaches with an example to illustrate.

1. Looking to Moral Principles—Deciding What's Right and Wrong (Drawing on traditional morality)

This *moral principles* approach is the one that is most wedded to the traditional ideals taught by our religious leaders, teachers, and parents about how we should act. These principles are the laws and rules we start learning as children about what's right and wrong— "Do this"…"Don't do that." When rules conflict, we learn other principles for choosing the higher value, such as when we learn that "It's wrong to tell a lie," but later discover that telling a "little white lie" may be all right, if it's done to protect someone's feelings or to keep someone from being hurt.

A good example of this "looking to moral principles" approach is the teacher who decides to enforce the school rules, no matter what. This happened to Alan when he was a junior in high school in a small town in Pennsylvania. His sister was going away to college, and his family decided to drive her to the campus. To take the whole family meant that Alan would be a week late going to school himself, but his parents wanted the family to be together and felt Alan wouldn't miss much school.

Alan, his parents, and sister had a wonderful time seeing her off to school. But when Alan arrived back at high school a week late, his English teacher asked him: "Where is your paper?," referring to the papers she had assigned the previous week. When she explained these papers were due today, Alan explained about his week's absence and how he did not know about the paper. "No one told me," he said.

But his teacher was adamant. Alan should have found out about the paper and been prepared. No exceptions. So she marked him down for not having his paper in on time, though he was able to turn it in a day late.

2. Applying Moral Strategies—Deciding What's Good or Bad or When the End Justifies the Means (Using a pragmatic or utilitarian approach)

The *moral strategies* approach represents the more pragmatic, practical approach many people use to make decisions and resolve ethical conflicts. It's the approach we as a culture tend to use, especially in work and business situations, since the emphasis is on what seems to be the best, most effective, or most useful approach in light of the potential outcome or consequences. It might sometimes be referred to as the utilitarian approach.

Someone using this approach might engage in a cost-benefits analysis, weighing what he would like to do for gain against the costs of doing it. Also, someone might consider the value or worth of the end goal in relationship to the methods he or she might use. If that goal is important enough, its attainment might be used to justify a less than ideal or acceptable means. Or if the risks of a negative outcome are low enough, this might justify using such a means, too. The difference between this and the "greatest good for the greatest number" approach described later is the focus here is on what is good for the individual or for the group making the decision, rather than the more altruistic social motivation underlying the "greatest good" approach.

Many examples of this approach can be found in everyday business and work situations. One of the most dramatic is what happened to the Challenger Space Shuttle. Everyone involved in designing the shuttle had a powerful drive to accomplish the mission of launching the shuttle and only a small window of opportunity in which to do so. At the same time, media and political leaders placed strong pressure on them to get it launched, and the eyes of America were closely watching the launch countdown. As a result, Lockheed, a company which worked on O rings for the shuttle, discovered a potential for weakness under stress, the company was under intense pressure not to call attention to the problem. Meanwhile the engineers, scientists, and administrators in NASA were under a similar pressure not to delay or halt the launch in order to investigate and correct this problem. Thus, the project participants who knew about the problem felt that the embarrassment that might result from not making the deadline would be worse than the seemingly small risk of the equipment malfunctioning. Besides, they imagined that the ring was such a minor part that probably nothing serious would happen.

The result of this cost-benefits, end-justifies-the-means approach, was the shuttle's go ahead. And, of course, everyone knows the grisly outcome. The O-ring failed and the Challenger exploded, killing all on board.

While this was an example of "the end/means" approach on a large social scale, in many cases, it is used by individuals who take chances or play the odds to gain a hoped for outcome. Sometimes it works; sometimes it does not. Typical examples might be: an employee up against a work deadline who decides not to run a computer test to check that there are no bugs in the system, though the usual procedures at work require this; the man who decides to cheat on his income tax or file an inflated insurance claim, thinking he won't be found out; or the woman who decides to hide a past abortion from a prospective suitor, thinking he will be better able to accept this after they are married.

Very often, such calculated risks work—the moral gamble succeeds. But when it fails the results can be very costly—such as the computer system that collapses resulting in a huge data loss because the bug wasn't discovered; the financial penalties or criminal charges that result when an investigation uncovers the truth after a false return or claim is filed; and the man who files for divorce after he finds out a truth he can't accept.

3. Evaluating the Situation - Deciding What's Fitting or Not Fitting (Following the appropriate rules)

This is the approach where the person looks at what is happening at the moment and decides the best thing to do given the circumstances. He might be guided by fairness, feelings of loyalty to another person, priorities of the moment, the attitudes of his peers, or the policies of his employers. The emphasis is on what is the most appropriate, suitable, practical, or optimum action to take now, based on present considerations.

Often, this kind of ethical response occurs in situations involving one's family or personal relationships, since clear guidelines or rules may not work well in complex situations which are often full of feelings and countervailing pressures. Also, the more strategic cost-benefits analysis that seems so fitting in the work and business environment may appear less appropriate here. Yet, while family and relationship situations provide a particularly fertile ground for such an approach, it can occur anywhere.

A good example of this situational approach is what happened to John. He had his heart set on a career as a doctor, and with the strong support of his family, he studied hard in high school to get into a good college. Once he was admitted, he continued working hard to get good grades to get into medical school. After he was accepted by the medical school he wanted to attend and was all set to go, his father got sick, and suddenly the family was strapped for cash. As a result, John knew his parents would now have trouble supporting him in school. He also he knew he would only have a

limited amount of time for working because of the heavy class schedule, so working his way through medical school was not the answer.
Though his mother told him the family could still manage to send
him, he knew his family would be depleting their already low bank
account, and if any unexpected emergency occurred, they would
quickly run out of funds.

Thus, though he desperately wanted to go to medical school
and his parents were still willing to send him, the situation created a
difficult moral choice for him. Should he do what he wanted for
himself? Or should he put the present needs of his family first? Should
he respond to self-interest or to family bonds of loyalty and love?
Finally, though reluctantly, he decided that what would be most
fitting in this situation was to put his family's needs first. His parents
really did need him at home to help economically, and seeking their
support for his schooling in a time of crisis would put his whole
family at risk. Moreover, he might have to drop out of school anyway if family support was no longer possible. Besides, the guilt of
not contributing to his family's problems was too great. He additionally felt that when the crisis was over, he could probably reapply
and be accepted again. So, taking all these factors into consideration, he decided to do what he thought was most fitting—to delay
his medical training until conditions were more favorable and help
his family first.

4. Following One's Intuition—Looking to One's Inner Voice, Inner Eye, Inner Knowing, or Gut-Level Feelings or Instincts (Using an intuitive approach)

Though one may use one's intuition to make any of the choices
already described—say by feeling a strong intuitive pull to follow a
certain rule, select a certain strategy, or decide that a certain action
is the most fitting under the circumstances—people think of an
intuitive response as a distinct approach. Such is the power of that
inner, intuitive, or emotional call that people believe they are responding to it, rather than trying to reason out what to do by weighing various factors, as in many choice-making situations.

In using the intuitive approach, people find that the knowledge or feeling of what choice to make can come to them very suddenly, like a flash of insight, illumination, or compelling impulse to do a certain thing. Often such feelings come in very personal or emotional situations, such as when a man decides to follow his heart and run off to marry the woman he loves, despite major obstacles. Such an experience may also occur for the person deciding about a future career or spiritual calling—the inner impulse propels making a particular choice.

The underlying ethical foundation for the validity of this approach is the view we can intuitively know what is right, good, or fitting, and act accordingly. Indeed, this often appears to be true—people follow their intuition and the outcome leads them to feel they have made the right choice. They feel good; other people affected by their decision feel good; the outcome is successful. Thus, the result validates and reaffirms their intuitive leap.

On the other hand, the potential danger of the intuitive, visceral response is that the person responding may think what he is doing is good, but the results may be very destructive, such as when a person is inspired to do something malevolent. An example is the parents who feel called by God to beat their errant daughter to exorcise her for what they believe was a sin.

Still, when the call of inspiration or revelation is for a beneficial purpose, the results can be very good. Cynthia had this experience when she got pregnant and was deciding whether to keep the baby or not. About six weeks into her pregnancy, she started experiencing some odd itching sensations, and went to see an internist and obstetrician. Both diagnosed shingles and advised that her baby would probably be abnormal. As a result, they scheduled an abortion, and Cynthia's husband and dozens of friends agreed. The best thing to do was to have an abortion and start again to have a healthy normal child.

However, the night before Cynthia was scheduled to discuss any concerns with a counselor at a final meeting before the abortion, she had a mystical experience which transformed her and changed her future. She was in the bathroom when she looked up through the skylight and noticed the full moon shining down on her. At that moment, she felt the fetus within her speaking to her, saying: "I'm all right. Don't do it. Don't have the abortion." At once, she sensed this living thing within her, and she emerged from the bathroom, feeling her inner voice had spoken to her, guiding her to do something different from what she had planned.

Yet, since everything seemed so finalized, she was still unsure when she spoke to the counselor. But, the meeting confirmed her mystical experience. The counselor encouraged her to listen to her inner voice, and this lone voice of support for her inner experience convinced her. Then, as she walked out the door with her husband, she noticed that the heavy rain when she went into her meeting had stopped, and there was a glowing rainbow across the sky. "It was like a confirmation of my inner knowing and my decision to keep the baby," Cynthia said.

She had the baby, and the result was a healthy baby boy, who subsequently grew up to go to college. The outcome reaffirmed Cynthia's decision to listen to her inner voice.

5. Following the Pleasure or Power Principle—Choosing What Has the Most Personal Benefit (Responding to self-interest)

The pleasure or power principle comes into play when people choose to do whatever gives them the most immediate satisfaction or gain at the time. For example, someone opts to have an affair, because he is powerfully attracted to a woman at work and hopes his wife and co-workers won't find out about it. Or, an employer decides to make his employees work overtime, because he has the power to make them do so and he wants to finish the project in time to take a vacation to the mountains.

This approach is different from the self-interested moral strategies approach in that the focus is on one's immediate desires rather than on long-term gains. In some cases, the two may go together very well, when there are both immediate and subsequent benefits. But in other cases, the long-term consequences may not be so favorable, as reflected by the phrase: "Pay now or pay later." In fact, sometimes the later consequences can be very severe (i.e.: unprotected sex now, AIDS or scandal later).

Often, people don't consider this approach to be a real ethical or moral position, because from their ethical perspective, they think the person acting for pleasure or power is immoral, amoral, or unethical. But, in fact, that person is taking an alternate ethical or moral position, even though they feel it is a wrong, bad, or unfitting one.

A widely publicized example of this type of approach is Woody Allen's relationship with Mia Farrow's adopted daughter Soon Yi, and his reaction to Mia and public opinion when the relationship became known. He had previously been a long-time lover to Mia, and they had adopted some children together, though they never formally married. However, while he was no longer in an intimate relationship with Mia and he had not adopted Soon Yi, when Mia discovered the affair, she felt outraged and betrayed. She considered Woody's actions incest, and once her charges tumbled into the tabloids and created a public sensation, most of the public and the media sided with her. Even though Woody protested that he never considered himself as a father to Soon Yi and his relationship with Mia had become a platonic friendship, the general opinion was that he had committed a grievous sin, and he was rationalizing his behavior with his excuses.

Meanwhile, despite this storm, Woody argued he had done the moral thing, since he and Soon Yi loved each other, citing the passions of the heart as an arbiter of what was morally right. Or as he commented: "The heart wants what it wants." And in the end, it would seem that Woody did largely weather the public storm successfully, despite some losses. He did continue his relationship with Soon Yi and later married her. He also went on to release several more successful movies, and despite some reverses in the courts, curtailing his visitation and parenting rights, in the court of public opinion, his state of disgrace seemed to eventually pass away. Perhaps it did so for several reasons—his talent as a film maker, his occupation in the arts which has a generally more tolerant attitude towards untraditional family and moral arrangements, and his enduring relationship with Soon Yi, suggesting this was not just a whimsical, self-indulgent fling, but based on a true calling of the heart.

By contrast, others who have followed the personal pleasure or power principle have been less successful, when their actions have so seriously hurt others that they have not gained forgiveness or have been penalized for committing a crime. Some examples are the "wronged" husband who beats his wife only to end up in jail and lose her; and the woman who spreads embarrassing but true private information about a rival, only to be embarrased as well when negative information is revealed about her.

Still, whatever the outcome, beneficial or not, opting to follow the pleasure or power principle is a moral choice. Whether it is a good one or not is the subject of debate, although often this determination is made in retrospect, when the choice turns out to have a favorable or unfavorable result.

6. Seeking the Greater Good—Choosing What Will Help the Most People (Being concerned about others)

This final principle is virtually the opposite of the pleasure/power principle in that its focus is on what will bring the most benefit for others. It's the most altruistic of the ethical approaches, since it emphasizes helping and serving others, and frequently these "others" are defined in a general, abstract way: such as helping the poor, the homeless, the indigenous peoples of the Americas, or the world as a whole. It's a stance that can easily blend into politics, as the person holding this viewpoint seeks to put it into action. This approach can also lead to peaceful or violent protest to change the current laws or system; or it might be expressed through journalism, public speaking, or other forms of outreach to influence others to attain this greater good. Though some may not agree with the choice of what the greater good is or the strategies used to achieve it, the search for "the greater good" is an ethical choice.

In some cases, the approach reflects a personal sacrifice in putting the group first, before one's own needs. One example is Magic Johnson's decision to come forward, announce he is HIV positive, and become a spokesman for AIDS. People have disputed how virtuous Johnson really was in making his announcement, since he engaged in sex with many partners, considered immoral by some. But importantly he did come forward voluntarily, when he could have kept his condition secret while he was still in good health, and he used his personal tragedy as an example to help others change their own behavior to avoid the disease. Thus, he chose the greater good for others, and still is active as a role model for others as of this writing. And even if his choice may have had some personal benefits (such as the praise and recognition he has received for this decision), overall, his emphasis was on the general good, particularly since the revelation brought with it some risks of personal losses (such as the loss of advertising contracts and endorsements, and the potential income loss as a result).

On the down side, however, this altruistic approach can involve sacrificing or hurting others in the name of "the greater good" or the larger society. The person making this choice sets himself up as judge of what is best for the larger group and who should be hurt or sacrificed to provide this benefit. This has occurred in the case of outing homosexuals, when certain people, including some newspaper and magazine publishers, have taken it upon themselves to reveal that some people who have kept their homosexuality a secret are gay. These self-styled "outers" have justified their right to invade others' privacy on various grounds—such as a gay politician who acts against gay interests should be revealed because he is a hypocrite or that revealing gays in high places will help open doors for others. Whatever the particular reason, it reflects the moral position that the chosen person should be exposed for the benefit of others, and that the individual making the choice to do so has the moral right to act in the name of this greater good.

APPLYING THE ETHICAL APPROACHES IN EVERYDAY LIFE

In summary, these are the six major ethical approaches that have been recognized as guiding our life—drawing on traditional morality, using a pragmatic or utilitarian approach, following the appropriate rules, using an intuitive approach, responding to self-interest, and being concerned about others. In addition, as we'll discover in Part II, there are two more approaches which people report using—creating their own rules and using a rational analysis to decide what to do. As a result, the usual way of thinking of these major approaches as a list from which people choose one or more strategies to apply in a particular situation turns into a matrix or map. I call this the Ethical Choices Map, and the intensity or importance of a particular approach adds a third dimension.

We'll explore how this works and how you can apply this approach in your own life in Part II.

PART II:

HOW PEOPLE RESOLVE ETHICAL DILEMMAS AND MAKE THE CHOICES THEY DO

CHAPTER 4

•

THE ETHICAL APPROACHES PEOPLE USE

When people encounter ethical dilemmas or make ethical choices to resolve problems, they usually do not think about how and why they are making their choices. They choose something because it feels right; because there seem to be more benefits than disadvantages in doing so; because that's the way things are usually done; because they will benefit and it won't harm others; because they will help others; because they have learned it is the right thing—or a combination of these reasons. They usually don't have particular rules, guidelines, or language for describing how they choose and why. Often, because they see things from their own ethical perspective, they don't understand why others feel differently, not recognizing that we all inhabit different moral worlds—and in many cases, these different views may, though conflicting, each be right. We can all agree that certain actions and beliefs are clearly wrong— antisocial acts for example, like mass genocide and wanton destruction for greed. But in most areas of life, there are shades of gray, and from different viewpoints different things are "right".

Making things even more confusing is that different cultures have different values. People also are exposed to different influences based on background factors—depending on where they were born and raised, the teachings of their parents, the religion they were brought up in and the one they follow now, if any. Other factors include their political leanings, occupation, education, and class status. Even personality style, approach to learning, thinking, perception, and general style of resolving conflicts all come into play.

I began to recognize these differences when I interviewed people from different backgrounds about how they made ethical choices. Gradually, patterns began to emerge as I met and talked with people in different occupations or in different life situations (such as being married or single). I then discovered that people who came from different parts of the country, had different religious upbringings, or who identified with different political parties or philosophies had different ways of making choices or dealing with ethical dilemmas. They even defined an ethical problem differently.

With very few exceptions, most people I spoke with readily acknowledged numerous conflicts. "You can't be alive and not have conflicts," as one man said. But especially intriguing was the wide variety in what different people viewed were "ethical" conflicts and dilemmas, how they approached them, and how they made a choice.

In the next chapters, I'll present the stories of how people define and resolve ethical dilemmas of all sorts, which you can use as a guide in making your own choices and resolving your own problems. But first I want to present the model of how people make ethical choices which emerged from these interviews.[1] I have used pseudonyms in the book in reporting their stories.

The model developed out of interviewing these people will help

---

[1]Briefly, the people I spoke with to develop this model, had the following characteristics. Though a small sample of the population, I included people from a wide spectrum of backgrounds, since these factors contribute to the ethical perspectives people have. The characteristics of the 28 people I spoke included the following:

• Half were women; half were men.

• About 20% were in their 20s and 30s, 60% were in their 40s, 20% in their 50s or in one case older.

• About 30% were single, 30% divorced, and 40% were married (or in two cases living with a significant other).

• About 35% were Jewish, 40% Christian (25% Protestant; 15% Catholic) and the rest embraced a mix of New Age spiritual beliefs, or had no religion.

• About half identified themselves as liberals, about a third were moderates, and a few described themselves as strong conservatives or radicals. Most, however, were not politically active.

• They represented a broad mix of geographical areas—about 40% from the East Coast, about 25% from the West Coast, and the rest from the Mid-West and the South.

provide a frame for understanding how people make their choices. It will also show how these choices relate to the background, personality traits, and other qualities which uniquely shape our lives.

THE WAY WE RESOLVE ETHICAL DILEMMAS: A MODEL FOR MAKING ETHICAL CHOICES

Using the six major categories for making ethical choices described in the previous chapter as the basis of my interviews, I asked people how they made their choices when faced with an ethical dilemma. It soon became clear people were very different in their approaches. Again, these six categories were:

• choosing traditional right and wrong categories (drawing on traditional morality)

• deciding what's good or bad to do (using a pragmatic or utilitarian approach)

• doing what's fitting or not (using a situational ethics approach by following the appropriate rules or customs)

• doing what intuitively feels right (using the intuitive approach)

• deciding what has the most benefit for oneself (responding to self-interest)

• doing something that most benefits others (being concerned about others).

Many people opted for a combination of approaches, or used different approaches at different times or settings—say being more pragmatic or more apt to follow the rules in a professional or work

---

• Most were well-educated—almost all college graduates, with about half doing some graduate work; 25% had Ph.D.s or other professional degrees.

• They represented a wide variety of occupational backgrounds, including artists, writers, therapists, a social welfare worker, nurses and medical personnel, a teacher, an academic, an architect, a scientist, lawyers, a tax consultant, managers and supervisors, sales and marketing professionals, advertising and PR professionals, a talk show host, a speaker/seminar leader, a political consultant, and a computer consultant.

setting, while being more likely to follow one's intuition in a personal situation. Some felt many approaches dovetailed together, such as one woman who said: "When I do what intuitively feels right and it benefits others, it benefits me, too."

DIFFERENCES IN APPROACHES

I also began to notice patterns in the kinds of ethical issues people raised or how they approached them, based on their occupations or their backgrounds. For example, for several artists and writers, a common theme was making a choice between being more practical (particularly when parents and significant others urged them in that direction) versus making the more idealistic, altruistic, and self-interested choice of pursuing their dream, which these people ultimately did. For several people who worked in large organizations, a recurring issue was whether to go along with the rules when they felt that people were being hurt by the organization's way of doing things; or should they try to change the rules by speaking up or by quietly finding a way to act more ethically. For those involved in politics, there were issues around making promises to gain support but not being able to keep them later, and some were disturbed by compromising deeply held beliefs by being a team player. People in other circumstances had other issues.

People's ethics also seemed shaped by their current social situation—whether they were single, married, or in a relationship with another person; whether they had to turn to their parents for help or were independent of them; or whether they had children themselves. Different types of relationships created their own special dilemmas (i.e., how much information to share about oneself in the dating relationship; whether to borrow funds from one's parents; and when to put one's kids' interests first).

There seemed to be a connection, too, between people's religious and political orientation, their geographic and family roots, and their ethical approach, even with the small number of people I interviewed. For example, those who identified themselves as liberals (and those who were likely to be Jewish or have no religion, and come from the East Coast) were more apt to be altruistic in their outlook and less likely to follow the rules in making their choices. By contrast, those who thought of themselves as moderates or conservatives (and who identified themselves as coming from Protestant and Catholic backgrounds and from the Midwest or West Coast) were more likely to be pragmatic and go along with the rules.

Then, too, another difference was how consistent the interviewees were in their ethical approach. Some were apt to separate the different areas of their lives in how they made choices, most notably acting one way in their personal lives and another at work. Those who held strong religious or political views, either liberal or conservative, tended to be more consistent in their ethical choices, while others were more apt to approach making choices differently in different situations, such as being more intuitive in responding to personal and social problems, and more likely to follow the rules and their self-interest at work.

Such connections are just suggestive of the vast differences between people of different backgrounds.

THE FOUR KEY DIMENSIONS IN MAKING CHOICES

So how do we make choices? What factors influence us, based on our personal, social, and other characteristics?

Based on the way people chose to use different ethical approaches and which approach they found the most and least comfortable, it seems four major factors or dimensions come into play, each with two opposite ways of making choices. These are like a continuum in which people may be more or less likely to respond in different ways depending upon the situation. Taking all four factors together, one can create a kind of Ethical Choices Map, indicating where each person is likely to be placed in given situations. The way people make these choices may also be related to other personal differences, such as personality type and ways of thinking, perceiving, and relating to others, as will be discussed in Part III.

The four Ethical Choice Factors—and the continuum of choices for each factor—are these:

Style of Choosing—from Rational (or logical or analytical) to Intuitive

Orientation—from Other (more altruistic) to Self (more self-interested)

Philosophy or Values—from Moralist (or traditionalist) to Pragmatic (choosing what works)

Attitude to Rules—from Follower (or team player) to Innovator (rule breaker or maker)

Combining these factors together results in the Ethical Choices Map, illustrated below.

Table 1:
ETHICAL CHOICES MAP

		Style of Choosing		Orientation	
		Rational	Intuitive	Other	Self
Philosophy or Values	Pragmatist	O			O
	Moralist		T	T	
Attitude to Rules	Follower		T	T	
	Innovator	O			O

The T's and O's on the map indicate the difference between the individual who has a traditional religious perspective (the T's) and those who differ in other perspectives (the O's). The person from the traditional background is basically a person who follows the rules, intuitively knows the right thing to do because these traditional religious and ethical teachings are firmly ingrained, and is taught to be very concerned about others and the larger community. As indicated, the T person falls squarely in the center core of the Ethical Choices Map. This is the person who might be categorized as being a Moralist and Follower, and having an Intuitive style and Other orientation.

The complete opposite indicated by the outer O's is the person who makes ethical decisions by deciding what works best, perhaps evaluating things from a cost-benefits perspective, breaks the rules or makes his own when it suits him, thinks through what would be the best thing to do, and makes a choice based on what's best for him. In other words, this is a person who is a Pragmatist and Innovator, who has a Rational style and a "me-me" Self orientation.

DIFFERENT WAYS OF MAKING CHOICES IN DIFFERENT SITUATIONS

People can combine different characteristics in each of these dimensions in different ways, so they can differ in some dimensions from the traditional moralist but not in others. For example, a person might have a strong intuitive sense of what to do and a very altruistic orientation, but often breaks the rules to create his or her own way of doing things. And he or she might often use a very pragmatic approach when doing so, rather than thinking of things in terms of what's right and wrong.

Though people might have a characteristic approach, they may make choices in different ways under certain circumstances. For example, a person who practices the traditional core values at home with his family and in personal relationships might often make decisions from a more pragmatic, rational, and innovative perspective to obtain the best career opportunities. A person may also change his approach over time, such as becoming more concerned about others and more tolerant and less judgmental of them with time.

It is important to realize that people may fall at varying points on the Ethical Choices Map, may be more or less consistent in how they use an approach in different situations, and may change to a greater or lesser degree in each of these areas over time. Furthermore, it is important to recognize that these categories are ideal types, representing the way people might be categorized as they approach ethical issues. More precisely, people might be placed along a continuum in each of these four dimensions. For example, rather than being Rational or Intuitive, people might tend to fall more at one end of the Rational/Intuitive continuum than another. Then in certain situations, they may change their approach. Similarly, people may vary in the degree to which they base their decisions on their self-interest or on the interest of others. Too, they may differ in the degree to which they follow traditional religious teachings about what is right versus working things out pragmatically, or in the degree to which they act as followers or rule-breakers and rule-makers.

What is clear is that there is no one right way in making ethical decisions. Perhaps we may be more apt to consider ethical the choices that fall near the center of the Ethical Choices Map, since they represent core principles of what's right and wrong and how to choose what to do. But under varying circumstances, people with different ethical approaches may consider their own approaches to be quite valid. They may have their own ways of justifying the ethical choices they make however they make them, such as deciding to go along with the team and follow the rules, even though they don't think these rules are right. A business executive or company employee, for example, may be bothered by some of the things he has to do, but he remains with the company anyway because of other considerations, say financial ones. Only when the demands become too great and create too much ethical conflict does he finally decide to leave.

On the other hand, many people may judge the person who makes decisions—by doing whatever he wants to do for his own self interest—as completely unethical. But this is another form of making an ethical choice, although it may have negative consequences for the person who chooses this way, such as finding that other people don't want to be with him because they find him "unethical." Or this self-interested person may find this strategy produces gains in the short run, but in the long run, results in negative reactions as he finds his social life and job prospects narrowing.

In short, the point of the Ethical Choices Map is to indicate how people actually make their choices, not judge them. One can come to a better understanding of one's own choices and the choices others make by using the Map.

In addition, this map presents a ethical portrait of how people react at one point in time, whether the categories are treated as either/or categories or as points at either end of a continuum. While one can use a single map to identify how one reacts generally, one can also distinguish responses under different conditions (i.e., personal life versus professional/public life), under certain circumstances (i.e., in relating to one's parents versus relating to one's friends), and in responding to different types of people (i.e., in relating to a person who is very altruistic versus relating to a person who is self-centered and will try to take every advantage if given the opportunity).

Thus, two other dimensions that cannot be reflected physically on the map are how consistent one is in one's ethical approach, and how one uses this approach in different situations or over time.

USING THE ETHICAL CHOICES MAP TO UNDERSTAND THE CHOICES PEOPLE MAKE

At the end of the book, in the Appendix, you'll find a copy of a questionnaire to help you measure your own ethical approaches. It's a questionnaire I used in my own interviews, and I will be using it to develop a more formal Ethical Choices Scoring Guide to compare people from different social, economic, racial, and ethnic groups, as well as comparing people with different personality and other traits to show how these characteristics shape our ethical choices.

In the following chapters, I describe examples of the types of ethical choices people make and how they make them, drawing on the stories of the people I interviewed. Yet, while these people come from largely mainstream professional and business backgrounds, all are very different in their ethical approaches and fall in varying places along the Ethical Choices Map. Just think how many more differences there might be if they came from even more varied backgrounds—in class, in culture, and in other factors as well. In the future, I hope to explore these possibilities, applying the Map to many other groups and cultures.

CHAPTER 5

•

THE TECHNIQUES AND PRINCIPLES FOR MAKING DECISIONS

Besides having a general approach to making ethical choices and resolving ethical dilemmas, people also use a wide variety of techniques, depending on how serious the problem is, how close it is to them (i.e., whether a personal, work, community, or societal issue), and their personal style. Some people also have underlying basic principles or guidelines that help them make choices. All of these factors change over time—influenced by the individual's age, stage of life, experiences, and current social environment.

In effect, the general approach described in the previous chapter intersects with these particular ways of dealing with ethical dilemmas, and together they influence how each person decides. Think about where you might fit yourself.

THE ZONES OF MAKING ETHICAL CHOICES

A way of think about how we apply the ethical approaches we use is to consider the situations we face in daily life like a series of circles around us. We are in the center, surrounded by issues of decreasing closeness to us. These are like radiating spokes on a wheel, circles around a bull's-eye, or locations which are increasingly distant from a central city. People have different priorities in what's important to them, but in general, as these circles of closeness radiate from us, they become less important. This level of importance, in turn, which affects the ethical approaches and techniques we use.

These zones surrounding us include the following:

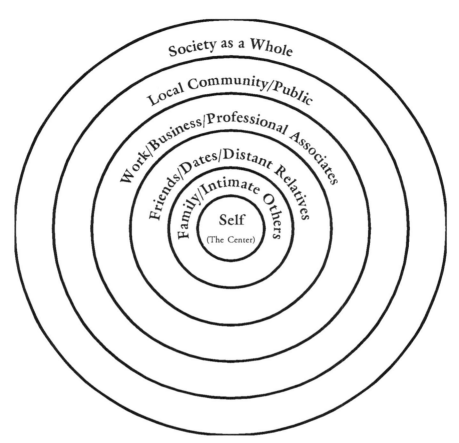

Figure 1: Zones of Ethical Choices

In general, those dilemmas closest to us involve the most power and emotion, since they are closer. We have more emotional and psychic energy invested in them, because they have more affect on our personal sense of identity and well-being, and they involve the people we care about the most. Yet, while most people recognize these common radiating zones, in that they see their family and intimate others as most important, followed by social and work roles, and lastly their community and society as a whole, some people have different maps of what's closest to them. One example is person who identifies very strongly with a social cause, making that an essential part of his or her being, though others find such matters less compelling. Another example is the person whose very self is invested in his work, so that he invests it with much more emotional energy than family and mates.

GUIDING PRINCIPLES

Some people have guiding principles they apply in resolving ethical problems in most or all areas of life, whatever the circumstance; while others may use these same principles in dealing with particular dilemmas, but use other approaches at different times.

In general, the people I interviewed who indicated they had firm guiding principles tended to have strong religious or spiritual beliefs, although they followed different religious traditions and ranged from being liberal to conservative politically. But whatever their religious or political orientation, they tended to hold their guiding beliefs more deeply and intensely than those without a strong guiding philosophy.

The major guiding principles they mentioned are ones taught by the major religions. And all of these ideals or values fall within the inner core on the Ethical Choices Map, which represents the principles of the traditional ethical systems. These are:

- Do what you can to help others.
- Avoid harming others.
- Follow the golden rule (do unto others as you would have them do unto you).
- Be truthful and fair.
- Seek balance in the way you act.

Some Examples of Following Guiding Principles

One woman with strong guiding principles, was Trudy[2], a black educator in her 40s who grew up in the South and ran for political

---

[2]A pseudonym, like the other names, which follow.

office several times as a conservative. These principles came from her religious background as a born-again Christian. As she described it:

> I try to do what's right, what I believe is right. I try not to do things that hurt other people, unless it's unavoidable.

Similarly, Lori, a teacher in her 40s, from a New York Jewish background and active in liberal social causes, reported following like guidelines. In her words:

> Basically, I'm guided by the question: "Does what I do hurt another person?" If I feel it would hurt somebody else, that would stop me from doing it. The Golden Rule. That's a principle I follow...It guides my way in the world.
>
> I do so, because I really believe we make our own heaven and hell here and now, and I'd rather live in a heavenly environment than a hellish one. I believe I have a major role in creating the kind of world I live in and the kind of world that we have out there. I want the world to work, and I feel the world would run better if people would follow the unwritten law of "Do unto others as you would have them do unto you."

Similarly, Andy, a salesman in his late 40s, originally from Hawaii and a self-described moderate had his own core principles to guide him. For him, the most important ones were seeking balance and having integrity in keeping with the principle of Karma. This way, he believed, one would always do the right thing and not harm others. As he explained it:

> My overall ethical approach is following the principle of karma. Karma is doing something out of integrity, based on recognizing that you get back what you put out. This means that if I produce a positive affect on someone, so they feel good and feel I support them, at some point in their lifetime, they will give me the similar experience in return. So that win-win situation produces good karma. On the other hand, if one does something negative that is harmful to people, that tends to create a negative karma, in that people won't feel receptive or supportive towards me.

Others identified certain fundamental core principles they had been taught to follow, most notably being honest, trustworthy, and fair. For example, Connie, an art director in her 40s from Los Angeles, who considered herself a politically active liberal, had this to say:

> For me what's fundamental in approaching ethical issues is being honest, telling the truth even when wrong, and being truthful with myself and with someone else, though that can be very painful at times. It's really important to me, being up front, trustworthy, and responsible, and being kind to people and animals. Then, I think people can communicate in an open, honest way, in which no one is hurting the other. And that helps to make human relationships work.

THE RELATIONSHIP BETWEEN MAKING ETHICAL CHOICES AND RESOLVING CONFLICTS

To some extent, the process of making ethical choices is like choosing among a repertoire of possible responses. As I discussed in a previous book *Resolving Conflict,*[3] there are five major approaches to resolving conflicts—being competitive or confrontational, avoiding the issue, accommodating the desires of others; collaborating by taking the time to fully discuss and resolve the matter; and compromising.

In resolving an ethical dilemma, one can similarly choose from a repertoire of methods. However, when ethical issues are involved, the process often involves a more internal conflict, in which people are torn between opposing desires and feelings of deep uncertainty and guilt.

The particular method chosen for each conflict can in turn be placed on the Ethical Choices Map, although it may not involve all four dimensions. For example, some people faced with a dilemma tend to use a more intuitive process of meditating deeply on the problem to imagine the best thing to do—a kind of Intuitive Pragmatist approach. Others who use this intuitive process do so to get a feeling for what feels right—more of an Intuitive Moralist approach.

---

[3]Gini Graham Scott, *Resolving Conflict,* Oakland, California: New Harbinger, 1990.

By contrast, those who are more logical in weighing the alternatives to make the best choice would fall into the Rational Pragmatist category. Or if someone uses reason to determine the morally right thing that would involve using a Rational Moralist process, though often moralists don't try to figure out what to do logically. Rather, they simply have a sense of knowing what's right because they have been taught these principles.

In any case, as represented on the Ethical Choices Map, these techniques for ethical decision-making reflect combining one's *style* of choosing and one's *philosophy*. Then, in a particular situation, one might take into consider other ethical choice dimensions. One such dimension is considering the benefit of that choice for oneself or others (i.e., deciding whether to do what is of most benefit to oneself or to others—the Other/Self Orientation). Finally, one might be affected by one's attitude towards the applicable rules (i.e., whether one should go along with the rules, break them, or create new rules—the Follower/Innovator Dimension).

By using this combination approach, in any particular situation, one's choices can be represented by a point in each of the four quadrants of the map. Also one can examine one's general tendency to make choices over time in a series of situations, thereby determining one's overall ethical approach.

Additionally, the Ethical Choices Map can be related to the Resolving Conflict model by combining the Other/Self Orientation and Attitudes Towards Rules categories. These two categories form a good fit with the Resolving Conflict Model, because this model is based on combining two factors that influence one's approach to conflict—how assertive one is in satisfying one's own concerns or the other party's concerns, and whether one is more oriented towards oneself or others. There is also a good fit between these two systems in that the Follower goes along with the rules rather than assert his own desires, while the Innovator is ready to break or remake rules if this is in his own interest. In other words, making an ethical choice involves some of the same considerations as resolving a conflict with others. The following diagram shows how these two systems can be combined.

Table 2:
THE RELATIONSHIP BETWEEN ONE'S APPROACH TO RESOLVING ETHICAL DILEMMAS AND ONE'S STYLE OF RESOLVING CONFLICTS

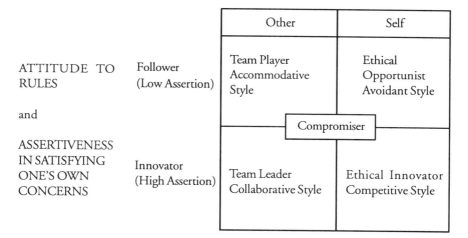

ORIENTATION TOWARDS
SELF OR OTHERS
(Used in Both Systems)

		Other	Self
ATTITUDE TO RULES	Follower (Low Assertion)	Team Player Accommodative Style	Ethical Opportunist Avoidant Style
and		Compromiser	
ASSERTIVENESS IN SATISFYING ONE'S OWN CONCERNS	Innovator (High Assertion)	Team Leader Collaborative Style	Ethical Innovator Competitive Style

Since resolving ethical dilemmas involves ethical considerations, not just a conflict with others, it involves two other dimensions as well— one's style of choosing (rational versus intuitive) and one's general philosophy about how to act (pragmatically versus drawing on fundamental moral principles).

In short, resolving these dilemmas can includes all four dimensions, categories, or quadrants of the Ethical Choices Map. The following chapters will describe each of these dimensions or factors in making choices in more detail. Again, these four dimensions are the following: Style of Choosing, Orientation, Philosophy, and Attitude to Rules.

CHAPTER 6

•

THE STYLE OF CHOICE PEOPLE USE

The style of choosing you use in making an ethical choice is whether you are more intuitive or rational in making your choice. While some people tend to be very intuitive in sensing, knowing, or spontaneously deciding what to do, others are more analytical in considering and weighing the options. Also, whether more intuitive or rational, some people are more intense and emotional, others more calm, cool, and collected.

Intriguingly, when I asked interviewees to describe their style, there was a clear split between the men and the women. Though this was only a small sampling and a somewhat larger majority were intuitives (about 60%), the differences conformed to traditional notions about how men and women think about things—the men were more likely to try to reach decisions logically, weighing alternatives in their mind, assessing costs and benefits, and thinking about priorities, and they were less apt to be emotional in going through the process. By contrast, the women were more likely to use intuitive processes, such as meditation, to think about what was going on in a more holistic way. The women were also more apt to report feeling more emotional intensity in reflecting on the problem, whether they did so more logically or intuitively, describing stronger feelings of guilt or suffering as they wrestled with what to do.

There also seemed to be a relationship between the kinds of jobs people had and whether they were more likely to be more logical or intuitive in their approach. In general, those who identified themselves with the creative, healing, or "people" professions (i.e., writer, artist, nurse, therapist, social welfare worker, teacher, sales, and PR) tended to be more intuitive, while those in the more scientific, analytical, or business management type of professions (i.e., computer writer, business manager, political consultant, architect, scientist, and academic) tended to approach ethical issues from a more rational perspective or, as a few indicated, they tended to use a combination approach. In this combo style, they used logic to decide when it was appropriate to use one's intuition and when it was better to use reason, and they applied that style accordingly.

However, there didn't seem to be any connection in one's style of making choices and one's religious background, strength of current religious involvement, or political identification as a liberal, conservative or moderate. Regardless of these factors, people seemed to differ in their approach. Rather, what seemed to be most closely connected with one's style of choice was gender and occupational choice—which are perhaps most closely related to personality characteristics and thus to one's style of making ethical decisions.

Here are some examples to illustrate the varying ways in which people apply rational and intuitive measures of resolving dilemmas. They reflect these associations with gender and occupation, in that most of people using the rational approach are men and in the occupations associated with being rational, while most of the people using the intuitive approach are women, and in the occupations associated with using one's intuition more.

THE RATIONALISTS

For the rationalists, an ethical dilemma is something to be weighed and considered. They look at the alternatives, think about the relative advantages and disadvantages of the possible outcomes, consider the pros and cons, examine the benefits and costs. Commonly, this is an internal process, although some may consult with a partner, close friends, or family members in assessing what to do.

In describing his approach, Dick, an architect in his 30s, explained:

> I tend to think through what I find most important and do my
> best to avoid having problems come up in the future. For in-

stance, I have my own ideas on how buildings should be built and how we should go through the whole process. So I tend to assess in advance and take on those projects that meet my own criteria. I avoid working with people or in situations that I think will present a problem down the road. By thinking things through, I try to get ethical and other problems resolved before they happen.

Similarly, Alan, a business manager in his late 20s, worked things out logically. For him, the approach was like using an internal weighing process in which he put the options he considered on a scale, which included costs, benefits and priorities to help him decide what to do. Usually, he did this weighing on his own, though he sometimes asked for input from his wife or other relatives. As he explained it:

> I have a very individualized approach to ethics and moral values, so generally I don't see any ethical or moral value being any more important than the other. As a result, when I make a decision to do something, it is the right decision to do, because I evaluate a decision from one end to the other...
>
> Also, I see a problem as a temporary moral dilemma. I look at it in the same way I would approach doing a business analysis at work or in any other situation. I map out what led me to that point. I map out the ramifications based on whatever decision I may make. Finally, if it's warranted, I will consult my wife, my grandmother, or my in-laws. Otherwise, I make my decisions on my own.

Alan prided himself on this highly logical, systematized approach which he felt came from being raised in a family of lawyers and scientists. As he continued:

> My grandmother was a practicing attorney for 55 years, and her first husband was a publisher of scientific books. So I was raised around all these scientists. And being raised like that, I have always viewed everything in a very logical pattern. It can sometimes be to my detriment, because I try to take all emotion out, which doesn't always work. But I try to approach ev-

erything logically. I try to map it out, and then make the choice and stick with it. And that approach has generally worked for me.

Others who spoke about being logical in their approach emphasized the importance of considering consequences and weighing priorities. They also spoke of choosing what situations to deal with based on what was most important to them—a matter of "picking battles," as a few phrased it.

Pam, a registered nurse in her 30s, emphasized priorities when she explained:

> I think about what's most important at the time to make the best choice. For example, at work, say one patient is screaming and another one needs a blanket, I'll consider what's more important right now. Or say I'm working with people on a political campaign, I think about what I want to accomplish and do that. I'll also assess the circumstances to consider what I can say or not say about what I think. Say I went to a Republican luncheon. Though I believe in free choice, I wouldn't start talking about abortion rights in the middle of the luncheon. I know that wouldn't go over, so I don't do it. But if someone asks me a direct question, I would give them my truthful answer. But I don't offer up opinions that would create conflict if I don't have to. It's like a camouflage I use, because it makes good logical sense to operate that way.

Kelly, a speaker and consultant in her 40s, spoke of weighing alternatives, using visualization techniques to imagine the consequences. Sometimes she even wrote down the pros and cons, letting the final decision emerge later through visualization based on this prior logical analysis. As Kelly described the process:

> I look at all the alternatives and think: 'Which will do the least possible harm to the people involved?' 'What are the possible outcomes?' I visualize in my mind or I project what the likelihood is.
>
> For example, I did this when I had a hard decision to make over whether to help a friend who needed money at a difficult

time in her life, when I was feeling financial pressures myself and had lent her some money before. I asked myself a series of questions to help decide: "If I refuse to give my friend money, how will it affect our friendship? How will it affect this person's ability to pay her rent? Will she find another source if I'm not there? And if I do give her the money, how will it affect my life.'

I also do this process in different ways. Sometimes I just do it mentally, thinking about the alternatives in my mind. I visualize seeing the scenes in my head. I see them play out like I'm being a playwright imagining the different ways the play might turn out. Or sometimes I do this process in writing, writing down the pros and cons over a couple of hours in an evening. Then, I'll let the situation rest for a couple of days, and when I come back to it, I'll make my decision, based on weighing all these factors.

In describing still another way of applying this rational approach, Henry, a social work supervisor in his 50s, emphasized the importance of future planning:

I think about things that could become problems in advance. I'm constantly preparing for what can happen. This way when dilemmas arise, they're very easy to resolve. Decisions are pre-made, situations are pre-thought-out.

It's like being on the highway preparing for the possibility of getting a flat tire. I know where my spare is. I know how to change my spare. I've got my phone card. So if I can walk to a phone, I can use my card to call and have the car towed. So I have a variety of different things I can do.

I regard dealing with ethical dilemmas the same way. The key is to be prepared and have a number of different options to choose from when the time comes to face the dilemma. As a result, as long as I can, I gather input, and I make the decision based on the information I have at the time. Then, once the decision is made using this approach, I feel comfortable that this is the best judgment I could make at the time given what I had. So I don't feel any need for second guessing what I decided later on."

For Don, a radio broadcaster in his 40s, an important key besides working things out logically was choosing the most important battles into which to invest his energy—both in personal relationships and in his efforts as an activist to create a better world. As he put it:

> I'm logic driven. I operate mostly internally, though I some-times consult with my partner, Suzanne, if I want input...Also, I pick my battles to decide where to put my energies and try to work through or change what I can based on what's the most important to me.

THE INTUITIVES

In contrast to the rationalists, who thought through and weighed their decisions, the intuitives came to their choices in a more holistic way, in which they got insights into what to do or had a gut level feeling about what was right. For them, it was much harder to put into words exactly how they resolved their dilemmas, because the way to act seemed to just come to them or felt right. Although they might sometimes begin by internally weighing the pros and cons or imagining possible consequences, they did so in a more haphazard way of now and then thinking about the issue. Then the decision came to them as more of a "Eureka" or "I feel it in my gut" re-sponse.

Bill, a lawyer in his early 50s, did this. After taking into consid-eration the prevailing rules or customs in a situation and thinking of the consequences in general terms, he would get a strong inner know-ing about what to do. He described it thus:

> I solve most ethical dilemmas I encounter in a practical way. I look at the problem and ask myself what is the practical conse-quences of doing one thing or another. I really don't do a lot of weighing of the scenario in my mind. Rather it's an intuitive thing. Always. Nothing weighs on me very long. It's a gut thing. If I don't feel comfortable with something because I can imag-ine some circumstance where I can regret it—and that comes to me as an intuitive flash—then I don't do it.

Other intuitive decision makers, notably some of the women I spoke to, used meditative techniques to resolve a problem. In the process, they weighed alternatives and looked at different sides of the situation, but did so in a non-analytic way. They viewed the possibilities in a contemplative, relaxed frame of mind, sometimes in a hypnotic, altered state of consciousness, in which they could see the situation and various options and outcomes, like watching a film pass before them on a screen. For some, when emotional feelings triggered by the dilemma were strong, this meditative process was a way to help calm down and separate themselves from their strong emotional feelings.

Karen, the head of an advertising agency in her 40s, described her meditative approach thus:

> I tend to meditate on things when I have to make a hard choice about doing something. For instance, suppose a company asks me about doing the advertising for some project. First, I want to decide if I want to do it, because I only want to work on projects or with people I consider ethical. If there's any question in my mind of whether it's a good or bad thing to do, I will say: 'Let me get back to you on that,' without making a snap decision. Then, I will really reflect on doing the project to decide whether it feels right and good to me.

Likewise, Iris, a psychotherapist in her 50s, used meditation, generally going to a quiet place where she could be alone with her thoughts, often walking along the beach near the ocean. This process helped her detach from her emotional feelings and better focus on the problem and what to do. As she described it:

> I do a lot of walking on the beach when I have ethical or moral problems to resolve. I meditate. I attempt to remove myself from the emotional feelings surrounding the situation. Then I can sit back, reframe the matter, and look at what is really going on. I try to look at things from a number of different sides, more than from just my side, in this quiet meditative frame of mind to decide the best thing to do. Sometimes the answer comes to me very quickly. But other times it takes longer, and I have to reflect on the matter for a long time.

The intuitives also differed from the rationalists in feeling the negative emotions associated with the problem more strongly, since they were more in touch with their emotions, whereas the rationalists tended to be more pragmatic and emotionally detached. Thus, for them, an emotional dilemma could at times trigger much deeper suffering in agonizing about what to do or feeling guilty.

This is what happened for Francine, a free-lance public relations consultant in her 40s. She had been brought up as a Catholic and now held strong religious beliefs associated with Eastern philosophy. Because she felt deeply steeped in guilt from her Catholic heritage, she tended to suffer a great deal when she faced a problem and tried to come to an intuitive understanding of what to do. As she described her process:

> My approach is more intuitive, more of a gut feeling I get if I feel right about something. But I also suffer an awful lot when I reflect on things to come to this decision. I really torture myself when I make decisions about anything that is meaningful, especially when I don't just look at how something is going to affect my current life, but take into consideration how it will affect others and what they need. I often do this because I'm looking at things from a larger spiritual perspective.
>
> That's what I did when things didn't work out with my husband and I was getting a divorce. In reflecting on the situation, I felt he had more financial needs than I did at the time, since he was having financial problems and I felt 'I'm strong. I can make it on my own.' So this approach led me to be magnanimous and move on, not asking for any support, because I put his own needs first.

Yet, while an intuitive may reach a decision differently than a rationalist—feeling more and seeing things more holistically—both experience the same sense of completion and no regrets after the decision has finally been made. As Francine commented:

> Once I finally have made my decision, I have learned not to look back and think if I had known this or that, I would have done it differently. You can't do this. You have to realize you are

who you are at that time, and that the decision you made at that time, right or wrong in hindsight, is what you had to do at the time.

For example, that's how I feel about having an abortion in my early 20s. I don't feel now I could have made the decision any other way. There was no way that I could have a child then, because I couldn't count on anyone helping me. Also, I felt I would resent the child and couldn't properly care for it. So I feel that's what I had to do at the time. So I can't look back and regret it, though I suffered in making the decision. It was the right decision at the time, though I would make a different decision now, since I'm in a different position.

THE RATIONAL INTUITIVES AND INTUITIVE RATIONALISTS

Still others more equally combine resolving dilemmas both rationally and intuitively. Those who are more intuitive than rational might be called Rational Intuitives, while those who are more rational might be called Intuitive Rationalists.

What characterizes both is their emphasis on having a variety of methods to draw on, so they can be alternatively rational or intuitive or a combination of both based on the situation. It is as if they have a repertoire of approaches to draw on to find the best approach to fit the situation.

Bret, a gay political consultant in his 40s, described himself in these terms. He spoke about being generally very rational in his approach, but when he felt very emotional about something, particularly in personal situations, he would act on a more intuitive, gut level basis. As he put it:

> When I'm personally and emotionally involved, whether it's a personal, professional, or political situation, it's much more difficult for me to recognize and deal with conflicts. Then, I respond more on an immediate gut level, such as if the issue deals with my relationship with a domestic partner or gays in the military. Then, sometimes I get angry and blow off the handle.
> But if I can look at something analytically, which I try to do,

then I'm able to weigh the various things involved and if appropriate, talk to other people or act as a kind of broker. As long as I don't feel emotionally involved or can be detached, I usually weigh what I would do personally and what's best for the organization, since I'm an organization person and the organization's strength is important to me too. I remove my own emotion and feelings from the process.

Similarly, Lars, an academic in his 40s, working on an M.A. in Philosophy, felt the rationalist-intuitive perspective advantageous in providing more options for problem solving, noting that:

The more options you have to deal with the circumstances, the more you are in control and the better the outcome is likely to be. For example, sometimes even if I feel angry about something, I will hold it back and not show my feelings at all to keep matters from getting worse.

As for Dave, a scientist in his 50s, the key to resolving ethical dilemmas successfully was in using a combination of approaches in a balanced way. As he observed:

I don't think you can isolate one ethical approach in a vacuum from the others. So I use a combination of weighing alternatives, being aware of the rules, thinking about what's right in a particular situation, using my intuition, or other considerations.

What I do depends on the situation. In my view, there are two basic kinds of ethical questions. One is the situation where you know something is good or bad and you know you should do what is good on a deeply knowing, intuitive level. That's what happened when my own funds were running low and I had some money in a trust account for my daughter's last year in college. I thought at one point that I could borrow some money from that account and then pay it back. But I realized that this would be doing a selfish thing instead of doing an ethical thing. So I didn't yield to that temptation and the money stayed in that account. But then there are other situations where nothing is clearly good or bad, so it's harder to decide. That's when I try to look at the down side and the upside and weigh things in a more logical rational way.

DETERMINING YOUR OWN STYLE OF MAKING CHOICES

People thus vary widely in their style of making ethical choices—from the person who responds in a highly intuitive way to highly analytical rationalist. In the middle is the person who combines both of these approaches as a rational-intuitive or as an intuitive-rationalist.

Still, there is a continuum in the way people generally respond, because we are all to varying degrees rational or intuitive. Additionally, we are all affected by the situation, our experiences over time, the person or group we are with, and other factors.

Conceived of as a continuum, this Rational-Intuitive Dimension or Scale looks something like this:

Intuitive-Rational Scale

Where do you fall on the scale? If you are more intuitive in your approach, you may be able to sense this by visualizing where you might be and seeing yourself someplace on the scale. If you are more rational, you may feel more comfortable seeing where you fall after answering a questionnaire and scoring yourself. If so, you'll find an Ethical Approaches Questionnaire in the Appendix. This includes questions on how intuitive or rational you tend to be and will give you a score on this dimension.

USING DIFFERENT APPROACHES IN DIFFERENT CONTEXTS

This Style of Choosing—rational or intuitive—is also strongly related to two additional dimensions that exist beyond the four categories of the Ethical Choices Map. These are the spatial and time dimensions—one's approach in different situations (spatial) and one's approach at different stages of life (time).

Although the sampling of people interviewed was small, the Intuitives, Rationalists, and those in the middle tended to show distinct differences in their approach to different situations. All of them tended to draw more on their intuition in the personal sphere, while they tended to be more rational in deciding what to do in the business/professional sector.

In addition, whatever their style, people tended to act more emotionally and more informally, with less regard for the rules in the personal sector, while they were more apt to follow the rules and act pragmatically in the professional/business arena.

A result of this personal/professional distinction is that many intuitives tend to hold back their natural tendency to respond intuitively to better fit in in the business sector, while many rationalists try to respond more intuitively and emotionally with family and friends. Still some respond the same way regardless of the context. As for those in the middle (the rational-intuitives or intuitive-rationalists), they adapt to the context, since that ability to adapt and choose among a repertoire of approaches is central to their overall way of making ethical choices and resolving problems.

RESPONDING DIFFERENTLY TO DIFFERENT SITUATIONS

These differences in response in one's personal life and one's professional or public life may be affected by many other factors—such as the length of a relationship, how close one feels to another person, and whether that person is in a dual role (i.e., both a friend and business associate). These differences occur because people generally distinguished between the two realms of life. As illustrated on the Zones of Making Ethical Choices Chart (described on page 61), one's personal life includes the three inner rings of the circle (including oneself, one's family and intimate others, and friends, dates and distant relatives), while one's professional/public life includes the outer three rings (including work, business and professional associates; the local community and general public; and finally society as a whole).

Again and again, the people I interviewed pointed up these personal and professional/public differences, emphasizing how they are more apt to use more informal, less rule-driven approaches in their personal life compared to more formal rule-based responses in the professional/public arena. A key reason is that the former involved more emotional relationships, and any problems that developed, particularly with intimate others and close family members and friends, were more complicated. Thus, it was harder to respond logically or rationally; the situations and the rules were less clear.

By contrast, in work and public settings there were more apt to be rules in place for relating and dealing with problems, such as codes of ethics in many professions, like psychotherapy and the law. Then, too, people were more apt to face practical, survival requirements, such as having to act certain ways or not say anything about something that offended one's sense of ethics in order to keep a job.

Yet even within these settings, Intuitives and Rationalists tended to respond somewhat differently. While the Intuitives found it somewhat easier to adjust to the clearer rules and pragmatic requirements of the workplace, the Rationalists sometimes found it hard to deal with uncomfortable emotional terrain in personal relationships.

BEING CONSISTENT FROM SITUATION TO SITUATION

The few interviewees who claimed to be consistent in both the personal and professional domains were Intuitives or Rationalists. Intriguingly, while the Intuitives reported having underlying spiritual or religious beliefs that helped them maintain this consistency, the Rationalists were nonreligious.

More specifically, though the two Intuitives believed in very different religions—one a conservative fundamentalist, the other a New Age liberal—both held such powerful beliefs that they carried them into their whole life and tried to apply them everywhere.

As Trudy, the conservative fundamentalist social worker, put it:

I'm pretty simple. What you see is what you get. I'm hardly changeable, whatever the situation. I try to apply the same basic ethical principles at all times.

And Andy, the New Age liberal marketing and sales manager, commented:

I've always been a proponent of the ideal that one could do the same all the time....In business, many times when people say, 'It's just business.' It's almost like there's an expectation in business that you'll lie. But I don't do that. I might perhaps stretch the truth in a situation, like talk about the benefits of my product a little bit more than if I was talking to a friend. But I would be honest with both of them—my friend and someone in business. I try to apply that same basic principle of being honest and fair with people everywhere.

As for the two Rationalists, who used the same analytical style in both professional and personal matters, they did not have core spiritual or religious principles guiding them to this consistent approach, since they were both nonreligious. But as rationalists, they tried to do the most practical, pragmatic thing they could, and determined this by weighing the alternatives or costs and benefits of one action or another each time.

As Pam the nurse noted:

I pretty much use the same ethical approach at all times. I weigh everything out and see what is the best thing to do, whether at work or on deciding on what to do about a relationship in my personal life.

And to quote Bret, the political consultant:

Just as I'm more of a utilitarian in deciding what to do in my work as a political consultant and political activist, so in my relations with my family, I've been very utilitarian too. I look at what's in the best interest for myself and others as I view it, though after that I bring in my intuition.

USING DIFFERENT APPROACHES IN DIFFERENT SITUATIONS

Most people, though, do use different styles to decide what to do in an ethical dilemma in different situations. However, while those who combine the intuitive and rational styles seem to readily choose different approaches to adapt, Intuitives often have to become more rational and practical-minded in the workplace. Conversely, while Rationalists have to let go of their more rational approach in their personal lives to have smoother relationships.

For example, Tom the physicist, who used a combination of approaches, found it relatively easy to shift from one approach to another in different settings, commenting:

> I think in the political arena and in business, you have to pay more attention to the written rules that others are supposedly observing. In personal things, you don't have to go so much by written rules but by your intuition. But then, if you go against something you've agreed to, you might be in trouble. So you've got to be ready to use both approaches—the rational and intuitive—in both situations.

By contrast, Alan, the business manager, who viewed himself as a very logical, rational person, permitted his emotions and intuitions freer rein after he got married. As he explained:

> It used to be that I only followed one principle, being logical, straightforward. But since I mellowed with age and getting married, I've let emotion take part more. So I will follow different paths. At work, I'll do what's best for the company generally, based on what logically seems to make the most sense. But at home, even if it's not good for me, I'll frequently do whatever is best for my wife, since she's working hard to get through school and I want to make sure she doesn't have to worry about anything but her grades. So I'll use all different types of approaches now in making ethical choices. I'm not so stringent anymore.

Alternatively, Francine the PR free-lancer, who was generally very emotional and intuitive, viewed the business world as the place where she had to follow the rules or make compromises, while she could be who she really was and respond intuitively in personal relationships. As she commented:

> With my family, it's a lot more emotional and intuitive, and I try to do what's best for everybody. At work, you can be much more objective and rational...For example, in some cases, when I had to choose between right and wrong, I found myself having to go along with what my boss wanted, although I would always state that I didn't feel what I did was necessarily correct. My boss didn't fire me, but I didn't get advanced because of it. But at home and in personal situations, I found it easier to really be me and make the choices and take the actions I really wanted to do.

STYLES OF MAKING CHOICES, ORIENTATION, AND THE SITUATION

In short, there seems to be a relationship between the way people approach making ethical choices generally (Rationalist or Intuitive) and the situation (i.e., business/public versus personal/private). Considerations about the rules of the road in different settings also come into play, as do concerns about doing what's best for oneself or for others, and whether to be more pragmatic or do what one has been taught is morally right.

At any given time, one or more of these factors may be more or less relevant, affecting how we respond, although some people are more apt to approach the issue logically or intuitively, depending on the situation. Too, some are more consistent than others in what they do. And over time, people often change in their perspective, while situations and relationships continually change, as well.

The following chapters will look at these differences more closely and discuss how the different approaches are applied by people with different perspectives in different settings.

CHAPTER 7

•

ASSESSING YOUR ORIENTATION

The self/other orientation is a central principle in traditional moral thinking, since we are taught that this be altruistic and help others orientation is the ethical thing to do. You can see this ideal elevated to a moral principle on the national stage, such as when it is considered more ethical to help faraway and poor countries where our national interest is not at stake, than to make decisions in the national interest (such as going to war in the Gulf because of oil). Similarly, we look up to spiritual leaders like Mother Teresa or public figures like Colin Powell who act to help others. On the personal level, this self/other orientation comes into play when we have to decide to do something for our kids or parents because we put their interests above our own or to do something for ourself (such as taking an undesired job to support our kids versus pursuing a risky dream of becoming the artist we want to be).

Yet while we teach the principle of putting other's needs first by being altruistic and doing for others, choosing to act in self-interest is an ethical choice, and often it is necessary for personal survival. In fact, being too focused on others' needs and not on one's own can be self-destructive, as described not only by some interviewees, but in the reports of many psychologists, journalists, and members of self-help groups. The co-dependent in an alcoholic relationship or the battered wife in an abusive relationship are examples of those who put others' needs first to an extreme.

This said, we all fall someplace on the Self-Other continuum in our orientation to resolving ethical dilemmas. On the Ethical Choices Map, this dimension is presented as a either-or distinction, although this dimension is really a continuum like the other dimensions. Our position on this continuum can, just like how rational or intuitive we are, change in different situations and at different times. Also, the importance of this dimension, relative to the other three dimensions on the Ethical Choices Map depends on the circumstances, as well.

THE SELF-OTHER ORIENTATION AND DIFFERENT SITUATIONS

When are people more likely to use one approach rather than the other? Generally, the interviewees were more likely to think of themselves when it came to career and business/professional issues and more apt to think of others when personal relationships, particularly children, were involved. A few, who were active in community and political issues, whether conservative or liberal, were also apt to think of ethical issues from a broader societal viewpoint, feeling that they should sacrifice their own interests at times to this larger cause.

There also seems to be a relationship between one's ability to think of others and one's economic situation. When one is in a more stable or higher-income financial situation, one is better able to consider others, much like a politician may devote himself to social causes or a philanthropist to doing good, because he has the financial support to do so. For example, Brett the political consultant, tended to put the needs of the organization first and engaged in political battles to help others, since he could support himself on a trust left to him by his mother.

By contrast, when one is in a lower-income financial status, one must be more self-oriented to survive, which some of the artists, writers, and entrepreneurs I spoke with emphasized. They tended to put their own career concerns first, so they could establish a secure base for themselves, before they could give as much priority to others' concerns.

Jerry, the lawyer in his 30s, who was still struggling to get his own legal practice established, pointed out that he had to put himself first now, though he hoped to be more socially concerned in the future. As he explained:

> Right now, I'm starting up a new business, so most of my energy is going towards my own gain. But as I get more stable in my own business and financial situation, I'm going to put more energy into helping other people.

Orientations can often change over time, too, particularly when one discovers a particular orientation isn't working well. Tom, the scientist, experienced this, after being more self-centered in the way he related to people, notably girlfriends, when he was younger. But after he found that approach didn't work very well and led to the loss of many relationships, he gradually became more concerned about others, and he more often put their needs and demands first, resulting in improved relationships.

Conversely, Francine, the public relations freelancer, felt that she was too likely to consider another's needs to the detriment of her own. That's what happened when she gave up her chance for a good financial settlement after she broke with her first husband, because she felt sorry for him. As a result, she had a hard time struggling, often living on the financial edge, as she tried to make a go of things in a new city. In retrospect, she wouldn't have made the choice she did, though she felt it the right thing to do at the time. By contrast, now she more often puts her own needs first, though still very concerned about others.

MALE-FEMALE AND OCCUPATIONAL DIFFERENCES IN ONE'S SELF-OTHER ORIENTATION

Another way to think of these differences in the Self-Other Orientation is to think of the distinction between Givers (other oriented) and Takers (self-oriented). There are commonly distinct gender differences in these approaches, since women have traditionally been taught to be supportive and nurturing, men to be achievement-oriented and competitive. And this is what I found in my small survey. The women I spoke with were much more likely to be altruistic, accommodating, and put other's needs first—and sometimes they felt they were doing too much of this, particularly in personal relationships, By contrast, the men were more apt to put self-interest first, especially in making work choices. However, at times they felt they were too self-interested to their detriment was in relationships, such as described by Jerry.

In turn, this difference between men and women in the Self-Other Orientation is very basic to the differences in the way men and women have been brought up to fill different roles—men the aggressive providers, women the more receptive nurturers trained to help others. From this traditional point of view, being self-oriented would contribute to the man aggressively going out and achieving success whether in the hunt or a modern day job. Conversely, being other-oriented would contribute to the woman being receptive and ready to assist and care for the male after he returned from being the provider. Of course, the traditional roles have changed and men and women share more equally in the home and workplace. But boys and girls still get different messages in growing up about the proper way to behave, contributing to these male-female differences in the Self-Other Orientation seen today.

One also might relate this Self-Other Orientation towards one's position of power. The more power one has, the more one can act to further the interests of the self—and traditionally, men have had more power. Conversely, when one has less power, one has to defer more to others, and thus be more other oriented. This distinction would likewise contribute to women more often being the other-oriented Givers, men the self-oriented Takers.

Although I had only a small sample, the women and men in the group reflected this common pattern. The vast majority of the women viewed themselves as other oriented—about 75% of them, while the rest saw themselves as a mixture of both orientations. None described herself as primarily self-orientated. By contrast, about half of the men were more apt to put their self-interest above the interests of others in dealing with ethical issues, and the rest split about evenly between being more other-oriented or balancing the self-other orientation.

In addition, there seemed to be a close connection between the types of professions people were in and their usual orientation. For example, those who worked on their own or had to be aggressive on the job were more likely to put their self-interest first (such as two writers, the academic, two lawyers, and the supervisor who described his government job as a battle zone where he had to repeatedly resolve conflicts between employees).

By contrast, those who worked in helping and people-oriented professions were more likely to put others first in making decisions. For example, some of the other-oriented people included the nurses, teacher, social welfare worker, and people involved in advertising, PR, politics, broadcasting, and sales. Those who had a more balanced self/other orientation included two therapists and the scientist, architect, computer writer, architect, and a nurse.

Here are a sampling of comments from people with these different orientations:

Those with a stronger other-orientation who found it worked for them:

Trudy, the social welfare worker who was active in conservative politics to contribute to society, had this to say:

> I believe that when you do things that are best for others, you are acting out of self-interest, too, when you are successful at the things that you are trying to accomplish.
>
> So I try to do what's best for the most people. I've always been like that. I got a degree in social welfare, because that's what I wanted to do. Now I'm running for political office, because I think that's very important to help others. I have had to give up a lot to do this—it takes all of my time. But it's worth it to me, because I want to do what I can to help my society.

And Nancy, the art director, who gained fulfillment in putting others first, said this:

> I tend to always think of the other person first and put myself in the background. But I like to help people. I'm very altruistic. I volunteer a tremendous amount to organizations I believe in.

That was the way I was raised. My mother did that. We believe in giving ourselves as part of our duty as people in our society, and I feel very good about doing that.

Those with a strong other-orientation who thought they gave too much:

Francine, the public relations free-lancer, who felt she often gave too much and didn't think enough of herself—especially in personal relationships, noted:

> I tend to do what will help the most people or act for altruistic reasons to benefit an organization a lot. But sometimes that's not the best thing for me. For instance, at work, I once went to battle for what was best for everybody and really fought for that. But I think that held me back from getting ahead and getting promoted myself.

Bret, the political consultant, who felt he sometimes thought too much of the team as a team player, noted:

> Being an organization person, I look at what's in the best interest of the organization, though sometimes I don't say no enough. So I overextend myself and I don't do what I've wanted to do for myself.

Those with a strong self-orientation, who found it suited their style:

Henry, the supervisor, who felt he needed to put self-interest first to survive in a competitive, dog-eat-dog world, explained:

> I'm becoming more of a mercenary as I get older, simply because I have to think more about making money. I won't cross certain lines, such as doing something that's blatantly illegal or I know will seriously harm someone. But I'm less altruistic now than I used to be, such as when I used to fight for my fellow workers in the union, because now I put my own interests and needs first.

Bill, the lawyer, who felt especially drawn by the attractions of status and high-self-esteem, stated:

> For me, personal benefit is important, though not in the sense of financial gain. I feel I'll get that in the long-run if someone perceives me as trustworthy. What's most important is prestige and feeling good about myself. Those things mean a lot to me.

Those with a more balanced self/other-orientation, who felt they had a good balance of acting to benefit themselves or others at different times:

Tom, the scientist running for political office, reported:

> I follow my self-interest when I want to do those things that satisfy me, sometimes for monetary reasons, but not always. But at other times, I love working on political policy and school issues, because I think they will bring great benefit to the children. And I'm involved in politics for the same reason—because I think there are better ways of going about things that will be beneficial to others.

Alan, the business manager, explained that he combined these two traits thus:

> I normally evaluate the situation and generally try to do what's best for myself and my wife, while staying true to my beliefs and the logical processes I use to work through any problems. For example, at work, I've given my boss a time commitment to stay on the job for two years, and I'll stick to that if I can, though it's not a formal contract. But since we're still struggling, since my wife's in grad school, if something came up with much better pay and opportunity, then I would break my word and say: 'I'm sorry, but I've got to do it.'
>
> On the other hand, I have a very strong altruistic streak in me and ever since I've been a child, I've been fighting for one altruistic cause or another. So while I want to do what I can to help myself, I'm also concerned about the whole community, and frequently I work with the big picture and a cause in mind.

DETERMINING YOUR OWN ORIENTATION

In sum, people vary greatly in the degree to which they are self or other-oriented in making ethical choices and resolving ethical dilemmas. They range from those who are more apt to consider their own interests almost exclusively to those who are more apt to put others first, and those who fall somewhere in the middle. Often this orientation is related to gender, with women tending to be more other-oriented and men more self-oriented. Occupational choice seems closely related to orientation, too. Additionally, different situations tend to bring out different responses, with people more likely to consider self-interest in the work and professional context, and to be more concerned with the interest of others when it comes to their own family. Then, too, some may be more oriented towards others when they think about how to help society as a whole.

So where do you fit? Again, think of this self-orientation as a continuum, in which the Self-Other Orientation Dimension or Scale looks something like this:

Other First	Other-Self	Self-Other	Self First
Orientation	Orientation	Orientation	Orientation

Self-Other Orientation Scale

Where do you fall on the scale? If you have a strong intuitive style of perceiving qualities about yourself, you may be able to sense where you fall by visualizing how you are most likely to respond in most situations and imagining where you fit on the scale. Conversely, if you are more rational in your approach, you may feel more comfortable determining your orientation by answering a questionnaire and scoring yourself.

CHAPTER 8

•

UNDERSTANDING YOUR PHILOSOPHY OR
VALUES IN MAKING CHOICES

Another big split in our approach to ethical choices is deciding based on practical, pragmatic or utilitarian considerations and doing what we have been taught is the right thing to do. Sometimes the choice is the same, but often it is not, because we have different priorities.

Often what's considered right is drummed into us through guilt, which is what the Catholics or formerly practicing Catholics I spoke with often experienced. But in a strongly secular society where guilt holds little sway and materialistic values reign, the power of practical and utilitarian thinking is strong, and that's how the majority of the people I interviewed made their choices. Only a few put much reliance in traditional moral teachings, although many felt influenced by a core of moral teachings they had been brought up with, whether these were linked to a particular religious tradition or not. Sometimes these were principles a parent had taught them, such as don't harm others, be nice to people, and follow the Golden Rule. Then, over time, these principles became incorporated into an intuitive feeling or inner sense of what felt right, which often led them to make the choice taught by traditional ethical thinking. But while some came to this choice intuitively, others justified it based on practical or social considerations—it made the most sense; it was sensible; it was the best way to further a relationship, get ahead, or achieve a desired goal.

However, while doing the most practical utilitarian thing was viewed as being goal oriented, effective, and efficient, those who used it did not generally regard it as a calculating, Machiavellian approach to making decisions. Rather, they saw this practical approach as a way to choose to do what was best under the circumstances, whether they made this choice logically or by intuitive means.

THE THREE MAJOR PHILOSOPHICAL APPROACHES

There are three major approaches based on this distinction of following traditional morality versus practical considerations, although as with other dimensions, this is more precisely a continuum. Each approach was embraced by about a third of the people I interviewed, crosscutting both gender and occupational lines. For the most part, one's philosophical approach seems to be more connected with the influence of one's religious or spiritual upbringing and one's current ties to a religious or spiritual tradition.

The three basic philosophical approaches are these:

- *The Moralist*, who embraces the traditional notions of right and wrong, and rejects the Utilitarian or Pragmatic/Practical Approach as ethically objectionable, because it is contrary to their intuitive feeling of right and wrong.
- *The Pragmatist*, who embraces practical considerations, often because he or she finds traditional moral teachings not relevant to current concerns or is not currently religious.
- *The Moral Pragmatist or Practical Moralist*, who combines a mixture of both approaches.

There also seems to be a relationship between one's philosophical approach one follows and one's primary Other-Self Orientation, in that those with an other-orientation are likely to fall in the Moralist category. By contrast, those who are more Self-Oriented tend to fall in the Pragmatist category. As for those in the middle, they tend to be split in their orientation—some slightly more Other-oriented, others with more of a Self perspective.

THE RELATIONSHIP BETWEEN ONE'S ORIENTATION AND ONE'S PHILOSOPHY OR VALUES

You can use the following chart to more clearly understand this relationship between one's orientation and philosophy. This chart takes the categories illustrated on the Ethical Choices Map, but instead of just showing two opposite approaches, the two combination categories in each dimension are included, too. This reflects that these differing perspectives are more like extremes on a continuum, rather than either/or points of view. As this chart highlights, while the Moralist tends to be Other-Oriented, and both responses fall within the core of traditional moral teachings; the Pragmatist tends to be Self-Oriented, and both responses fall outside of this core. By contrast, those with a mixed approach fall somewhere in the middle.

THE RELIGIOUS AND SPIRITUAL MORALISTS: THE POWER OF MORAL AND SPIRITUAL THINKING

Some of the people who strongly embraced the teachings of traditional morality and strongly rejected the more pragmatic utilitarian approach had a strong spiritual or religious anchor in their lives, which contributed to their commitment to doing the right thing. By contrast, others came to this moralist position for more social or personal reasons. To distinguish them, the first group might be called the Spiritual and Religious Moralists; the others the Secular or Emotional Moralists. I'll discuss this first group here; the other group in the next section.

All of the Spiritual and Religious Moralists were strongly Other-Oriented. Yet while they shared a spiritual or religious anchor in common, they came from vastly different spiritual or religious traditions. Trudy, the social worker, was a born-again Protestant; Don, the broadcaster, was raised as a Catholic but now had a secular orientation; and Andy, the sales manager, was raised as a Protestant, but now was involved in Eastern and New Age traditions. Their widely divergent political views also show that people on different poles of the political spectrum can identify with this approach, in that Trudy was running for political office as a conservative, while Don was speaking for liberal causes as a broadcaster, and Andy, who considered himself a moderate, was not politically active at all. He was more interested in getting people to change personally rather than working towards political and social change.

SOME EXAMPLES OF RELIGIOUS AND SPIRITUAL MORALISTS

Trudy expressed her attraction towards doing what was morally right due to following traditional religious principles thus:

> Everything I do has one general approach. I try to do what's right; what's the best for everybody involved. I'm totally opposed to the 'ends justifies the means' approach. A lot of people follow this, particularly in the political arena. They tell a lie about one thing or another, such as about gun control or school choice, to convince others of their point of view because they feel the end justifies the means... But that's the problem with our political process today.

Don, a now secular nontraditional moralist, explained how he came to embrace a similar approach:

> Following the principles of right and wrong is fairly common in my process. I'll say what I think, even if it isn't popular, such as when there was a controversy over the mural of Malcolm X at San Francisco State. The prevailing sentiment was this was a racist picture, which it was, and should be covered up. But I believed in the artist's freedom of expression, and spoke out about it, because it fit my sense of what is right.

While Andy arrived at the same perspective, he explained his rationale for embracing it in New Age karmic terms:

> Though I don't think there's a right and wrong in the traditional religious moral sense, I think there's an energetic conse-

quence to making decisions from the point of view of lessons. That's what karma means. So if you act only in terms of current practical advantages, you'll experience negative consequences which is the karmic lesson, which is designed so people will pay attention to what they are doing. That's why I look at things from this long term karmic view; I think you have to look at the long-term consequences.

THE SECULAR AND EMOTIONAL MORALISTS: DOING THE RIGHT THING FOR SOCIAL OR PERSONAL REASONS

In contrast to the Religious or Spiritual Moralists, the Secular or Emotional Moralists generally made choices for moral reasons and rejected utilitarian concerns for two different reasons. They felt that other people or larger social concerns should come first, or they were drawn intuitively or emotionally towards doing what they felt was the right thing.

Like the Religious or Spiritual Moralists, almost all the Secular or Emotional Moralists were Other-Oriented and included both men and women from different religious backgrounds, although none was actively practicing any religious tradition. While all expressed varying degrees of concerns for other people or society that steered them away from a utilitarian orientation, they were not influenced by current spiritual or religious concerns like the Religious and Spiritual Moralists.

SOME EXAMPLES OF SECULAR AND EMOTIONAL MORALISTS

Terry, the artist and academic, reflected this moralist and anti-pragmatist point of view in his feeling that he was drawing on traditional Judeo-Christian principles, though he reinterpreted them into a modern global perspective, which expressed his strong concern for the underdog and exploited. As he described it:

> I use basic traditional Judeo-Christian principals, but I feel they
> have to be interpreted into the twenty-first century. You know

there are certain fundamentals, such as it's wrong to kill and it's wrong to steal. But sometimes you have to determine what is killing, what is stealing, and other principles in terms of the modern age. Still, these are good basic principals that I was raised on, and I think the basic principles other cultures use are as valid, too.

At the same time, we have to realize there really is no complete right and wrong. There is a lot of gray, and when there is, we need to have compassion and mercy, as well. So we should be open to dialogue, since different things have different values. We have to look at all the possibilities and implications.

Karen, the advertising company owner, traced her moral roots to her upbringing in a Jewish family, and rejected utilitarian thinking, when it was used to justify what she considered unfair dealings in business or immoral practices in society. As she explained:

> I don't know about what's taught in the Bible, because I never read it. But I was brought up very much by the golden rule, to do others as you would have them do unto you, and I tend to run my life that way.
>
> I also don't use the utilitarian or pragmatic approach in making my decisions to justify something I think is wrong, such as war or representing a harmful product in my business. I don't think the ends justify the means, and I won't do it.

As for, in Francine, the PR consultant, her strong moral core came from being brought up as a Catholic, though she wasn't a practicing Catholic now. She also found it difficult to be pragmatic because she tended to become too emotional about things that were important to her, and her emotions strongly influenced her actions, often leading her to do what was impractical but felt good. As she told me:

> As much as I don't follow the Catholic Church today, I still have a lot of stuff ingrained me...Though I rebelled a lot in my teenage years, as I got older, I found the lessons I had learned were still there. So that's one reason I don't believe that the ends justify the means, and for the same reason I don't use a cost benefit approach towards weighing things. I'm not good at ra-

tionally sorting things out. I'm far too emotional for that. Sometimes I have tried. But almost always, I end up going by my feelings at the time, and I make my decision by what seems right at the moment.

THE PRAGMATISTS: DOING WHAT WORKS

Unlike the Moralists, the Pragmatists place practical or utilitarian concerns high in making ethical choices. They are interested in doing what works, whether they come to this alternative by rationally weighing and analyzing or feel more intuitively that something is the sensible, effective, or most practical thing to do under the circumstances.

Moreover, they give little or no weight to traditional religious or spiritual considerations. They did not practice the religion they had been brought up in, described themselves as atheists, and in one case followed a mystical spiritual discipline that stressed self-mastery and control, though their backgrounds represented a wide mix of religious practices growing up. They also had a range of political orientations, from conservative to liberal. But there was a male-female difference, in that the men were somewhat more likely to be Pragmatists than the women, perhaps because men are generally raised to be more results oriented; while women are more apt to be concerned about relationships and the process of getting to the goal.

Some Examples of Pragmatists

Here are some examples of the way the Pragmatists described their outlook of making practical ethical decisions.

Some of the men I interviewed had this to say:

Dick, the architect, commented:

> I tend not to follow any religious teachings that I can think of. Instead I tend to do a combination of things that will be effective in a particular situation. I'll break or question the rules if necessary, use my intuition, do what's best for me or the client, as appropriate, whatever works in the situation.

Bill the lawyer, said:

> Following the moral principles of what's right or wrong is not a motivation for me. Rather, I ask myself: 'Does it work?' If something is illegal or unethical because of legal or professional purposes, I won't do it, because it can come back to haunt you later if you do.
>
> I also try to get my clients to look at things that way. I try to get them to be practical. For example, I'll sit down with my clients, even sometimes with the other side, and say: 'Look, here are all the things we can do. But what are the outcomes if we do this or that, and what are the relative advantages?' Thus, I try to focus on what makes the most sense under the circumstances, as well as what's legal and ethical to do.

Henry, the supervisor, stated:

> I don't think there's any such thing as right or wrong unless it involves legal matters. My feeling is that as long as something doesn't physically hurt somebody, fine.
>
> Rather, I tend to look at the results of an action, and in some cases, I think that the ends justify the means, as long as no one is getting hurt, and there's some gain in doing it. And that applies in my personal life as well as my life professionally.
>
> For example, if I see a woman I want to make love to, I think the ends justify the means in trying to convince her to do that with me, as long as I'm not using force or alcohol. Or at work, I wouldn't take a job with a company that's going to cheat people. But if the company has a product and doesn't know if it's safe or not, and I feel the product is safe, even though the environmentalists do not, I would be willing to work there if I felt it was a good job offer.

Alan, the business manager, explained:

> To my mind, there are very few true moral principles, perhaps since I didn't have a religious background. To my mind, one should just go with straight logic, and think about what is bad, what is good, essentially what causes the least or most harm.
>
> I believe very strongly I am 100% responsible for what I do, and generally I like to work things out logically to decide what

works and produces the best results when there's a problem to resolve.

Here are some examples of what the women with a more Pragmatist outlook said:

Kelly, the speaker and PR consultant, said:

> I don't believe in organized religion, so I don't follow traditional moral teachings. I think you have to look at the complexities of a given situation. Things aren't that simple that you can just apply these traditional principles.
>
> Also, I think about the results and what's good or bad in certain situations, since I have a strong logical side to me, and I weigh things back and forth in deciding what to do.

Iris, the psychotherapist, emphasized how pragmatic considerations were especially useful in work and everyday dealings in the community:

> I don't follow the traditional principles of right and wrong, because I figure there are a lot of ways to look at something. The traditional principles are too black and white for me.
>
> Instead, I use other ways of deciding what to do, including considering the consequences or results. What I choose to do may not seem like the most ethical or honest thing to do, but if it will be effective, I'll do it.
>
> For example, one time my husband rolled his truck over a couple of years ago, and after I asked him "What happened?" he said: "I think I might have run a stop sign." If true, that would mean the accident was his fault and there might be a problem with insurance and the police. So I told him: "Oh, don't tell them you aren't sure. Tell them you stopped like you should, and if they think differently, let them figure it out." And so that became his story.

FOLLOWING A MIXED APPROACH: THE MORAL PRAGMATISTS OR PRACTICAL MORALISTS

Finally, those who mix the Moralist and the Pragmatist points of view are the Moral Pragmatists or Practical Moralists. This approach seems to cut across religious backgrounds, political ties, and gender, since the group in this category was quite mixed in background. This approach even seems to cut across the self-other orientation, in that the interviewees had very varied orientations. While the majority were primarily other oriented, others fell in the self-other or self-orientation categories.

Jerry, the lawyer, expressed this middle approach, when he said:

> I look at decision-making as a kind of balancing act. I don't think there's any cut and dried formula. It depends on having a good balance, whether it's a political, social, or business situation. I think you have to balance going for the goal with the means used, as well as your own self-interest with that of others. You want to get where you're trying to go, but you want to try not to hurt other people on the way if possible. So you have to keep the means as well as basic principles of right and wrong in mind, too.

Ari, a registered nurse, felt she had come to this balanced point of view due to the strong influence she experienced from Indian and New Age teachings. As she commented:

> I think the ten commandments are inherent in every religion in the world and I try to live by those, such as not to steal. But I also take into consideration the consequences and results.

And Pam the nurse expressed this middle approach, when she said:

> I don't really go by the Bible in any formal way, but I do have a strong sense of right and wrong, and I'm sure it comes from that, since I was raised as a Catholic. For example, I believe in basic principles like you shouldn't steal things or hurt people. Besides, there's nothing to be gained by that behavior.
>
> At the same time, I'm very pragmatic, too. I think the ends justifies the means a lot of times. For example, though I'm not supposed to prescribe pain medication as a nurse, sometimes I'll do it when the doctor isn't around or hasn't authorized it, because I don't want to see a patient suffering.

ASSESSING YOUR OWN PHILOSOPHY OR VALUES

In sum, people vary greatly in their own philosophy or values—whether they make ethical decisions primarily from a moral perspective drawn from religious, spiritual, secular, or emotional sources, are more practically oriented, or tend to combine and balance the two perspectives. Often this philosophy is related to orientation, in that those with a more moral perspective tend to be more other-oriented, while those with a more practical bent tend to act out of self-interest.

Then, too, like orientation, philosophy seems to be related to gender, in that women tend to be other-oriented and more likely to respond from a moral perspective. Conversely, men tend to be more self-oriented and more likely to make decisions based on utilitarian and practical considerations.

In addition, there is a distinction between the philosophy or values one uses in the personal and public spheres, just as there is in one's orientation, because orientation and philosophy are closely linked. In general, people are more likely to use practical and utilitarian considerations in a work and professional context; and more apt to apply a more moral perspective in dealing with family matters or in thinking about social issues and society as a whole.

So where do you fit? Again, think of your philosophical or values outlook as a kind of continuum, in which the Moralist-Pragmatist Dimension or Scale looks something like this:

Moralist-Pragmatist Scale

Where do you fall on the scale? As in assessing where you fall on other dimensions, if you have a strong intuitive style, you may be able to sense where you fall by visualizing how you are most likely to respond in most situations and seeing yourself someplace on the scale. Or if you are more rational in your approach, you may feel more comfortable answering a questionnaire and scoring yourself.

CHAPTER 9

•

RECOGNIZING THE RULES WE FOLLOW

The fourth major factor influencing our ethical choices is whether we follow the rules we have learned are appropriate for a particular situation or whether we break those rules and make our own. This is the difference between being a "Follower" or an "Innovator." Often, we choose to innovate, creating new rules because we feel that's the practical, sensible thing to do; so Innovators may tend to be Pragmatists, as well. Additionally, since Pragmatists often act for their own benefit, Innovators may tend to be self-oriented, too. But other Innovators might choose to create new rules because others are doing what they feel is not "right," so they act innovatively to right the wrong. An example is the whistle-blower who pulls the plug on a seemingly corrupt and harmful way of doing business. Then, too, a person may take an innovative action to help others, so innovating can be for altruistic or other-oriented reasons, as well.

Normally, though, we are taught to conform, to go along with the group. Even though in the United States, we place such a high value on individualism and independence, we still expect people to follow the rules to achieve and gain success. The idea is to win, but play by the rules. That's why there's a strong pressure on people to be a team player, go along with the peer group, and fit in, and a powerful dislike of the person who goes too far in his or her own way. We make things hard for the whistle-blower, the turncoat, the eccentric, the deviate, the spy. We want people to stand out and shine, but not too far or in undesirable ways. Then, we react by disparaging and rejecting the person who has crossed the line.

This pull in two directions can create ethical choices over what to do—should one follow the rules or not? This consideration, in turn, intersects with other factors affecting our choice: What's right and wrong? What's of most benefit to others or ourselves? Additionally, our style of choice—rational or intuitive—comes into play in deciding how to weigh these options or in sensing what feels right or good in a particular situation: going along with the rules or creating new ones we feel are better.

In some cases, the rules are very clear. And in certain professions, there are formalized, often very detailed, rules of ethical conduct. For example, lawyers have an extensive professional code of ethics with rules governing numerous situations. And other professions, including doctors, therapists, police officers, and journalists—have well-developed codes of ethics, too.

In many other situations, especially in personal relationships and in the family, the rules are much less clear. Moreover, as times and technology change, the traditional rules change, too, and often heated debates result over what the new ethical codes for behavior should be, such as in current controversies over human cloning, and rules about privacy in an information age. In response, new growing fields have arisen to deal with the ethical implications of new technologies, such as medical ethics and bioethics.

Additionally, principles about what's considered "ethical" differ from society to society, and within different social, cultural, racial, ethnic, and economic groups. Part of the confusion today is in deciding what rules apply when the codes of different groups come into conflict with each other. There is confusion when individuals with different opinions about the appropriate rules come into conflict, too.

Another source of confusion is that the applicable rules are often unstated. They are not written down, and sometimes not even formally discussed or expressed. Rather, everyone seems to know or take them for granted. Then, too, adding even further complications, there may be a distinction between the formal rules—what's written down or verbally agreed upon, and the informal rules—what everyone does in practice, such as in the office. It's like the laws against speeding. You're not supposed to drive over 55 or 65 on the freeway, but if the road is clear and straight, everyone goes much faster.

Thus, when any ethical dilemma comes up, the question of what rules to follow often arises—although the applicable rules may be more or less formal, stated or unstated, outwardly agreed upon or quietly practiced. While Followers are more apt to go by the rules, whatever they are, if they can figure them out, Innovators are more apt to improvise by applying or creating rules more spontaneously to suit the situation. Another complication is that one may tend to follow the rules in certain types of situations—such as at work, particularly if one is an employee with little power; while one may be more of an innovator in other settings—such as in one's family and personal life.

THE THREE MAJOR APPROACHES TO THE RULES

As in the case of Orientation and Philosophy, there are three major ways of relating to the rules:
- *Being a Follower*—determining the rules in a particular situation and going along with them;
- *Being an Innovator*—questioning the rules and being ready to create new ones;
- *Being a mixture of Follower and Innovator*—seeking the middle way between following the rules and creating new ones when it seems necessary and sensible to do so.

THE RELATIONSHIP BETWEEN ONE'S ATTITUDES TOWARDS RULES, PHILOSOPHY, AND ORIENTATION

One's attitude to the rules appears to crosscut gender and occupational lines for those I spoke with. There also didn't seem to be much connection with one's religious background or political orientation. Individuals of various backgrounds showed varying attitudes to the rules, with one exception: liberals were more likely to be Innovators.

However, there did seem to be a connections between one's attitude towards rules and one's philosophy and orientation. In general, the Innovators were likely to be strongly moral and not pragmatic in dealing with dilemmas, perhaps because they were willing to speak up and create their own rules regardless of the practical circumstances. On the other hand, the Followers were more likely to be pragmatic or seek a balance between following the rules or not—a practical approach to the rules.

One's approach to the rules and one's Self-Other Orientation also seemed to be linked. Generally, Innovators were likely to be oriented towards others, Followers more self-oriented, perhaps because those less concerned about self-considerations might be more willing to risk breaking the rules which might bring social censure and personal criticism.

So what are people likely to do in different situations? Here's how the interviewees responded.

THE FOLLOWERS

While those who viewed themselves as Followers came from a wide variety of backgrounds and orientations, they shared a desire to go along with the rules of whatever situation they were in. If they didn't like the situation, they would seek out another situation where they felt more comfortable. They were strong and loyal team players if they worked in an organizational setting, such as Trudy and Bret, who were active in politics. Some wanted to go along with what their community of peers did, even if that wasn't what the code of their profession advised, such as Gaby, the therapist. And some didn't want to make waves to better get along with people, such as Sam, the writer, who worked as a stand-up comedian on the side.

Here are some of their comments, reflecting their desire to conform, belong, and fit in.

Trudy:

> I generally follow the rules or the customary practice in a particular situation or with a particular group. If I'm in a group of people who believe a certain thing or are involved in a certain activity, I will go along with the group for the most part.
>
> For example, when I'm traveling, I try to follow the custom wherever I go. Or say I'm at a meeting and don't like what's

going on. I won't disrupt the meeting by making a scene or storm out, even though I might disagree. I believe in respecting the other person and that means going along with their rules when I'm in their environment.

Bret:

> I think you have to be conscious of what's suitable or not in a particular situation to get along. I try to do this even when I run into things that really offend me. In many cases, I believe in putting those things on the shelf, and trying to work with others in that situation if that seems beneficial in the long run. But there are other times when things are so objectionable that I will leave or object. So for me it's a combination of following along with the rules where it seems appropriate; trying not to be bothered by some things that disturb me so I can continue to work with the group if that seems feasible; or finally, moving on to find a situation where I feel comfortable, if something bothers me too much.

Gaby:

> I think of ethical dilemmas as related to rules. In the various psychotherapy organizations I belong to, we have ethical guidelines and I try to apply these when a conflict comes up. But in my family, I'm much more spontaneous and informal.

THE INNOVATORS

In contrast to the Followers, who were very aware of the rules and tended to follow them, the Innovators spoke about being rule breakers. Their style was to question rules and authority, wonder why things should be as they were, and go their own way. Bucking the rules was often not the most practical thing to do, but most tended to want to do the right thing as Moralists, rather than Pragmatists. Accordingly, they often spoke up or acted based on what they believed, which in many cases made them gadflies in confronting their organization or others they felt were doing wrong. Some did so because of a desire to help other or society in general, rather than thinking about the possible negative consequences to themselves.

There was no difference between the men and women I spoke to. About half of each group described themselves as Innovators—about half as Followers. But politically, the Innovators differed from the non-Innovators, since they were more likely to describe themselves as liberals, perhaps because of the "stir the boat" and social cause orientation of many liberals. Also, many Innovators described themselves as growing up in a nonreligious background, no longer practicing a traditional religion, or being currently involved in a less traditional practice, perhaps because these qualities left them freer to break and make rules.

Here are some of their comments, reflecting their free-spirited outlook.

Connie, the art director, a liberal from a Jewish background:

> I'm not likely to think about the rules in making an ethical choice. I say, rules are to be broken. I'm a free spirit, and I usually go against the grain in that area.

Dick, the architect, a liberal from a Protestant background:

> For the most part, I tend to question the rules, rather than follow them. There's no specific set of people or rules that I'm subservient to. Since I went to college and broke away from my family, I have been going through a constant process of breaking the rules or not wanting to live by other people's rules.

Don, the radio broadcaster, a liberal from a Catholic background:

> I'm a little bit schizophrenic when it comes to rules. I went to a deportment school at one point, so I know how to be polite, and I like to be gracious and considerate. On the other hand, I like to be a rule-bender, and I always ask myself if that rule applies to me, whether it's coming to a stop at a stop sign or making professional decisions about what to say on the air.

In some cases, this attitude of being an Innovator was very effective, such as when Karen the ad agency owner urged clients to break the rules to use a new approach in marketing a product, or when she warned them against following certain practices, like copyright infringement, that might result in legal problems.

But in other cases, being rebellious and ready to question the rules and authority resulted in conflicts, as Francine, the PR freelancer, reported:

> My parents always taught me a 'don't follow the crowd' kind of thinking. I've done that, but it's created problems for me sometimes. In my previous work situation, it came up all the time. I was pretty much the lone wolf and very unpopular in some cases, because I didn't go along with the crowd.
>
> For example, when I used to work in a large organization, I'm not a nine-to-five person, but I was forced into doing that. I worked better if I came in a little later and stayed later, say to nine or ten o'clock. But people resented it, because I didn't follow the crowd.
>
> Also, if something bugged me, like I saw someone treated unfairly, I would say something. A lot of people just close their eyes and might talk about a problem among themselves, but they never bring it up to their superiors. Or if they have a problem with another person, they don't talk about it with the person. But I deal with people more directly on a one-to-one basis, which sometimes creates a conflict when I confront someone. It's stood in the way of some of my promotions. However, I believe in saying something and standing up for what I think is right, even if it means breaking the rules and causing some trouble for me.

THE MIDDLE WAY: THOSE WHO BALANCE BEING A FOLLOWER AND AN INNOVATOR

Finally, some people fall somewhere in the middle between being an Innovator and a Follower. They tend to go along with the rules in some situations and break or make the rules in others, depending on circumstances and what's most important to them at the time. It's a group characterized by its diversity in background, with little difference between men and women or individuals of different political or religious backgrounds. The one difference that stands out is that the balancers in following the rules also tend to be balancers in their Self-Other Orientation and are more likely to be Pragmatists or a combination of Moralist and Pragmatist. So they tend to follow a middle road in other ways, too.

For example, Tom, the scientist, noted:

> I usually try to respect the interests of the people that I'm with and usually follow their customs unless I have a reason for not doing so.
>
> For example, I did this when I was rude to a woman the other night at a singles dinner. She used the expression: "People of color," and I've always found that expression offensive. I never reacted negatively in public to anybody before, but I took her to task for this. So that's an example where I broke the rules of politeness and rebuked this person in front of others, because I felt strongly that something needed to be said.

Similarly, Lori, the teacher, emphasized how she usually tried to follow the rules, but at times would break or bend them if they didn't make sense to her under the circumstances. As she put it:

> I always try to fit in, to follow the customs of the group. But I'm not so sure I would always follow a rule that is set out by somebody else if I can't see the purpose of it.
>
> For example, when I was substitute teaching, there's a rule that says: "Substitute teachers have to stay a half hour after the kids leave." Oftentimes, I'd get my work done and there was nothing I had to do, and I was really angry about having to stay that extra half hour. So I didn't stay that whole half hour. In fact, if I could leave exactly when I was finished working, I would.

As for Alan, the business manager, who prided himself on his rational thinking, thought it made perfect sense to balance out following the rules or breaking them as the situation warranted. As he observed:

> I was raised to believe in individuality and that my thoughts are important. I always attempt to respect and follow along and work with other people's beliefs, value systems, and customs. I don't put them down if I don't agree with them. But my decisions and the way I work ultimately are my own. I feel I am

responsible for dealing with the consequences, so I will never sacrifice my thoughts, my beliefs, my ideals, my moral values, or my processes for the sake of others. So I try to find that balance point in following the rules but remain true to myself.

Similarly, Henry, the supervisor, sought a similar balancing act, though he did so from an intuitive, "feel good" perspective. As he commented:

Whether I follow the rules or customs or not depends. I'm very intuitive and I'm very comfortable around a lot of different types of people. Normally, I try and go along with what people want, what's comfortable for them. There's no point in doing it differently unless something is to my advantage or my safety. And then I will.

In turn, many balancers took this approach towards the rules because they thought of rules as merely guidelines, to be followed or not as appropriate under the circumstances. For example, Jerry, the lawyer, explained his outlook thus:

I'm very pragmatic in considering whether following customs and rules are in my self-interest or not. I make decisions about what's right and wrong for myself and don't defer to expert decisions. Instead, I think in terms of whether following customs will get me on someone's good side, say by making them more comfortable or relating to me better, and therefore more open to a business or other relationship with me. So it's a totally pragmatic approach.

Likewise, as a lawyer, I go along with the codes of my profession for practical reasons. One reason is I'm scared of getting caught and having unfavorable consequences if I don't do something the right way. Also, I think in business, most of the rules and regulations are intended to protect the integrity of the profession and make sure the clients don't get ripped off, so that's one reason I follow them.

It's the same in my personal life. For example, I don't do anything in private that's illegal, such as using drugs. But if I disagreed with a law strongly enough and it didn't hurt anyone to do so, then I would break the law.

ASSESSING YOUR OWN ATTITUDE TO THE RULES

As people vary greatly in style, orientation, and philosophy, so they vary in their attitude towards rules—from those who tend to follow them (Followers) to those who tend to break them or make their own (Innovators). Few people I interviewed tended to be very rigid or rule-bound, most falling somewhere in the middle or being Innovators, though people in different fields or with different backgrounds might be quite different. For example, one might expect those with military or law enforcement backgrounds or people with a strong conservative political or religious views to be more rule oriented, which was generally true of the people I interviewed. In other cases, one's attitude towards the rules might be more related to personality characteristics, such as I found, too.

People are also apt to make a distinction between how one acts in one's professional and personal life, being more likely to follow the rules in one's work, particularly if one is in a profession with a detailed ethical code, such as therapy or law. By contrast, people are more apt to follow a more informal, spontaneous style in adapting and changing the rules to fit in family and personal situations.

Where do you fit? Again, think of your attitude towards the rules as a continuum, in which the Follower-Innovator Dimension or Scale looks something like this:

Follower-Innovator Scale

Where do you fall on the scale? If you have a strong intuitive style of determining what's so, you may be able to sense this by visualizing how you are most likely to react to the rules in most situations and imagining yourself someplace on the scale. Or if you are more rational in your approach, you may feel more comfortable assessing your attitude by answering a questionnaire and scoring yourself.

CHAPTER 10

•

THE RELATIONSHIP BETWEEN STYLE, ORIENTATION, PHILOSOPHY, AND ATTITUDE TO RULES

Whether you have a more intuitive or rational approach to making your choices, there appear to be some connections between your style and the three other factors: orientation, philosophy, and attitude to rules. Despite the small number of interviewees, certain patterns stood out.

STYLE AND ORIENTATION:

- The Intuitives were more likely to be Other-Oriented.
- The Rationalists were more likely to be a mixture of Self and Other Oriented.

STYLE AND PHILOSOPHY:

- The Intuitives were more likely to be Moralists.
- The Rationalists were more likely to be Pragmatists or a mixture of Moralist and Pragmatist; none were strict Moralists.

STYLE AND ATTITUDE TO RULES:

- Both Intuitives and Rationalists varied greatly in their attitudes towards the rules; in each group, most tended to be a mixture of Followers and Innovators.
- Intuitives are often Innovators.

WHAT THESE CONNECTIONS MEAN

These relationships are intriguing, because the Intuitive response falls in the central core of traditional moral and ethical values. So do being Other-Oriented and being a Moralist, and these three approaches seemed linked to some degree.

On the other hand, while being a Follower is linked to traditional moral and ethical values, most of the interviewees fell outside the traditional ethical pattern in their attitude towards rules. Whatever their style, orientation, or philosophy, most were either Innovators or a mixture of following, breaking, and making the rules. Perhaps a reason for this is that in our complex modern society with so many different rules in different settings, it helps to be able to adapt and change. Perhaps the spirit of individualism and independence in American life encourages this flexibility, too.

There also seems to be a link between being a Rationalist and being more Self-Oriented and more Pragmatic. These characteristics seem to go together well, in that rationally working things out and pragmatically weighing costs and benefits are strategies one might use to help decide what's in one's best self-interest or to find a practical solution that works. Certainly, using one's intuition can help achieve one's goals, though intuition often comes into play in less goal-directed situations, such as when one is deciding if something *feels* like the right thing to do or when one is *relating* to other people.

Finally, the Intuitive-Innovator connection seems like a natural one for many people, in that intuition is often associated with innovative leaps. It's associated with coming up with new ideas, with considering new possibilities, and, yes, with imagining and creating new rules.

USING THE FOUR DIFFERENT DIMENSIONS IN RESOLVING AN ETHICAL DILEMMA

In summary, as described in the preceding chapters, you incorporate four different qualities in making ethical choices or responding to any ethical dilemma—style, orientation, philosophy, and your attitude to rules. In any given situation, these factors (which I have also described as dimensions or categories) are joined together in different combinations, and you may be more or less likely to use a particular quality in that situation or more generally. Also, you may differ in which qualities you are more apt to use in professional or personal situations, or in relating to different people in your life. You may change over time as well, as you enter different social situations at different stages of your life.

The Ethical Choices Map is designed to help you better understand where you have been or plan how to change yourself and how you respond in the future. This way, by having an expanded repertoire of choices, you can better decide what to do to better make choices and resolve any ethical dilemmas you face. The following chapters will help you do this.

PART III

APPLYING THE ETHICAL CHOICES MODEL IN YOUR OWN LIFE

CHAPTER 11

•

PUTTING IT ALL TOGETHER: APPLYING THE ETHICAL CHOICES MAP

THE EVER-CHANGING ETHICAL CHOICES MAP

To most simply illustrate the Ethical Choices Map, I have described each of the dimensions using polar opposites, creating a chart divided into 16 sections, although this is a simplification. If each category is divided to reflect the way many people fall somewhere in the middle in each of these categories, the chart would be divided into 36 sections. Or if each of these dimensions is more accurately described as a continuum, then one's position can be even more precisely located on the Map.

Still another consideration is that one's position on the Map only reflects one's pattern of choices under all circumstances, reflecting a cumulation of one's approach to making choices in a number of situations. These might be in one's professional life and personal life generally, or in certain types of situations—such as dealing with co-workers, employees, supervisors, or business associates at work, or relating to family members, friends, social acquaintances, and members of the general public.

But these situations might be examined separately in that people may be more or less likely to use one style, orientation, philosophy, or attitude to the rules in different situations or relating to different people (such as being more rational and formal in the work setting; more intuitive and informal in personal relationships).

The dynamics of choice can thus become very complex, so rather than one overall Ethical Choices Map, one might imagine a series of Maps which apply under different circumstances. These individual Maps, such as a Map for work, a Map for dealing with the general public, and a Map for relating to friends, then combine together to create the overall Map.

MAPPING ONE'S ETHICAL CHOICES
IN DIFFERENT SITUATIONS

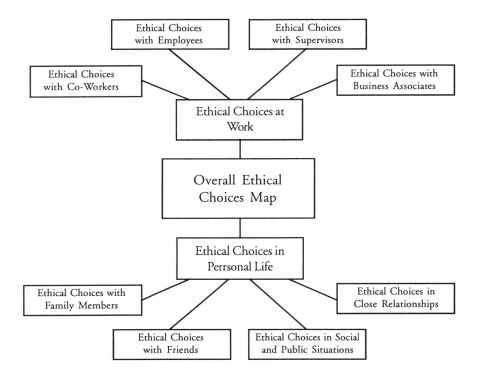

Additionally, one might think about this Map—or series of Maps—as an ever changing Map of the ethical terrain over time. For example, all of the people I interviewed spoke of the changes they experienced in their ethical perspective as they grew up and at different stages of their life. They saw themselves as very different as teenagers than as young adults, since they were now independent and had to assume certain responsibilities. Then, in their 30s and 40s, many interviewees described how they changed again, often becoming more tolerant, mellow, or "realistic" about what to expect from others.

Thus, besides a series of Maps in space representing different aspects of one's life, one might have a series of overall and special situational maps going back in time. These Maps might be represented by a series of boxes for different situations, looking something like the diagram on the preceding page.

Then, the time element might be represented by having a set of these maps for different time periods, like a series of slices through a tunnel of time. One could then compare changes in patters of choices for different periods.

APPLYING THE ETHICAL CHOICES MAP TO DIFFERENT GROUPS AND CULTURES

While each person will have his or her own pattern on the Ethical Choices Map—whether it is an overall Map or one that represents different situations and times in one's life, this Map can also be used to show how different groups and cultures differ in their approach to making choices or dealing with ethical dilemmas.

For example, I noticed similar patterns in some of the people I interviewed who came from similar ethnic backgrounds, parts of the country, or occupations. Though everyone is unique, social and cultural backgrounds and occupational and lifestyle choices contribute, too, both in shaping the ethical dilemmas one encounters and one's way of dealing with them.

For instance, a recurring dilemma for the artists and academics I spoke with was whether to pursue one's true dream of following an artistic or academic career or choosing a more secure, financially remunerative path. They faced numerous ethical dilemmas, since pursuing their passion meant making some hard decisions, such as asking their parents for continued help, despite being at an age when one is expected to be financially independent—in their 30s and 40s. Following their dream also meant not being as good a provider as expected for the men making this choice, so they had seek help from wives or significant others or persuade them to live at a lower standard of living than accustomed, while they tried to realize their dream. When I interviewed them, the artists had already made the decision to follow what felt true for them—living a life based on integrity rather than compromising as they had done in the past, though they had to borrow money or scale down their lifestyles to do so. On the other hand, the two academics I interviewed had both come to terms with not being able to pursue the full-time research and writing career they wanted, because they had to make a living. Instead, they took jobs they didn't really like and pursued their academic dream on the side. But other artists and academics might make opposite choices.

Significantly, though, all faced similar ethical dilemmas because of their life circumstances (facing an uncertain financially insecure career path), but they made choices using different styles that seemed related to their occupational background or personality characteristics. For example, the two artists used an Intuitive style in dealing with the dilemma. By contrast, one academic who specialized in text and philosophical analysis used a Rational approach, while another academic who was also an artist used an Intuitive style.

In the same way, certain types of occupational backgrounds seemed to contribute to people's attitudes towards the rules. For example, the people in professions with clear ethical codes (such as the therapists and lawyers) or those who worked in large organizations (like the supervisor, business manager, and scientist) tended to be very concerned about rules, describing themselves as Followers or a mixture of Followers and Innovators. By contrast, those who worked alone or in the entrepreneurial or creative professions (such as the ad agency owner, sales manager, the artists, the academics, broadcaster, and the writers) tended to be Innovators.

Political, and social factors also came into play. For example, a number of the interviewees who identified themselves as liberals or came from the East Coast (mostly New York) used an intuitive style in dealing with dilemmas. By contrast, those I interviewed who identified themselves as political moderates and conservatives or came from Midwestern and Western cities mostly used a rational approach.

Thus, certain patterns seemed to be associated with various background characteristics. So it seems likely that different patterns are associated with different social groups, if one looks at such characteristics as occupation, political affiliation, where raised, place of residence, and other factors.

One might also take into consideration ethnic, religious, and cultural backgrounds. For example, those from Hispanic and Asian backgrounds tend to place a very high value on the family, and this might influence them to make different ethical choices from many of the people I interviewed who tended to be more individualistic in their approach to life.

Then, too, if the Ethical Choices Map is used in different cultures in different countries, one might find still more differences.

In short, the Ethical Choices Map not only provides a personal guide on how we respond to ethical dilemmas, but it can provide a portrait of different groups and cultures by combining the profiles of numerous people from different environments and comparing them.

CHAPTER 12

•

ASSESSING WHAT'S MOST IMPORTANT

While all four factors—style, orientation, philosophy, and attitude towards rules—influence all of your decisions, certain factors are more or less important when you make choices generally or make a particular decision.

This means that not only will you fall somewhere on the Map based on your location on each of the four factors, but each Map will have a third dimension—how important or influential that particular factor is for you.

To visualize this, imagine each Map is like a flat plain or field stretching out all around you. Your overall Map is where you usually stand—and your Maps for certain types of situations (i.e.: work versus personal life) are like cities or towns on a map, with the larger cities and towns representing the areas of life that are most important to you. The particular situations (i.e., choosing to take a job or not) are like neighborhoods or blocks within the city or town. As for the time dimension, just imagine photos taken of that location at different times showing you standing at different places on that map, showing the way you and the site change over time.

To visualize the importance of a particular factor, imagine mountains or valleys rising above or dipping below the plain. If the plain is flat where you are standing, that factor is of average importance in how you make choices generally, in certain types of situations, or in a particular situation—now or in the past. But as the factor becomes increasingly important in contributing to your decision, the height of the mountain increases. Conversely, as a factor becomes less and less important, the valley becomes deeper and deeper. Taken together, the various points where your scores fall on an Ethical Choices Map become like hills and valleys dotting each map.

It is too complicated to show these variations in intensity on a simple map or chart. However, an easy way to identify these differences is to star those factors that are especially important to you with one, two or three stars depending on how important they are. The unstarred factors will be of least importance to you.

Graphically, to take a sample map, the results will look something like the Ethical Choices Map below. It illustrates an example of one person's overall results—someone who tends to be relatively rational in style, pragmatic in thinking about the consequences, self-oriented, and more of a follower than an innovator. Of these the most important factor is being pragmatic (P***), followed by going along with the group as a team player (F**), and then being self-oriented (S*). Least important is the way the decision is reached.

Table 3:
IMPORTANCE OF CHOICES ON THE ETHICAL CHOICES MAP

| | | Style of Choosing | | Orientation | |
		Rational	Intuitive	Other	Self
Philosophy or Values	Pragmatist	X P***			X S*
	Moralist				
Attitude to Rules	Follower	X F**			X
	Innovator				

In different situations or at different times, other factors may be more or less important. So, if you do a series of charts to show how you respond in different setting, each chart might show a slightly different pattern of one, two, three or no stars, reflecting what's important (*), very important (**) most important (***), and less important (no star) to you.

The chart on page 120 indicates the different areas in which you might make choices, so you can compare how you differ in different areas of your life. The starting point is the overall Ethical Choices Map, representing a cumulation of your choices in all aspects of your life. Then, you can look at how you make ethical choices in more specific areas, such as your work and personal life. Should you want to make any further breakdowns, you can choose those situations that are most relevant to you, such as how you make choices in specific areas of your work or personal life. For instance, at work, you might look at any differences in how you make choices in situations involving employees, co-workers, or supervisors. In your personal life, you might look at differences in how you relate to family members or friends or in public situations.

You might also consider comparing how you change over time in different areas of your life. To do so, simply make an Ethical Choices Map for your life generally or for different areas of your life at different time periods. Choose times when you have gone through major changes and periods of growth and compare the maps for these different times. Also, try making a map or series of maps now and do this again in the future (say in six months or a year), and see how you have changed. Likewise, you might continue to make these maps every few months and notice any trends.

THE DIFFERENCES IN WHAT'S MOST AND LEAST IMPORTANT

Just as people are unique in where they stand or score on each factor, so they vary widely in what's most and least important to them. For some people, one factor is especially important—such as using their intuition, working everything out logically, knowing the rules and following them, *or* doing the right thing. For others, two or three factors influence them the most—such as using their intuition, doing what will help the most people, *and* doing what's practical. Others use a combination of everything—and they may fall in the middle of the continuum on most factors, so they truly choose among a repertoire of influences.

I began to discover patterns as I asked people which factors were most and least important to them. Most people listed one, some two or three, and a few emphasized a combination of factors. Most people were also able to identify one or two factors that were least important, unless they felt all factors influenced their decision. But everyone differed in the particular factors they identified.

There also seemed to be a connection between how strongly people responded a certain way and how important they felt that factor was to them. For example, several people who identified themselves as strong Intuitives placed the highest priority in relying on their intuition to help them decide, while those who used a combination of the Intuitive and Rational style identified several factors as especially important to them.

MOST IMPORTANT

For most people I interviewed, the intuition was the most influential factor, regardless of how they rated in the other dimensions. About 60% rated it highest, although many rated it most important in combination with a few other factors—most notably being concerned about others or doing what seemed the right thing to do. In fact, several people suggested that the intuition encompassed all the other factors, providing them with an overall gut feeling or insight about what to do. For instance, some typical comments:

From Connie, the art director:

> I would have to say the strongest desire for me is the unconscious—being in just the purely intuition mode. That's where I really feel most confident.

From June, the tax consultant:

> My gut instinct. That's what I use the most. I just feel it in my gut, in my stomach. There's a sense of peace. When there's turmoil in my gut, I know I'm not looking at something the right way, because something is making me uncomfortable.

And Jerry, the lawyer, provided a rational, legalistic explanation of why he used his intuition the most:

> My top choice is my intuition. The reason why is that often I don't have time to go through a checklist of the various pros and cons to decide. So I use intuition as a catchall, because I think the intuition is a distillation of experience and knowledge that doesn't get processed through the linear mind, because that takes longer. So using the intuition gives you a sort of Gestalt of what you know.

The only people who didn't emphasize the importance of the intuition—by itself or in tandem with other factors—were those who tended to be very rational and pragmatic.

The other major factor that most people mentioned as especially important in making decisions was being influenced by what would help others. This was mentioned by a third of the interviewees, though most considered this a key influence in combination with the intuition.

LEAST IMPORTANT

When it came to deciding what factor was least important, many people had more difficulty deciding, because they used a combination of approaches, which included everything. Still, most did identify one and sometimes two factors as the least important influence to them. Least important for about a third of the group was the teachings of traditional religion or morality about right and wrong, perhaps because this was largely a non-practicing secular group. The other factors mentioned by about 15% of the group were following the rules or thinking things through pragmatically on a cost-benefit or utilitarian ends-means basis.

ASSESSING WHAT'S MOST AND LEAST IMPORTANT TO YOU

How would you rate what's most and least important to you? If you think back to the Ethical Choices Map—for your overall responses or for particular situations, rate each of the dimensions on importance by assigning one to three stars based on how important it is for you. Then compare how you have rated each of the dimensions.

For example, if you have given only one dimension a three stars rating, that's the major influence for you. If you have two or three dimensions with three stars (or all with two stars), then you are bi- or tri-modal in making your decisions. Or if you have identified all of the dimensions as about the same importance, then you follow a combined approach in what you consider important.

If you want to compare what's most and least important in different situations (such as in work or personal situations), do the ratings for each of these situations separately and compare the differences. You can use the chart below to rate what's most and least important to you.

RATING WHAT'S MOST AND LEAST IMPORTANT TO ME

[Rate from 0 (least) to 5 (most) important]

The Four Dimensions in Making Ethical Choices							
Style		Orientation		Philosophy		Attitude to Rules	
Intuitive	Rational	Self	Other	Moralist	Pragmatist	Follower	Innovator

CHAPTER 13

•

MAKING CHOICES IN DIFFERENT SITUATIONS: IN YOUR WORK AND PERSONAL LIFE

Different influences or factors in making ethical choices also come to the fore in different situations. A major distinction is that people are more apt to use intuitive and informal methods in making choices in their personal life and more apt to use more rational and pragmatic means in their professional and work life.

Kelly the speaker and consultant reflected this approach when she observed that:

> In personal relationships, I'm more likely to follow my intuition and do what feels right. I would be especially likely to do this if there is a lot of emotional energy between me and another person. But if it's more of a business situation, I get very much into my logical mind, and I'm more likely to weigh things to decide what's the best thing to do.

A few reported being very consistent in their approach, whatever the context. Some did so because they had strong feelings of right and wrong to guide them, which derived from a particular religious tradition or from a strong social conscience and a concern with personal integrity in all dealings. As Karen the ad agency owner observed:

> I don't think I would be more likely to use one approach than another in my family, relationships, at work, or in public. I apply the same criteria in making decisions. I think the golden rule applies generally, so I would say I don't switch for different audiences. I think my approach stays pretty much the same.

Some who were very pragmatic and utilitarian carried that over into most situations, personal as well as professional, such as Bret, the political consultant, and Pam, the nurse. As Bret put it:

> I would say I'm pretty consistent in the way I make decisions in most situations, whether they're political, personal, family, or other situations. For example, in my relations with my family, like in recently administering the estate, I've been very utilitarian, looking at what's in the best interests of everyone, as I view it. Then I use my intuition to make the final decision.

And Pam observed:

> The ethical approach I use is pretty much the same in different situations. I normally weigh everything out to see what seems to be the best thing to do.

But most people observed that they differed in the priority they gave to different factors in different situations.

For example, Terry, the academic observed:

> I think I'd be more likely to use an ends justifies the means approach in a life or death situation where someone's life was at stake. I might stretch the rules a bit to save that person. In other cases, it might be easier to know what's right or wrong. For example, say I captured a burglar in my house and I had a gun in my hand. If he was unarmed, I would be less likely to shoot him.
> But I'd be more likely to follow the rules in a social situation, and more likely to use my intuition to know what's right in a matter of faith. I might be more likely to give more weight to self-interest in making a business decision that would affect my family. And if I had a great deal of power, I would put more importance on trying to help the most other people I could.
> In short, it would depend on the circumstances, what factors would influence me the most.

Tom, the scientist said he paid more attention to the rules in work and public situations, whereas he used his intuition more in personal and family matters, explaining:

> I think in the political arena and in business, you have to pay more attention to the written rules that others are supposedly observing. In personal situations, you don't have to go so much by written rules, but by your intuition. But even then, if you go against something which you've agreed to you might be in trouble, such as not doing a task you said you would do.

For Don the broadcaster, being more flexible in work situations was a matter of making trade-offs, whereas he was more likely to hold onto his core principles in his personal life. As he put it:

> I do compromise and trade off more in my work than I do in my personal life.

In turn, a key reason for compromising, according to Andy the sales manager was that politics in the workplace made it harder to be straightforward and open in business. As he explained:

> As much as I might want to have the same ideal of integrity in business as in my personal life, I sometimes might stretch the truth or selectively report something in business, rather than being as open and direct as I would with a friend. It's because the expectation in business is different; it's more competitive; and I don't feel as close to the people I work with as the people who mean a lot to me in my personal life.

ASSESSING HOW YOU CHANGE IN DIFFERENT SITUATIONS

In sum, though some people try to be consistent in making ethical choices in different situations, commonly people vary greatly in what factors influence them. Paying attention to the rules and to what works tends to be more common in professional and work situations, while people are more apt to respond based on their emotions in personal situations, and they may feel more flexibility in how they can respond, too. This is because in personal relationships, others may be more tolerant and forgiving, although in some cases, the rules of social protocol are very important.

How do your own ethical approaches change from situation to situation? You can try rating the factors that are most and least important to you in different situations and compare the results to your overall approach. You can use the chart on the following page to do so. Rate what's most and least important to you on a scale of 0 (least) to 5 (most important).

RATING WHAT'S MOST AND LEAST IMPORTANT TO ME
[Rate from 0 (least) to 5 (most) important]
The Four Dimensions in Making Ethical Choices

Overall Response in All Situations Generally							
Style		Orientation		Philosophy		Attitude to Rules	
Intuitive	Rational	Self	Other	Moralist	Pragmatist	Follower	Innovator

Professional and Work Situations Generally							
Style		Orientation		Philosophy		Attitude to Rules	
Intuitive	Rational	Self	Other	Moralist	Pragmatist	Follower	Innovator

Personal Situations Generally							
Style		Orientation		Philosophy		Attitude to Rules	
Intuitive	Rational	Self	Other	Moralist	Pragmatist	Follower	Innovator

Particular Situations: _____							
Style		Orientation		Philosophy		Attitude to Rules	
Intuitive	Rational	Self	Other	Moralist	Pragmatist	Follower	Innovator

CHAPTER 14

•

HOW OUR ETHICAL CHOICES CHANGE OVER TIME

Besides changing in different situations, the factors influencing choice change at different ages and stages of our life. It can get a little complicated to see this on the Ethical Choices Map, but if you can imagine a different series of Maps laid over each other—and over time, there are new roads, new locations, some places from before are larger or smaller or no longer there.

This is because our ethical choices, and the Ethical Choices Maps reflecting them, are influenced by changes in society and in ourselves. As we grow and change, so does the social world around us. We are affected both by our own maturation and by social changes in our culture.

THE EFFECTS OF DIFFERENT SOCIAL TRENDS AND GROUPS THROUGH TIME

Our attitude towards rules is especially influenced by our social and political context—whether we choose that environment personally or find ourselves in it. In the 60s, for example, the trend in society was to question the rules—"Question authority!" was one of the watchwords. But now there is a swing back to seeking to restore structure, law and order. This shift is part of a continuing back and forth pendulum swing in our society between liberalism and conservatism. Like permeable sieves, we draw in these currents and are influenced by them in making our moral choices.

Then, too, the people we associate with affect what we do, while our past choices may draw us to particular friends and associates. These associations have a powerful affect, since some groups are more rule conscious and rule following than others—such as conservative groups that dress conservatively and respect authority and tradition. By contrast, other groups are much less committed to following tradition or create their own rules, such as more liberal political groups or groups of creative artists and musicians.

As social conditions and the people we associate with change over time, so do our attitudes towards rules. At the same time, the maturation process, which tends to make people more law-abiding and conformist with age, affects our attitude, too.

These social influences and personal maturation likewise affect our orientation and philosophy. For example, some social periods and groups are more other-oriented; others more oriented towards a "What's in it for me?" self-benefits approach. These social differences influence us accordingly.

As an example, the 60s was a very other-oriented time. People were encouraged to think about the potential for changing society; and many people joined new groups with communitarian and humanitarian goals, such as communes, collectives, and political activist groups. As members of these groups, people were encouraged to put the interests of the group first.

By contrast, starting in the 1970s, the shift turned towards "me." This was the time when people began to flock to personal growth groups, typified by the rise of new growth centers like Esalen in Big Sur, California. Though groups proliferated, the emphasis was on "How can I develop and grow personally?"; the ideal was to put aside overly burdensome "obligations" and feelings of guilt instilled by traditional religion and morality, now seen as burdensome, to find the true "me."

Then, in the 1980s, this "me" shift intensified, coupled with the emphasis on success, achievement, and money. The ideal was now personal mastery and power, expressed in symbols of success. As one since discredited financier, Ivan Boesky, put it as a college graduation speaker—"Greed is good."

Meanwhile, this change in orientation was accompanied by a

change in philosophy. There was a shift from the more moralistic principles of doing what is right that predominated through the 50s and early 60s, to the more pragmatic approach that was especially characteristic of the 70s' emphasis on the self and the 80s focus on success and achievement. This change led to a push to do what worked to achieve success and fortune, not necessarily what was right.

And now in the 90s, there is a swing back to more conservative and community-oriented values.

In turn, the social groups one affiliates with over time reflect these patterns to a greater or lesser degree. For example, groups of people in business are more likely to reflect this pragmatic, self-orientation, since a key business value is to do what is most efficient and effective to achieve the bottom line. By contrast, groups of people in the arts or those who support social causes are more likely to reflect a moralist, other-orientation, since such groups are focused around expressing ideas and social concerns. As society itself shifts to strengthen different groups—such as in the 60s, when social movements proliferated, or in the 70s, when me-oriented groups did— these influences affect us. They affect us more personally and strongly if we are members of these groups, and more indirectly and less powerfully when we read about or learn about these changes in the news on TV. In either case, though, they have an effect.

Even where we live at different times in our lives affects us, particularly in our orientation, philosophy, and attitude to rules, since different parts of the country and different neighborhoods show different patterns on the Maps, too. For example, certain regions are associated with being more conservative and more supportive of traditional morality and religion (like the South and Midwest), while others tend to be more liberal and less traditional (like New York and California). I found corresponding patterns in the people I interviewed. Though they might not be practicing a particular religious tradition now, the interviewees from Midwestern and Western cities outside of California were more likely to be more traditional or moderate in their Ethical Choices profiles, though moving to California where I interviewed them shaped their attitudes, too, making them more liberal than they had been.

By contrast, our style of choosing—being more intuitive or rational—seems more likely to be set like an internal rudder, reflecting our way of seeing and responding to the world. As a result, once it is set when we are young, we appear to be more apt to continue to respond to making ethical choices this way, and are less likely to be influenced by other individuals, groups, or social changes.

THE AGE EFFECT

Besides this changing social landscape, and changes in the groups we belong to and the places we live, age plays a part. We are shaped by our experiences at the different stages of our life.

In the interviews, people mentioned certain common markers when they noticed changes in how they responded ethically to different situations. Although some psychologists, such as Jean Piaget have identified stages of ethical thinking, beginning with early childhood, the interviewees, when asked about changes in their ethical approach, started with their teenage years. This was like a launching place for them, when they first became aware of their personal ethical compass that had been created by the earlier influences on them. The other major periods they identified, which had different age ranges for different people, were:

- *Young Adulthood*: the first years of independence or taking on responsibilities as young adults. This was a time when they were still single and more freely exploring what to do, just starting careers, or first taking on the responsibility of being parents (from about 18-21 to 25-35);
- *Adulthood*: the period when many felt more settled in careers, marriages, or in family relationships, and generally assumed more responsibilities to others (from about 25-35 to 35-50);
- *Entrance to Mid-life*: the period when they felt even more established and were no longer struggling to establish a career or identity for themselves (from about 35-45 to 50-65).

THE TEENAGE YEARS

Generally, the interviewees described their teen years as a time when they were especially self-oriented and pragmatic. Some noted this as a very rebellious time, when they were not likely to follow the rules or be responsible. They described it as a time when they moved away from the traditional core moral principles to strike out on their own, as part of the adolescent process of finding one's own identity. At the same time, while seeking their self-identity, many interviewees wanted to closely identify with their peer group and go along with the crowd by following the norms of their high school or college crowd.

For example, Trudy, the social worker, now in her 40s and very committed to core moral principles as a born-again Christian, went through such a period of searching. This floundering was especially intense in her case, since she was in her late teens in the late 60s, a time when not only teens but society as a whole was going through an extended rebellion against authority. As she describes it:

> I went through an "ends justifies the means" phase in the 1960s and 70s. I was 18 in 1968, and as people started reevaluating right and wrong in society, I went through the process, too. Looking back, I think I lost a lot in doing so, because now I think all that craziness was destroying our society. So that's why I'm now coming back to how I was raised.
>
> But when I was going through this phase, it created a conflict for me, because there was no strict right or wrong. This creates a situation where you have to reevaluate every issue as to whether it's right or wrong, whereas if you have a basis for right and wrong, you don't have to evaluate everything. You know what's right or wrong at the time.
>
> What led me to stop going through this "ends justifies the means" phase in the 70s was I was watching these TV shows where these young black kids were talking about how they were going to be released from jail and what they were going to do. They claimed what had happened was not their fault, and I realized they would probably end up back in jail, because no one taught them anything while they were there. In other words, they were coming up with excuses, thinking the reason they

were in jail is not because of something they did, but because society was very bad to them. And that meant they could go steal.

So they were using the ends justifies the means rational. They stole because they were poor, and this gave them the right to do so, because society let them down. That's when I realized how this thinking was harmful, because I don't think being poor is a good reason to steal, and they were using this as an excuse not to take responsibility for their own actions. Then I realized that this thinking wasn't just destroying them but all of us, because they were using this thinking to justify victimizing other people. So that's when I turned away from that kind of thinking.

Similarly, Jerry the lawyer, in his early 30s, from a nonreligious background went through the same rebellious "I don't care about the laws" period as a teen, before he gradually changed to become a more ethical and responsible adult. He explained:

My ethics definitely have gone through changes since I've been a teenager. When I was about 18, I didn't care at all what the law said. I used to think that the ends justified the means in my actions, and I used to be much more self-centered. I was always looking for shortcuts, always trying to get the most done with the least amount of work, and I didn't particularly care if I was following laws or rules.

But as I've had more experience in life, my ethics have changed a lot. I've gained more and more respect for the law, and I found it more and more in my self-interest to follow the laws.

In some cases, this period of change as a teen began with the discovery that things weren't as ideal as one had been brought up to believe. This is what happened to Henry, the supervisor, when he went to college and fought in the Vietnam war. As he described it:

I was raised, like most people, with all the Golden Rules. You didn't do this. You did that. But then I went to college, and I got a dear John letter from the girl I had been seeing and hoped to marry, which tore me apart. Then I went into combat, and saw how man can treat man. I saw butchery, I saw death, I saw my own men killed. I had to make decisions about who lived and who died, when I decided who went out on patrol, since that was almost certain death. And then I had to write letters to their parents about how they had died.

So for me, that was a real wake-up as to how things were in the real world. I had to let go of some of those old ideals about how everyone is supposed to be honest and treat everyone as they would want to be treated.

Likewise, Alan, the business manager, now in his late 20s, and very other-oriented and rules-conscious, went through a very self-centered rebellious period as a teen. Later, he felt the need to shape up and become a responsible "moral" adult, shortly before he got married. As he described it:

I got involved with drugs and drinking as a teenager. It started the summer I turned sixteen and went on until I was about nineteen, and I still drank for about a year after that. Then I stopped and I've been clean ever since. When I got involved, I was at an age when all my friends were doing it, so I tried it and did a lot of experimentation, though I'm very much against it now.

What led me to change is when my 14-year-old brother came home and saw I was on something. He told me that I was too smart to ruin my life with drugs. It was the catalyst I needed, and about two weeks later I quit. He got me thinking, and I saw that the drugs and alcohol were undermining the values that I hold important, such as having self-reliance and making clear-cut logical decisions.

I realized after I had started doing drugs, I started falling apart. I started taking advantage of friends and family and lying to them. I became very arrogant and thought myself better than other people. Also, my grades dropped off, and I used the drugs as an excuse not to do the work.

Once I realized what was happening, I stopped the drugs cold turkey, and I pulled out of the whole punk rock scene that I had been involved in. One thing that helped me to do this was my decision to get married. I had to take on a whole range of new responsibilities for a wife and family.

YOUNG ADULTHOOD

This is another period when many interviewees noticed a change in their ethical approach, though people defined when this period began and ended depending on their current age and critical changes in their own life—from 18 to 21 at the low end to 25 to 35 at the other. People had a range of experiences, from feeling freer to explore themselves and the world beyond their peer group, to settling down in a job and taking on family responsibilities. These lifestyle choices shaped by personal values, in turn, shaped later values and ethical choices.

Young Adulthood: The Explorers

For some young adulthood was a time of continued self-definition, when they sought to discover who they were and what they really wanted to be. They were very self-oriented, yet imbued with a humanitarian altruism or idealism about what could be. For example, Eric, now a computer writer in his late thirties, went through this period for about 10 years after high school, until he became more achievement-oriented in his mid-20s. He settled down into a more balanced combination of working hard to achieve an idealistic goal in his mid-30s. Each time he changed his circumstances, so did his values and his approach to making ethical decisions which flowed from these. As Eric explained:

> In certain periods of my life, different values came to the fore. From about 1973 to 1984, when I was 18 to 29, I'd say my value was open-ended learning. I just wanted to explore life and pushed everything else aside. I wanted to travel all over the world, and other things didn't matter much—security, a career, developing relationships. It was easy to do at the time. I had almost no conflict with pushing other things aside.
>
> Then, at some point, I said: "Uh, oh, I've got to make a living." I realized something had to change, because I couldn't keep doing odd jobs. So I shifted into wanting to make money, and I started facing decisions around building up some kind of security and financial basis. But after several years, I felt I was

too focused on that. I didn't feel this approach was healthy. So when I was about 36, I shifted again to a more balanced perspective.

Young Adulthood: Taking On New Responsibilities

For many, young adulthood was a time of putting aside being less responsible and self-oriented to take on more responsibility and show more concern for others.

This was the experience of Janet, now a writer in her 40s, who had been a public health nurse. After a brief period of feeling free just after college, she had a child, settled down, and became very concerned with her child's welfare. As she described it:

> While I was in nursing school in Florida, I just wanted to live life, and I didn't think about money at all. I felt as long as I could make ends and get by I was okay. But when I was 21, I fell madly in love and I decided I wanted this child. That was my turning point. I got married and I had my daughter while still in school, and at first she was almost like a doll to play with. I took her to class with me, to the library, and even wrote my papers with her sitting in her little infant seat, as I studied from 9-5.
>
> But gradually, I became a more serious mother. Before I wasn't at all concerned about money. But now I had somebody to take care of, and as my relationship with my first husband drifted apart, I realized I had to depend on myself and be more responsible. So I shifted gears and the power of motherhood took over for a long time. All my decisions on where I was going to go, what I was going to do, was based on being a good mother. I spent more time at home to care for my child, and I postponed going to grad school until she was several years. I wanted to make sure she had a lot of love and support. That was my priority.

Young Adulthood: Becoming More "Ethical" and Judgmental

This concern for others in young adulthood was sometimes coupled with a more judgmental attitude. This was the case for Alan, the business manager, who went through a period of drug and alcohol abuse as a teenager, but now quickly rejected from his social circle anyone who used drugs or alcohol or had what he considered serious ethical failing. A few older interviewees also described young adulthood as a time when they became more critical and judgmental of others; whereas as they got older, they became more tolerant and accepting, or "mellow," as one interviewee put it. Here are some sample quotes reflecting these attitudes:

From Karen, the nurse now in her 30s:

> When I was in college and in my early 20s, I used to be much more judgmental about things, whereas now I'm more inclined to see both sides. Like at work, if somebody does something wrong or does something I don't agree with, I used to jump all over them. But now, I'm more likely to think: "Well, maybe they have a good reason for this." I'm more tolerant now than I was then.

Andy, the sales manager, now in his 40s, echoed a similar refrain:

> When I was younger, I felt like I was looking for perfection in the way people acted. If somebody lied to me, I would blame them totally, though now I believe I contributed to that process, too. For example, if somebody lied, the lie was often something I was willing to believe though I knew better, or I wasn't paying attention, so I contributed to what happened.
>
> That's why I'm more tolerant now. I think as you get older you get more tolerant. You start looking at what happens more philosophically or with more understanding when somebody does something that earlier might have seemed wrong. So now I tend not be so judgmental, as I used to be.

For Bill, the lawyer, now in his early 50s, this shift to a stricter standard of judgment in young adulthood was also tied to becoming a lawyer. Later, like others, he became more tolerant as he got older. As he reported:

> Though I was more rebellious when I was younger and identified with my peers who were also critical of the system, by the

time I reached my thirties, I was more involved in the legal system of ethics. I was much more strict about that. I took the establishment perspective more seriously, so say, if an attorney did something I considered unethical, I was a little righteous about it. But as I got older, I became more forgiving. For example, if someone does something that I consider unethical, it doesn't necessarily mean that I'll never forgive or forget. Perhaps this because I now feel that people do their best to get through their lives as best they can, so we're all struggling.

Young Adulthood: The Pressure to Achieve and Succeed

For many, particularly the men, the young adult years was a time when the push to achieve and succeed came to the fore, and this led many to become more self-interested and pragmatic in making decisions. For some, this meant paying more attention to the prevailing practices of their field, even though such practices might not be considered "ethical" by outsiders, especially in the competitive business world.

For example, some who started working in the business world explained that they had to put aside old ideals of being honest and fair to adopt the more cut-throat competitive ethics of their business environment to survive. Otherwise, business associates, suppliers, and others with a "predator" approach to life could quickly take advantage of them, if they continued to act in a more "ethical" way. So they soon switched to this more predatory approach, at least in business, though some eventually left the field, since they did not like having to act this way. This is what occurred for Ben, the writer in his 40s, who experienced a series of business battles in the advertising field when he worked in Philadelphia in his 20s and early 30s. As Ben explained:

> I was ambitious and wanted to get what I wanted to get. I also felt that I was in a den of thieves and the only way to deal with thieves was to steal from them. Then it all balances out in the end.
>
> For example, I found ways to get extra money from my vendors, who were increasing their own bills to customers. When I

first came into the business, I had certain ideals about how things should be, including ideas about dealing fairly with people. But I soon found I couldn't do this. People repeatedly cheated me, didn't pay the bills they owed, or strung me along for awhile before they broke deals. So after awhile, I realized I had to do the same sort of thing if I was going to make it and do well in the business. I had to play the same kind of game.

ADULTHOOD

In the next phase, adulthood, starting around 25 to 35, most of the interviewees talked about becoming more settled and responsible. This occurred because they now had families and children, had settled into careers, and had a clearer identity of who they were. While some talked about continuing to be more ambitious, self-oriented and competitive in the workplace, they also talked about having more concern for others generally. For some, this renewed concern for others was linked with being less personally ambitious and more realistic or more accepting about what they could do. But other interviewees in their 40s and 50s who had come to adulthood in the 1970s described being drawn into the self-growth movement, which had led them to become more self-centered and less concerned with responsibility to others. Now, though, they felt this was a wrong-headed choice which they rejected, feeling it was destructive to themselves and society. They felt they should be more concerned about others and the community as a whole.

Adulthood: Being More Ambitious, Competitive, Self-Oriented and Pragmatic in Work

This continued concern with being achievement-oriented, resulting in a more self-oriented, pragmatic approach in the workplace, was typified by Ben, the writer who ran an ad agency in his 30s and early 40s. In the struggle for continued success, he engaged in what he now considers questionable ethical deals. However, back then, he justified these actions as the way to be successful in an environment where other people did such things. As he commented:

I played the game along with everyone else to survive. For example, once I was doing PR work for a hospital and I worked with a guy who got an assignment to develop a program to promote health plans. He told me the job would go to the lowest acceptable bidder, so all I had to do had come in low.

As a result, I went to all my vendors and to the artist and photographer I worked with, and we figured out what we would do. I knew I could beat anybody because I didn't have any overhead. While I didn't always get the job, most of the time when I came in low through inside information, I did. So overall, I found being ambitious and doing what it takes to win was what I needed to do to survive.

Adulthood: Settling Down

While continuing to succeed at work in a not-so ethical world was a big influence for some interviewees, many became more responsible and ethical in other ways as they became more settled.

Pam the nurse, now in her mid-30s, described doing this after overcoming an earlier problem of alcoholism in her 20s and early 30s:

> I feel I'm more clearheaded and not as wild as I used to be. I'm more involved in social causes and trying to help other people now. Probably part of the reason is because I'm sober now. I was pretty wild and reckless when I was younger.

Jerry the lawyer, now in his early 30s, similarly saw himself as more ethical because he took others' interests into consideration more. He felt he could do so now, because he was more established in his career and didn't have to be so cut-throat to make it. As he observed:

> I feel I'm more ethical now, since I've learned from experience that it's in my best interest to be this way. It makes me feel better emotionally. I don't get into trouble, and I'm more likely to get what I want.

Adulthood: Becoming More Concerned About Others and More Realistic and Accepting About Oneself

Some felt they became more concerned about others in adulthood, since they became less ambitious and more realistic about how far they might go in their profession, such as Dick, the architect, now in his early 30s. For him, becoming more altruistic provided a better balance than being overly focused on self-interested career goals. As he explained:

> Now my goal is self-sufficiency. When I started out about 10 years ago, I was more ambitious, perhaps because I felt I could accomplish more. I had visions that an architect might be capable of molding people, because the way you create a community can have a great deal of effect on the people who live there and the ways in which they interact. But I discovered there are so many road blocks to making any changes, that it's not worth the fight. Any time there's a proposed change, everyone is so entrenched in the way we already do things that people tend to be resistant. They want to hang onto their original ideas. So I have become more realistic and less ambitious about what's possible.
>
> At the same time, scaling down my ambitions has meant I can be more ethical in what I do in working with clients. I can pay more attention to their concerns and do what's best for them, because I'm less interested in making a lot of money and getting ahead myself.

Adulthood: Going Through the Self-Growth Movement

While a number of interviewees, now in their 40s and 50s, went through the self-growth movement in the 1970s and early 1980s while in their late 20s and 30s, now they considered their participation an ethical wrong turn. They changed their view because they felt this movement had led them to become too self-centered and more likely to downplay or ignore the concerns of others. In retrospect, they felt this attitude led them to see all ethics, morals, and values as self-created, based on what feels good to me now; and they felt this focus on the self led them to lose their moral compass. As a result, they felt they lost sight of fundamental and generally accepted notions of right and wrong, becoming more present and pleasure oriented, and less willing to take responsibilities for things they didn't want to do.

Their reversal between then and now was dramatic. Now they rejected the "me-me" attitude as limiting and destructive to personal relationships, to the community, and to society as a whole. They used terms like "lost," "unrealistic," and "self-destructive," to describe their feelings about their earlier experience. They contrasted their "lack of ethics" then to their more "ethical" honest, altruistic, and socially aware now. Though they had very different social and religious backgrounds and embraced varying political viewpoints, all had been influenced by this general societal shift to glorify the self, and had come to reject it for similar reasons.

For example, Trudy, the conservative born-again Christian social worker observed:

> I went through the ends justifies the means phase at the end of the 60s and 70s, when people started reevaluating right and wrong, and then in the 70s, when people began asking "What's in it for me?" I think I lost a lot by going through that process, because it created a conflict for me. There was no strict right or wrong. I felt like I had to reevaluate every issue. I was caught up in this from about when I was 18 in 1968 to about 1984 when I was 34.

Dave, the moderate scientist from a Presbyterian background noted:

> From about the mid-70s to the mid-80s, I was caught up in what some people call 'pop psychology.' There was this new set of rules and ethics; a new way of living. It was very much me-me and for the moment. It was acceptable to be promiscuous, and after I was divorced when I was 39 in 1981, I had a lot of different girlfriends.
>
> Though I was previously more traditional in my lifestyle and ethics, I became much more individualistic, though now I'm more conservative and traditional again. As the 80s went on, in my 40s, I began to learn from my own experience that being

too selfish was hurting myself. For example, these relationships would backfire. So I began to think that all this pop psychology was nonsense. Besides, this attitude is not based on science— it's just based on somebody's ideas about new ways to behave.

So I gradually came back to doing what I feel is better for others as well as myself, trying to have a more balanced perspective.

And Kelly, the speaker and PR consultant, from a liberal non-practicing Jewish background, had this to say:

I've been part of the New Age through the 70s and mid-80s when I was in my 30s and early 40s, and I subscribed to some of its basic principles, such as if you did certain things, you could achieve all this abundance for yourself. The idea was to work on your personal growth, and then you would have this wonderful life in which you could get all you wanted and more. Just work hard enough, and you would get it.

But now I feel that this thinking promised a lot more than it delivered. I and many people I know didn't become that successful, and I think this approach created problems of commitment and trust in relationships. People were more likely to think only of themselves and not care about others, so I found a lot of problems in keeping relationships going. I guess we all have to live and learn.

Thus, while in adulthood many people focused on settling down, taking on responsibilities, and becoming more self-oriented in building a career and more other-oriented in close and family relationships, some people, caught up in the self-help movement, became highly self-centered and less responsible. It was as if they continued the me-oriented focus of adolescence into adulthood. However, towards the end of the 1980s and in the 90s, as the self-help movement lost steam and the people who embraced it aged themselves, they rejected this approach to life.

MID-LIFE ADULTHOOD

This mid-life adulthood period begins variously from about 35 to 50. Those I spoke to who experienced this phase talked about having achieved a mid-life serenity, in which they felt a greater sense of balance in their life. It took different forms, however. For some, this stage was characterized by becoming more ethical generally, in that they became more altruistic and more concerned with doing the right thing, rather than having a more self-interested or pragmatic philosophy of life.

For some who had been more ambitious and achievement oriented, this stage reflected a phase of being less concerned about trying to achieve and more accepting of what they had. For others who had been through the self-growth phase, this stage reflected a rejection of this more self-centered approach to life, as well as rejecting the focus on success. To some extent, this changed attitude reflected a response to the times, as the success and self-growth emphasis of the 1970s and 80s gave way to the more communitarian public service spirit of the 90s. Then, too, this new outlook reflected the experience of getting older and moving into another stage of life, when the struggles of the prime years of adulthood were over. Now people felt ready to relax and enjoy what they had more—and a few felt they now had time to pursue a more idealistic youthful dream that had gotten lost in the struggle for making it, being married, or taking care of kids.

Some felt they had achieved a new maturity and balance because of their experiences, which helped them learn some basic life truths about what works or doesn't for themselves and for society generally. In some case, this realization led them to become less altruistic and cause oriented, when they felt the causes they had pursued hadn't been effective. But some became more interested in social and political action, because they wanted to contribute to society, drawing on what they had learned when younger. Additionally, some thought their experiences led them to become more tolerant and understanding, since they had come to recognize and accept the failings in themselves and others, and they had encountered many different points of view, leading them to have greater respect for others' viewpoints.

Mid-Life Adulthood: Mellowing Out and Becoming More Altruistic and Concerned About Others

Ben, who had been especially ambitious before, reflected this shift to a more relaxed, balanced type of approach at mid-life. In his case, it was triggered by a near-death experience which reminded him of his own mortality and suggested he needed to stop, relax, and enjoy things now. As he explained:

> I've reached the point in life where I'm not that concerned about personal benefit anymore. I'm more concerned about what I can do to benefit others. Perhaps the reason I've come to feel this way is because I had a near death experience in heart surgery. After that happened, I felt like the worst thing that could possibly happen had already happened to me.
>
> So I'm at a stage of my life where I'm sloughing off burdens; trying to cut back and relax more. I used to think it was okay to hurt other people, when I was trying to achieve something for my own gain. Or I would be brutally frank with people, because I felt the truth was more important. But I realize now the need to be more solicitous of the needs of others. Now I sometimes do things for altruistic reasons, such as contributing to a writers' organization I belong to. There's nothing I have gotten personally from the group, but I contribute because I get a great satisfaction from helping. Now I like helping for its own sake, not seeking any gain for myself, and I never used to do that before.

Similarly, Karen, the ad agency owner in her 40s, felt she had become more other-oriented in recent years, noting that:

> Acting for altruistic reasons and to help others or humanity has become increasingly significant for me. Lately I've been seeking to work with non-profits, though they don't pay as well, because I admire what they do. Being in my mid-40s, I want to leave behind a legacy of helping to influence the world to make it a better place. I want to leave a legacy behind for the good.

Mid-Life Adulthood: Becoming More Self-Oriented

Yet, while mid-life may be a time of thinking more of others for many, some who had put aside earlier dreams for more practical work or other considerations found mid-life a time when they could do more of what they really wanted. As a result, they found themselves more self-oriented, while guided by more intuitive "do what's right" feelings, rather than more rational pragmatic considerations. Then, too, some felt they weren't as bound by customs and rules anymore; they felt freer to think and act for themselves.

This shift to recapturing earlier dreams was particularly true for Janet, who had once been a public health nurse and very other-oriented, committed to helping patients and raising her daughter. But in her 40s, with her daughter grown, she felt able to drop out of nursing to do something more personally satisfying, that would contribute to others, too—launching a series of writing and art projects with her husband. As she explained:

> When I was younger, just finishing school, I was very idealistic about nursing, wanting to do good. I felt like as long as I could make ends meet, that was enough. Then, after I got married and had my daughter, I became more serious about financial responsibilities and being a serious mother.
>
> But in the last couple of years I switched again. After my daughter went off to college, for the first time in my life, I didn't have to worry about someone else. So I stopped working as a nurse, and I feel like I'm going back to where I was before when I was in school. Back then, I wanted to do something creative and was more footloose and fancy free, and now I feel like I can do that again. So I'm thinking of myself more, doing what I want to do—but at the same time, I want to do something that will help others. I want to help people understand themselves and others a little better, as well as express myself through art.

Others who felt freer to be themselves and break away from customs and rules included Sam, the writer, in his early 50s, and Andy, the sales manager, in his late 40s.

Sam commented:

> I consider my personal gain more now. When I was younger, I used to think about the customs or rules more. I think it's because I was more timid then. I wanted to follow along with others and not make waves, since that might create trouble or people wouldn't like me. But now, if I don't think someone is right in what they are doing or I think they are putting me at a disadvantage in some way, I'll say something.

Andy explained his reasons thus:

> When I was younger, I would try to please people more or take on responsibilities I didn't want, and sometimes I resented doing things I didn't want to do, because I felt an obligation to others to do them. But now, I feel freer and don't feel the resentment, because I'm more apt to ask for what I want and get it.
>
> At one time I thought that being nice would avoid such conflicts, because being nice is supposed to make others like you. But if you don't stand up to others, they won't have respect for you, so just being nice doesn't work. That's when I realized that in order to say yes to somebody and get them to like you, one also has to have the ability to say no to them. So now I feel freer to be myself and say and do what I think.

Mid-Life Adulthood: Feeling a Greater Sense of Balance, Maturity, and Tolerance

Those who felt they gained a greater sense of balance, maturity and tolerance from what they had learned earlier in life felt better now for various reasons.

Sam, the writer, in his early 50s, who had become more self-oriented and pragmatic, reported:

> When I was younger, in my late 20s and 30s, I was more political. I felt we shouldn't be fighting in the Vietnam War, and I joined a group of people that stopped paying taxes, because we felt this was in support of a moral cause. We thought it the moral thing to do.
>
> But then I saw what we were doing was inefficient. For ex-

ample, several times the government attached my bank account, took money out of my bank, and charged a big fee each time for processing. So I abandoned protesting by not paying taxes after awhile. The others did too. We saw the government was getting more money from us when we didn't pay than if we did. Though we had made a moral point and converted people to join us, it was really inefficient.

Then, I became less involved in other causes, too. I found it frustrating, and I became interested in doing more practical things to earn money and benefit myself as I got older.

Connie, the art director, now in her early 40s, felt she had learned through trial and error to achieve her current feeling of synthesis. As she commented:

> I feel good now about my code of ethics. I've learned that trusting, being truthful, and not lying, cheating and stealing are really good things. Though I was taught these things when young, I've learned them myself through the mistakes I've made and the hurts I've experienced, rather than someone telling me that.
>
> For example, I had a very painful experience when I borrowed some money from my father and didn't return it, breaking a firm promise I had made. I let some friends persuade me my promise wasn't important. But my father was very angry and disowned me for several years, because my actions broke a basic bond of trust. I also made other mistakes in spending time with the wrong people who weren't honest and led me to put feelings of greed first, such as a business partner who cheated me when we developed an art center together.
>
> Thus, through trial and error, making mistakes, and life generally, I have come to recognize many things that are true about basic ethics and values, which I now consider very important.

Francine, the PR freelancer, also in her 40s, described how she had learned to become more tolerant through her own experiences. She reported:

> Now I'm not as adamant about what I feel is right and wrong. I'm more open to the fact that there's right and wrong from everybody's point of view. We all have our own way of looking

at things, and everybody does their own justification about why they are right, and maybe they are. I've had to look at my own thinking, and sometimes I have come to realize that what I used to think was wrong.

For example, in my own divorce, I blamed my ex-husband for leaving, thinking the one who leaves must be bad, because you should try to work things out. But now I realize that there are times when it's better to separate and go on. So if something's not working, I'm more accepting. Things are what they are.

In short, I have become more tolerant for things being what they are, which isn't necessarily perfect or ideal. Also, I've become more tolerant because I'm trying more to see ethical decisions from other people's view.

And Lars, the academic interested in philosophy, in his mid-40s, echoed the same note of gaining tolerance as he aged, noting:

As I get older I have found the concept of what's ethical and moral not as sure. I used to be more self-centered and thought of the world as revolving around me. I used to think that what I thought was right. But now I'm more tolerant, and I feel a conflict with others can be reduced by having more humility. Although I still have my own beliefs, I don't expect others to necessarily adhere to them. I have learned that conflict often comes from the inabilities of people, especially close partners, to have this mutual acceptance. So I feel there's a need for mutual tolerance, and I've become more tolerant.

SUMMING UP

In sum, as these accounts illustrate, people draw on many different influences in making their ethical decisions in different situations. Their approach also changes over time, since making ethical choices is a continually dynamic changing process. It depends not only on an individual's personality, background, and experiences, but on the circumstances he or she encounters at different times in life.

Certain early influences play a part in establishing an early core of ethical beliefs, primarily drawn from the teachings of traditional religions and morality. But thereafter, the individual is influenced by many other factors as he or she moves through life—from the attitudes of peers to prevailing community codes to professional and work norms and notions of ethical behavior.

A key influence is the maturation process as a person ages. In general, a person is more self-centered and impulse driven as an adolescent, becomes more motivated by achievement considerations as a young adult, and becomes increasingly concerned about others, taking on responsibility, and settling down in mid-life. Still, some mid-lifers may have the time to become more self-interested again as they have less responsibilities and feel freer, often when their own children grow up.

I'll briefly look at the early influences and core beliefs that provide the initial foundation for making ethical choices in the next chapter.

CHAPTER 15

•

BACK TO THE SOURCE:
THE EARLY INFLUENCE OF
PARENTS AND PEERS

While ethics are continually changing in time and in different situations, what about the source of these ethics? How influential are parents and peers in shaping ethics as people grow up and providing a foundation for who they are today?

Most of the interviewees credited their parents with providing the basic principles of right and wrong that are part of our Judeo-Christian heritage—such as don't lie, cheat, or steal; and follow the Golden Rule of do unto others as you would have them do unto you.

However, as they face the real world, children find the idealistic principles don't always work. They are tempted to do things they know they shouldn't—things their parents have told them not to do. They are then tempted to lie to avoid getting punished for that—the classic "No I didn't take the cookies you told me not to take" routine. After they get discovered and are punished for doing something or for lying about doing it, or both, they may avoid doing it in the future. Or sometimes these experiences lead to learning how to lie and deceive better.

In time, as children grow up and their experiences and ideals increasingly diverge from their parents' teachings, especially in their teenage years, they increasingly follow the code of their peers. It's a process I wrote about in *The Truth About Lying*.[1]

------

[1]Gini Graham Scott, *The Truth About Lying*, Novato, California: Smart Books, 1994. Available from www.trafford.com and Changemakers.

Yet, even though people often stray to a greater or lesser degree from these core principles, many continue to feel their influence, and through experience or mellowing with age, many are drawn back to these ideals. As described in the previous chapter, they have found these principles work better for them in promoting better human relationships—or they have lost the more competitive urge. Instead, they are more oriented towards helping others and giving back to the community—the other-oriented ideals basic to traditional moral principles.

The interviewees echoed these themes regardless of their particular religious backgrounds—or even if came from non-practicing or nonreligious families. They all described learning basic notions of right and wrong from their parents or other authority figures, like teachers, when they were children. The one key difference was that those from a Catholic background spoke about the powerful feelings of guilt transmitted to them by their parents and the Catholic Church when they did anything wrong. Others spoke less about guilt and more about the negative consequences if they were caught or if what they did wrong didn't work.

THE IMPORTANCE OF PARENTS

Again and again, the interviewees emphasized the power of their parents' early teachings. Even if they had moved away from their parents' ideals or developed their own ethical approaches from experience, they credited their parents with shaping them today.

Pam, the nurse, very much a pragmatist now, observed:

> As much as I hate to admit it, I have been influenced a lot by my parents. They were Catholic, working class, and they brought me up with a typical right and wrong approach. I've been influenced by my grandparents also. They gave me some basic ideas about what's right and wrong, and then I think about whether these ideals will work or not in a particular situation.

Likewise, Don, the broadcaster, now something of a freethinker and rule-breaker, commented:

My parents influenced me a great deal. I regard them as great sources of curiosity, personal strength, confidence, independence, and a sense of conviction about what is right or wrong. They had very high standards and a sense of morality with a God-based structure. My father combined a no-nonsense military exterior with a Christian base, while my mother was very religious. They sent me to a Catholic grade school and Jesuit high school, and they were successful in instilling in us a sense of values. They acted like these came from God and that the world has always been this way. At the same time, they both gave us the permission to question authority, which I still do.

While many parents taught by admonition—or occasional punishment, when their child did something wrong—many used themselves as an example by the way they lived their own lives.

June, the tax consultant found teaching by example especially important, since this is how she learned most of these principles. As she commented:

My parents were not very articulate people. But we learned to live by their example. They were good, decent, honorable people.

And Trudy, the social welfare worker, found these traditional principles a place to come home to after being influenced by the self-growth movement and pop psychology. As she explained:

Today I'm pretty much influenced by my parents, especially my mother. She was a perfect type of person. She always did for other people, and she had to because she had ten children. She did everything she could to take care of her kids. That was her total priority in life. She was a genuinely nice person and she always tried to do what was right.

So she influenced me a lot. Then, too, we were raised in the church, although my father wasn't very religious. But my mother took us to church on Sundays. Thus, though we weren't an extremely religious family, we were steeped in the basic values of our Christian religion, and were especially influenced by my mother.

KEY EARLY TEACHINGS

What were the key core values learned from their parents? The most commonly mentioned ones were:

- Be honest, don't lie, cheat, or steal
- Be responsible and self-reliant
- Have a strong social conscience.

Be Honest, Don't Lie, Cheat or Steal

The interviewees repeatedly noted the need to be honest and truthful, and don't lie, cheat, or steal, whatever their own religious and cultural background.

Andy, the sales manager, commented:

> Though they weren't particularly religious, my mom and dad believed in telling the truth. My mom was pretty idealistic, and my dad was pretty practical. Even so, he advocated being pretty straight forward with everyone.

And Janet, the nurse, noted:

> I think my sense of honesty comes from my father. My mother used to call him George Washington, because he really overdid it. But this principle is with me today. I have difficulty, even if I say something to protect somebody, telling a little white lies, though most people tell them. But I get all flushed and it shows. Yet I'm glad they taught me this value, because I think trust is critical to having good relationships with others.

Be Responsible and Self-Reliant

Another theme which many interviewees reported, especially the men and those from Protestant or nonreligious backgrounds, was the importance of personal responsibility and being self-reliant. In turn, this ideal contributed to them having a more rational approach to making decisions, and at times it led them to break the rules when that seemed the most practical thing to do.

For example, Dick, the architect, with a very rational, pragmatic, and innovative approach to dealing with ethical issues, observed:

> I feel there was a great deal of influence from my father, who is the kind of person who doesn't seem to need anyone else. He could survive on a desert island just fine. He doesn't have any ego or anything to prove to anybody, and doesn't care about having wealth and fame and prestige, so he always felt freer to act as he felt was right, and he encouraged me to be more self-reliant.

Andy, the business manager, commented:

> Though I was very much on my own when I was young, since my mother was ill and my father was fairly distant, they influenced me a great deal. They taught me the central core values that guide me today—to be responsible for myself, to be self-reliant, and to be resilient in the face of adversity.

Have a Strong Social Conscience

A few interviewees, who were especially altruistic or socially concerned, attributed this to their parents, who set this value as a model for them. Their parents described this as an ethical ideal or higher state of ethical development, and taught them to strive towards this. Now these interviewees still did, although this approach sometimes put them at odds with others who were more pragmatic, self-oriented, and rules-conscious. A number of the interviewees attributed this to being raised in a liberal Jewish family, which placed a great emphasis on being socially concerned and helping the down and out.

Ari, the public health nurse who worked in the jails, described learning the ideal of being socially committed in this way:

> My parents had a great influence on shaping my attitude of altruism today, because I came from left wing parents who were very concerned with humanity and doing good for your fellowman. So that's very important to me now, although being ac-

cepted by my peers and following the rules is, too. But sometimes, this desire to do the right thing and help others has gotten
me in trouble, such as when I've tried to point out something
wrong, which is hurting a lot of people. I've found that officials
and managers often don't want to hear that—but if I think it's
important enough, I'll press on, and I think that comes to a great
extent from my parents.

Similarly, Karen, the socially concerned advertising agency owner,
attributed her decision to work only with "ethical" clients on worth-
while products to her parents. She commented:

> I feel the way I am very choosy about what I do and who I work
> with comes from my parents. My parents were highly ethical,
> and I've done a lot of reading in philosophy and ethics, too. One
> of the things they taught me, which I believe strongly, too, is that
> each of us is responsible, while we're here on this earth, to make
> it a better place. That's really important to me.

Sam the writer, spoke of this humanitarian impulse from his parents,
too.

> I think my father had a big influence in instilling the general
> principle of treating people nicely. I remember when I was a kid
> there weren't many homeless people on the street, and if some-
> body on the street was begging, my father gave him some money.
> He said that when somebody says he's hungry, you've got to be-
> lieve them. That made an impression on me, and later when I
> got older I found I myself drawn into various social causes.

Reinforcing These Values Through Experience

After learning these key principles when young, the interviewees often tried testing them, and they found these values were reinforced
when they did the wrong thing and were caught.

For example, Karen, the art director, though taught to be honest,
frequently misbehaved, only to be reminded of the need to be truthful again. As she reported:

I was raised with a very strong sense of honesty and never lying or cheating. But sometimes I learned the hard way, by getting myself in trouble, getting caught, and then knowing that it was wrong. I tested myself a lot. I was taught and told to do things a certain way, but I always wanted to make sure, to test it out myself. Then I would get in trouble, say by stealing from people or from stores—small things like candy bars. Later, after I had to face the consequences, I would tell myself: 'You know, my mom was right.'

Rebelling; Learning from Experience; and Returning

Others described going through periods of rebellion as they grew up, but still recognized this early influence affecting them decades later. Sometimes they found when they rebelled that being "unethical" didn't work, because of the negative consequences.

For example, Francine, the PR freelancer, observed:

From the time I was very young, I rebelled against everything my parents ever told me, and I thought they had no influence over me. In fact, I feel I did this because my parents, particularly my mother, were so rigid. Her attitude was that everything was black or white, right or wrong, and her way was the right way, while your way was the wrong way.

So I struck out to find my own way, and I feel I became strong in my own beliefs, although I still question myself a lot, because I was always the one that was wrong when I rebelled and my mother was right. But while I did rebel and tried to find my own way, I find in my later years that my parents were good people and instilled good values in me.

And Lori, the teacher, had a traumatic experience when she didn't follow some principles her parents had taught about being honest. The consequences led her to not do that again. As she described it:

Though my parents had told me all about being honest, I started shoplifting when I was a kid. I found it easy to simply take a lipstick or something else I wanted, and at first, I got away with it. But one time, when I was 13, I was caught with three other kids.

When the shopkeeper told my parents, they kept wringing their hands, saying to each other and me, "What have we done wrong? What have we done wrong?" It so crushed me that I did something so terrible to hurt my parents so much, that I felt it wasn't worth it to do this again. So I never shoplifted after that.

OTHER EARLY SOURCES OF ETHICAL PRINCIPLES: RELIGIOUS SCHOOLS, TEACHERS, AND BOOKS

Besides parents, the interviewees noted other major early influences that included religious schools, teachers, peers, and personal experiences. While some found certain experiences, such as going to religious and particularly Catholic school, helped to reinforce their parents' message, in many cases, other influences pulled them away from their parents' teachings or led them to question what they had learned.

For example, Bill the lawyer, from a Catholic family, found his many years in Catholic school especially influential. These school experiences contributed to his continuing concern with applying ethical principles to the law. As he reported:

I was educated in a Catholic school for eight years. We were taught a lot by allegory, through stories of these various saints. Each saint had a little moral tale to tell. I took these things very seriously as a child, and even when I no longer believed in the stories of the Church, I still was influenced by the system of ethics that was left over as a residue. I think that's where my strong sense of following ethical principles today comes from.

I found these teachings much more of an influence on me than my parents, though they weren't opposed to any of these teachings. They just weren't the primary source of what I learned.

Learning from school and reading was another major source of influence for some, such as for Kelly, the speaker and PR consultant. As she explained:

I didn't get much guidance from my parents in my childhood about right and wrong. Their approach was more to expose me to a lot of things, like books, so I could come to my own reasoned judgment. Now, although I'm still very intuitive and want to do the right thing, I still do that. I weigh and evaluate everything to decide what to do.

I think my education in school also had a lot to do with shaping my thinking. Reading and literature had a great impact. And being with people contributed, too. I learned from many different sources.

THE INFLUENCE OF PEERS AND PERSONAL EXPERIENCES

Many interviewees noted that their peers and personal experiences shaped the development of their ethical ideas, too, although these influences tended to lead them away from the core principles of morality that their parents, teachers, or religious school training sought to impart. Instead, some found at an early age that their peers encouraged them to be rebellious, question authority, break rules, and test limits. Some found that their real world experiences contributed to their becoming more pragmatic and more concerned about their own self-interest, or led them to create their own code of rules to follow.

For example, Sam the writer, found that as a young child his peers led him to have a playful irreverent attitude towards rules that carried over into his later life. One result was a "question authority" streak that remained with him. As he noted:

> When I was 6 or 7, my peers would get me to do pranks with them. It contradicted what my parents were telling me to do about being nice to people. But we never did anything harmful. We did things like making phone calls to people and when someone answered, we would hang up. We had a playful spirit of mischief, not really harming anyone, but just teasing them...being a little bad, but not too much. Now I think that some of that spirit stayed with me, such as when I tweak authority as a part-time stand-up comic.

As for Ari, the public health nurse, an early experience paved the way for her developing an attitude of questioning authority, which sometimes led her to become a whistle-blower when she saw people weren't doing their job. As she commented:

> I've always had a fear of authority, which led me to follow the rules to get along. But at other times, I've wanted to stand up to that authority and challenge it, too.
>
> I had an early experience that made that a very important principle to me. I was a little child, about five or six, and I was marching in a May Day parade with another little girl of my age. All of a sudden, this policeman rode up on a horse, and he reared up the horse in front of us. Then, he backed us against a store-front and called us names, like 'commie pinko,' because at that time, in the mid-1950s, my parents were left-wing activists, and there was a lot of hostile feeling against people who did this. So I had a powerful experience as a very young and helpless child of being intimidated by a very powerful person on a gigantic animal, before he left us alone and we went back to the parade.
>
> That experience stayed with me, and I've always felt both submissive to and wanting to question authority at the same time.

Sandi, the government researcher, also had an early experience that strongly influenced her future outlook. It contributed to her becoming both a rule breaker and a follower, depending on what seemed to be the most practical at the time. As she explained:

> When I was in 7th or 8th grade, I met a girl named Patty from a divorced family, who was a lot of fun and she told great, fascinating stories. But my parents didn't want me to associate with her, because she lived in a run-down part of town, and they thought her mother, who worked in the local dime store, was weird and nuts. But I still saw Patty in school, and one day she invited me to go horseback riding at a stables where she worked. I really wanted to go, though even the mention of riding scared my parents. They were scared of my getting hurt.
>
> I decided to go anyway, and I told my parents I had done something else. The experience was great, and several times after that I went riding with Patty again, giving other excuses.
>
> So after that, I often did what I wanted without telling my parents or I made up a story about doing something else I knew they would approve. I never did anything bad, but I learned to

stretch the truth when necessary to get what I wanted, because it worked very well for me to do this. And later, I used this approach of breaking the rules or creating stories in my work to create a more successful, competent image of what I could do, which helped me get ahead.

Jerry, the lawyer, similarly had some experiences which helped shape his largely pragmatic, innovative outlook today. As he described what happened:

> Until I was about 20, I unconsciously took my parents as the gospel, and I adopted my father's politics and my mother's values pretty much hook, line and sinker. My father's politics were pretty liberal, while my mother emphasized being chivalrous to women, such as letting them decide what movie to see and where to go on a date.
>
> But as I got older, I started thinking through things myself and drawing on my own experiences to create my own ethical system. Though I sometimes came to the same conclusions as my parents, I was more comfortable thinking things through and finding what works and doesn't. One example is when I realized it makes sense to treat other people like you want to be treated, because if you treat them badly, people will tell others what you've done and that can hurt you.
>
> So I feel that ethical injunctions from any kind of authority, the Bible, the law, science, or whatever, may be fine. But I want to know the rationale behind why that approach should be followed. That's why I don't do or not do these things just because they're something I've been told to do. Instead, I do things because I've thought them through and have come to realize it's a good idea to act in certain ways, since it's in my own self-interest. After all, we're a capitalist country, guided by self-interest. It's what makes the economy work, and in my view, it's what makes systems of ethics work, too.

CONCERNS ABOUT THE DECLINE OF ETHICS IN TODAY'S WORLD

Some interviewees additionally expressed a concern about what they considered a decline of ethics in society today. They believed a reason for many social problems today is that we have drifted away from following basic moral teachings. Though they did not always use these principles themselves, they felt such principles were important and ideally should be followed.

Don the broadcaster expressed this notion when he observed:

> My parents tried to imbue me with their high standards and a sense of morality, drawn from traditional Christian values. I didn't buy into that totally and my experience in the secular world since then has been very different. People very often don't act in terms of those values.
>
> However, I see a lot of social decline in the world around us, and I consider this a painful evolution, away from what we used to know. There's an ongoing tension between these basic ideals and secular influences.
>
> Personally, I can navigate between the ideal and the actual; between the basic moral teachings I've learned and the secular. I consider having these foundational principles a valuable base point to carry with me into day to day situations, though I may be influenced by other factors.
>
> Yet, while this split works for me, I think it has contributed to the decline we see around us. In general, people don't take these old principles seriously, and that's seriously fraying the fabric of society, because people aren't showing the basic integrity or concern for each other that's part of these traditional teachings.

Jerry, the lawyer, similarly had concerns about where society was going. As he explained:

> I believe our notions of ethics not only help us individually, but as a society, since they lead us to pay attention to the concerns of others. They move us towards becoming more aware of others and what we can do to help one another. And that's in our self-interest, too. For example, ethics discourage individual greed by encouraging us to think of others, and that's good for the planet, too, because it helps to preserve our resources. It makes sense rationally and pragmatically, and that's why I think we all should be more conscious of world problems and lead a more simple lifestyle today. It's the ethical thing to do.

SUMMING UP

In sum, as the accounts of the interviewees reflect, we are shaped in our ethical approaches by numerous sources. One is our parents, who are a primary source of many of the traditional core ethical values that we hold and pass on. Many of these values are derived from the Judeo-Christian principles that have shaped Western society. Among these are the core values represented by the four inner boxes on the Ethical Choices Map, which include doing the right moral thing, following the rules, intuitively knowing the appropriate thing to do, and doing for others.

In practice, parents do not always follow these principles or successfully teach them to their children. Also, in growing up, people encounter many other influences which lead away from traditional values. While some influences, like religious school, or reading about ethical ideas, may help to underline core values, many other experiences pull people in another direction, such as participating in activities with peers or in the competitive workplace. As a result, as a practical matter, people may find they are more successful if they follow their own self-interest, and sometimes engage in deception to do so, question or rebel against authority, or determine through rational means the best strategy in a particular situation.

All of these factors, in turn, contribute to shaping the ethical choices people make today in many different situations. The next section focuses on the wide range of choices people make in the various arenas of everyday life.

PART IV:

RESOLVING ETHICAL DILEMMAS
IN DIFFERENT SITUATIONS

CHAPTER 16

•

INTRODUCING PART IV: MAKING ETHICAL CHOICES IN DIFFERENT SITUATIONS

In Part II, I described how the Ethical Choices Map reflects four major influences which guide the person in making an ethical choice or resolving an ethical dilemma. As noted, these represent style of choice (intuitive/rational); orientation (other/self), philosophy (moralist/pragmatist), and attitude towards rules (follower/innovator), with each person falling somewhere on the continuum in each of these qualities. For simplicity, I have divided these into either polar opposites or a three-way split reflecting the person's primary orientation.

To recap, the core ethical principles derived from religious and spiritual traditions provide that an ethical person should have these characteristics: be a moralist (do what's right), be other-oriented (be altruistic and help others), be a follower (follow the rules—which presumably are good and appropriate ones), and know and accept these as right (knowing this intuitively).

I also pointed out that individuals and groups with differing social characteristics and geographic boundaries, and even cultures as a whole, can be characterized by different patterns in how they rate in each of these dimensions. Further, individuals, groups, and cultures can vary over time, and the influence of varying factors differs in different situations.

How do these patterns of choice change in different situations? What factors are more or less important? And what kinds of situations create ethical dilemmas?

The people I spoke with helped to answer these questions as they described the ethical dilemmas they faced in their own lives—in their families, with spouses and significant others, with their children, at work and in business, with friends and in social situations, and in society in general.

This section highlights these dilemmas and choices, and discusses how these different situations influence us. These situations can be categorized generally by how close they are to us—reflected by where they fall in the Zones of Ethical Choices, as illustrated on page 61. These zones start with the self and radiate out through the zone of family and intimate others to friends and relatives, work and business associates, the local community and general public, and finally to society as a whole. For any person, these zones may be more or less important.

In considering how people make decisions in different situations, I will start with the way these zones are commonly characterized—starting with the self and going outward, like a bull's-eye, as illustrated in the Zones of Ethical Choices diagram. These differing situations are discussed in the following chapters in Part IV.

CHAPTER 17

•

MAKING ETHICAL CHOICES
ABOUT ONESELF

WHEN MAKING PERSONAL CHOICES BECOME ETHICAL DILEMMAS

Ethical dilemmas about oneself largely revolve around questions of personal identity, such as: "Who am I?" and "What should I do?"

When someone is making a choice like what which job to take, where to move, and whether to seek a promotion or not, ethical considerations don't always come into play. But these questions can become ethical dilemmas when they raise issues about personal values or ethics.

For example, a person who is deciding whether to go to graduate school to become a business executive or a doctor may have to consider not only which subject is most interesting but the relative importance of the values associated with each profession. For instance, the person deciding might view a businessman as being primarily motivated by self-interest and being pragmatic and rational (although some business people may be very altruistic, moral and intuitive in their approach). Conversely, he might consider a doctor to be very altruistic with a more humanitarian intuitive approach (although a particular doctor could be very self-interested, acquisitive, and guided by pragmatic considerations). Yet, for the person deciding, what's relevant is how he or she views his or her own identity. So the choice of a professional goal can become an ethical dilemma based on the conflict between what choosing a business or medical career means to that person.

Besides the identity question, the choice can involve other ethical issues. Say the person's parents are pushing him in one direction—that could raise questions about loyalty to one's family (the Self versus Other Orientation) if his preference is different from what his parents want him to do. Or there could be economic considerations if the person deciding has his own family to support or needs to borrow money from his parents or friends to pursue a choice he really wants versus one he likes less which would be more practical economically (a conflict between self/other and moral/pragmatic influences).

By recognizing these competing pulls from different ethical dimensions in a situation, one can better sort out what the trade-offs are to better make the decision. For example, a comparison of the meaning of choosing between becoming a doctor versus persuing a business career might look like this:

Becoming a Doctor	Going into Business
Attracted to role's values (altruistic, moral, intuitive)	Less attracted to role's values (self-interested, pragmatic, rational)
What I want (self-orientation)	What my parents want (other-orientation)
Financial difficulties now Need to borrow (less pragmatic/rational; moral conflict over loan)	Financial advantages Can earn money now (more pragmatic/rational; no moral conflict over loan)

As this example illustrates, clarifying and weighing the competing ethical concerns can help one better decide how to make a personal choice.

ETHICAL ISSUES IN MAKING PERSONAL CHOICES

Some examples of common ethical issues that come up in making personal choices include the following:

1. Idealism versus pragmatism for those drawn towards a career choice that is personally fulfilling but doesn't provide a sufficient income (such as art, writing, academic teaching and research).
2. Choosing or declining a project that conflicts with one's personal values or ethics (such as accepting work for a client or writing a book on a certain subject or from a certain viewpoint that is morally at odds with important personal principles).
3. Taking on or declining a project one has accepted after one gets a better offer (such as when one is choosing to accept a job, participate in a business venture, or sign a music or book contract).

In each case, the basic conflict is between doing something that appeals to one's self-interest while confronting competing ethical concerns (such as the need to borrow money to finance a low-income career choice; the need to earn money by doing something considered personally distastefully, wrong or illegal; or the need to break a previous promise to do what one really wants).

In turn, the difficulty of choosing, the way the person decides (i.e., rationally, intuitively, or a combination of both), and the decision made, depend on various factors. Among them are the person's own priorities in orientation, philosophy and attitude towards the rules in making choices in general or in certain situations; the perceived importance of the situation; the influence of friends or family members who are aware of the problem; the types of resources and options available to the person; and other considerations.

Often people making decisions aren't aware of these competing factors that contribute to their choices. Rather they go through a period of uncertainty when they are pulled in different directions by competing claims and feelings of upset and confusion. Then, after more or less consideration, they make a decision, and afterwards feel motivated to act to realize their decision or they drop it and move on to something else. Either way, they experience a feeling of resolution that the conflict is over, so they can put it away and move on.

To illustrate the process in making key personal decisions, following are some examples of decisions the interviewees made and how they made them.

THE IDEALISM VERSUS PRAGMATISM DILEMMA: DOING WHAT I WANT VERSUS WHAT I CAN AFFORD, WHAT'S MORE PRACTICAL, OR WHAT OTHERS WANT

The interviewees facing the idealism versus pragmatism dilemma were all drawn to career goals that appealed to them personally because these occupations were creative, interesting, or contributed to society. But then they confronted the question of what to do about money. Could they afford to do what they really wanted? Could they or should they rely on others to help them? Or should they do what was more practical—or perhaps try to do what they wanted on the side? The interviewees faced different variations on these questions and came to different decisions based on their own priorities and life circumstances.

Terry, the would-be academic, artist, and writer, in his early 40s whose ideal was helping humanity, decided after much agonizing to get a job. As much as he didn't want to, he did so for survival, because had no other alternatives to fall back on. As he explained:

> Right now is a time of transition for me after being in school, and it's time to go out and make a living and look at what I want to do.
>
> I had some friends urging me to take this job or that because I need the money. I didn't want to do that, and looked at what I really want to do. I see myself as basically a creative person, and I want to be in a position where I can be a benefit to people. Status isn't important to me. I see myself as an artist and writer, too. I very much want to do something, like going to El Salvador to help the people there, or getting involved in human rights work. So I turned down a lot of dumb just making money jobs.

But now, I've just about run out of resources. My funds from being a teaching assistant and from unemployment are almost over. And I don't have friends I can turn to—they're in a similar low-income situation, and I couldn't pay them back for a long time if I tried doing what I really want now. That's why I finally have to do what I have struggled against doing for so long. I feel like I'm putting my real life on hold, but I have to do it. I've gotten to the point where for now, I have no choice, though if I can, I'll try to write and help society on the side.

Janet, the former public health nurse in her 40s, and Eric, the computer writer in his 30s, similarly went through a struggle between doing the more practical thing or opting to embark on a risky writing and art project together. But, unlike Terry, they opted to pursue their dream. Janet explained her choice thus:

I felt very frustrated working in the health care system, especially in my last job for five years. I never felt I could really be idealistic and involved in what I wanted to do for the good of other people, which is what health care is supposed to be. The hospital always had its own other agenda, which was to follow the rules and regulations in the most economical way possible. I always felt like I was compromising myself, going through the motions, and though I tried to complain a few times, mostly, I learned to live with the situation.

Then a new president came in, and I felt the new management was really undermining patient care by not providing all it could in serious life threatening conditions. At one point, I even went to personnel to complain about a head nurse who was now in charge of me, but I got no support. So I started feeling worse and worse about the whole situation. I kept asking myself, 'What am I doing here?', and what made it even worse is that with the reorganization I had even more work to do—I was supposed to do what three nurses usually do.

Finally, about two years ago, I realized I had to do something to end this situation. And what made it easier is my daughter was now grown up and on her own. So I didn't have that responsibility anymore and as much need for money. Plus I had saved up money from my years of working as a nurse.

That's when I started asking myself what I really wanted to do, and I realized I wanted to do something creative, which is around the time I met Eric, and we started to work and live together. I felt freer, like when I was in college—more footloose and fancy free. So I started making decisions based on what feels right to me.

And that meant deciding to leave my job in public health nursing and work on an art and writing project with Eric. It deals with trust and self-trust, which has become very important to me. In fact, one reason I'm doing this now is because I have learned to trust myself and do what I feel is really right to do.

In much the same way, Eric came to put aside a more secure job to do something creative to contribute to society. As he explained:

For me the choice was between wanting to be creative and expressing myself and having a more organized, structured, secure life. Before I decided to work on this project with Janet, I was working on books about buying computers, and this decision became a choice between money and freedom. I was doing the work on the books for money but never really liked this, because I'm not into computers that much.

But after I made a bunch of money from these books, I said 'No more' and decided to do what really speaks to me. I still needed some more money to work on this project, and that meant going to my family for some support to help see me through. And they did contribute. I didn't feel that good about going to them; but I felt I had already started this process of choosing freedom and just needed a little more time. So I went to them, and about a year ago, Janet and I started working together on something that means a lot to me. Now I'm glad I made the choice I have, even though it's been hard financially and life is a lot less secure.

THE MORALITY VERSUS PRAGMATISM DILEMMA: DOING WHAT I BELIEVE IN VERSUS WHAT I HAVE BEEN ASKED TO DO

Another big personal identity question for some is when they are invited to participate in a project—say as an employee, manager, or partner—but they disagree with it on moral or value grounds.

Though the decision may involve less survival considerations than the broader "Who am I?" career choice question, the decision can still raise serious economic questions, when the person has to be willing to earn less money and scale back his or her lifestyle to do the "right" thing. Also, the choice may become even more difficult when one sees others in one's field doing what one hesitates to do, or when friends and family members urge making the more remunerative choice. It can be hard to decide which should comes first—Doing what seems "right," or doing what seems most "practical"? Or perhaps one might still find some kind of compromise, rather than being forced to make an either-or choice.

CHOOSING WHAT SEEMS RIGHT

A key factor in making the choice, as in the career choice question, is whether one has the financial ability or support of others to choose what seems right, as well as the willingness to earn less. The interviewees who choose "morality" over "profits" were either in a financially secure position, so they could easily turn down what didn't seem right, or they were willing to adjust their lives to earn less than otherwise—or do both.

This was the case for Karen, the ad agency owner, and Dick the architect. Both had been doing well economically, had a partner who helped with financial support, and were more concerned with acting with integrity than earning more.

In Karen's case, she launched her venture with the ideal of only taking on the kinds of projects she believed in, not just accepting a client's agenda. Thus, if she didn't like the prospective client's message, she wouldn't work on the campaign, and she was willing to make less as a result. In turn, she was better able to make this decision and follow her value of doing the right thing first, since her businessman husband could support her financially. As Karen put it:

> Of course, we need a certain amount of money, but my husband brings in most of that. So lately, I've been making more decisions on what personally is enriching and feels good, rather

than making a decision that could bring in a large dollar amount. What's more important to me is getting excited about what the project is and whether it feels good and whether I'm going to learn from it. So I've chosen to make a little less, and since I'm in a long-term marriage and my husband has a secure job, I've been able to do this.

Dick made a similar choice in the architecture business—with a little help from his wife. As he explained:

I much prefer doing the work that I enjoy, rather than doing the work I have to do to pay the rent. I've seen a number of people who are willing to do whatever comes along, and if it pays money, they'll do it, regardless of the impact on the city or the environment. But I'm more interested in doing what I want and make less money.

One of the things that has helped me do this is having a fairly steady income level, so I don't have to worry much about making money. It also helps that my wife has a decent job that pays very well. She is comfortable with this arrangement, so that's helped me in making the choices I have.

MAKING CONCESSIONS FOR FINANCIAL REASONS

Others who don't have the financial underpinnings or help of others may have to put moral considerations aside to make the more practical choice, as much as they don't want to do so.

That's what Sandi the government researcher decided. Being single, she had to depend primarily on her own earning power, although in a pinch, she could borrow from her parents. A key problem was that in her field, she had to depend on research projects getting funding, and she often spent time between jobs looking for work. During this down time, one option was taking on low paying temporary jobs working for clerical temporary agencies. Or she could do something where she could make much more money, though she didn't think it was right to do—writing student term papers for a local company to put herself through grad school. Even when she began doing this, she knew it wasn't right, and she knew a local man who advertised this service had been investigated, fined, and threatened with jail if he did this work again, though he continued to operate surreptitiously. Yet, when she hit a dry streak in her own work, she sometimes did take on such projects. Since she badly needed the money, she made a moral concession. As she commented:

> I know what I'm doing is wrong, and I don't like to do it. I've told myself at times, I won't do it again. But when times get tough and the research work dries up, I feel I need to do something to get work. I don't feel particularly comfortable doing these papers, but from time to time, I do them on a small, quiet scale, until I the regular work I do is available again. But I would never advertise and do this work openly. I only do it for another company or by referral. I feel I'm at least protected this way, while I know I'm doing something wrong.

FINDING A MIDDLE GROUND

Still others caught in this morality versus money crunch have found a middle ground, such as not doing the work they don't want to do themselves, while turning it over to an assistant or associate, so they don't lose the money. That's what Kelly the speaker and PR consultant did. As she described her situation:

> One time I took on a client because I needed the money, though it was a difficult decision. I do publicity for a lot of authors, and this author wrote a book that was very well written. But I didn't agree with his philosophy. In fact, I was on the opposite side of the issue. He wrote about alternative healing and advocated the approach of conventional medicine that alternative healing is deadly. But I happen to be very much into alternative healing, and I see the two as compatible. Or in many cases, I think the alternative approach is the better one.
>
> So though this was a well-presented book, the approach went against my beliefs, and I didn't want to represent it. But at the time I needed the money. I waited as long as possible to see if I could get other clients, but I couldn't, and finally I took this person on and agreed to promote his book.
>
> Then I dealt with the problem of not believing in his ap-

proach by hiring someone to call the TV and radio stations and the papers instead of myself, because I felt I needed someone who could sound sincere and convincing. But I did all the writing, because I can write better. I told him I only had time to do that, and said I would hire an expert telemarketer and I got him a really good person. This way I was still able to do a really good job for him by hiring a person who could get behind his book and be convincing though I couldn't, and I did the part I could.

I think that's the basic dilemma most people face unless they are independently wealthy. At times, we all have to prostitute ourselves to earn a living. Sometimes people say: 'Do what you love and the money will come.' But that's naive. It doesn't always happen. I once almost went bankrupt trying to do a radio show I loved, so now I realize there are times it is necessary to make compromises and take on projects I don't really like or believe in to pay the rent.

THE SELF VERSUS OTHER DILEMMA: BREAKING AN AGREEMENT TO ACCEPT A BETTER OPPORTUNITY

What to do when one is offered an opportunity, accepts it, and then gets an even better opportunity is another personal identity dilemma for some. Should one honor one's original agreement, which is usually considered the ethical, right thing to do? Or should one be more pragmatic and take the better offer? The supposedly right thing is to keep the promise, which involves putting the other person's needs first, since he or she is now depending on this promise. But the more pragmatic approach—at least in the short term—is backing out to help oneself.

While some people do honor a promise, though it means turning down something they really want, the interviewees ultimately did choose what was best for them personally. Still, they agonized long and hard about making this decision, and then found various justifications for their actions—a common approach when one feels one isn't doing what's right but wants to excuse or explain it.

Sometimes, even a seemingly pragmatic choice can backfire, when it provides a short-term advantage but leads to long-term problems, such as not being hired in the future because of a negative evaluation by the person experiencing the broken promise. Still the short-term solution cam be tempting, as the interviewees found.

DOING WHAT'S BETTER FOR ME BY
BREAKING AN AGREEMENT

Tom, the scientist, and Iris, the therapist, were two of the interviewees who faced this "Should I turn down the job after I've made an agreement?" dilemma, and both ultimately declined after a long period of consideration. Ultimately, they each decided to do "What's best for me?" after agonizing for some time over possible options and outcomes.

The process they used to decide was like they were creating an ethical balance sheet in which they considered their obligation to the person or company making the offer, along with their priorities and obligations to others, such as family members, who might be affected by the decision. Also they factored in their own preferences. Though they didn't like breaking a promise, on balance they opted to choose what they considered the best opportunity. A major factor was that they felt the person or company let down by their decision was more impersonal to them, and they felt less loyalty to them than to their family or themselves.

Tom described using this process when he was offered a job in another country, was ready to go, and decided to stay home. As he commented:

> Ethical dilemmas usually boil down to: "What's best for me in the long run?" though we usually have to think about what's best for others, too. In my own case, I felt an ethical dilemma when I took an early retirement from the lab where I worked, and I was looking around to find another full-time job. I had been communicating with some people in Germany, indicating that I might be interested in working there, and eventually they offered me the job.
>
> Then I started thinking about my situation if I accepted the job, and I realized that I have my elderly parents living nearby

and look after them a little now. In an emergency, I might need to look after them more. Then, too, I had my political activities which give me a lot of personal satisfaction, although I have been working to help other people by seeking elected office.

I anguished over what to do for about two or three weeks. In the meantime, the company thought I had accepted their offer, and was sending me electronic mail every three or four days about what kind of work I would do.

Finally, when I decided it wasn't going to work, I told them. But I managed to present my decision so I maintained a good relationship. Basically, I told the man who wanted to hire me about my considerations, explaining my feelings of commitment to my parents and my political party. Then I tried to show him what I could still do for the company, even though I was turning down the job. I said, 'I'm willing to be your consultant, and come over there several times a year. And I can help you find a young physicist who could do what you were trying to hire me to do.'

So though the company manager wasn't pleased by my backing out myself, I gave him something in return. I feel I did the best thing under the circumstances, and I'm glad I did.

Similarly, Iris the therapist had a struggle when she decided to quit a job she had just accepted, after she learned she had to make an additional half-hour commute. She described what happened:

I recently quit a fairly responsible job I was hired for running an employee assistance program for eleven government agencies with 2500 people under me. After I was on the job for three days, I learned the company was moving within a year into a tough area of San Francisco where I didn't want to work. It was hard for me to make the decision to quit or not, because I was replacing the person who hired me, and I knew when I took the job, she was planning to move to Nevada at the end of the month. So I knew the company had only a short period to train her replacement.

Thus, when I got this information about the move, I spent two sleepless nights considering what to do, because I would have an extra half-hour commute each day to a bad area, but I felt guilty since I felt an obligation to the company, too.

Finally, though, I decided I had to back out, because I would have to live with my decision day after day. So I went and told the woman who had hired me that I had to quit because I wasn't willing to move to the company's new location. I felt uncomfortable telling her, but I had to do it.

THE BACKFIRE EFFECT OF DOING WHAT'S BEST FOR ME

While the "what's best for me" approach can sometimes seem to be beneficial compared to keeping a promise to someone else, there can be a backfire effect. That's because the person who feels let down might do something to retaliate to the person who disappointed them. Though many people let such incidents go, some don't, and reactions can range from being miffed to acting to damage the reputation of the person they are angry at or worse. So this possible reaction should be factored into weighing the pros and cons of what to do, and it's another reason for the value of being other-oriented in traditional ethical systems. This value promotes good relations with others. By contrast, when this value of considering others isn't taken into account, the best choice for oneself in a self-other conflict might provide a short-term advantage, but have negative long range consequences because of the other person's reaction.

That's what happened to Ernie, a business associate of Joyce's, an entrepreneur in her 40s, after he let her down. Joyce invited Ernie to lead a program with her, because they had successfully done a workshop together on another subject a year before. Ernie said he was eager to do it, though he was busy with other projects. However, when the time came to prepare, Ernie was still very busy, and he repeatedly put personal and family matters first, thinking Joyce could change or postpone arrangements to accommodate him. Initially, Joyce did make some changes, but after the problem continued for several weeks, Joyce cut him out of the project. As Joyce explained what happened:

> I tried to tell Ernie for a couple of months what we had to do, and he seemed to agree. Though he was busy with many other

activities, he said he felt this project was important enough that he would make time and do what needed to be done. He seemed especially eager, since he saw this as an opportunity to set up a national program to promote his ideas.

However, when I told him about the time requirements for our project, he acted as if what I said was unimportant. He seemed to think I could readily change the deadlines around to suit him, but I couldn't and he didn't take me seriously when I tried to explain this. So he did what he wanted to do, which included spending a couple of weekends with his young daughter when he had custody from his ex-wife, instead of working on the project, since he felt his obligation to his family came first. Another time, he postponed a crucial planning meeting, to see his girlfriend, since she had the night off and he hadn't seen her in a week because he had been busy with his regular work.

The last straw came when Ernie told me he had to be out of town for a few days just before we had to present the workshop. Though he assured me he would have everything ready for the presentation, I felt I couldn't count on him any longer, despite our success in working together in the past. So I told him I had to work on the program myself and cut him out of it entirely. I felt I had too much riding on doing a good workshop to keep trusting him after he had let me down so many times.

I think Ernie felt he was doing the ethical thing, by being available for his daughter and seeing his girlfriend who he hadn't seen in a long-time. But each time he did, he let me down and broke his promises to me. Afterwards, he really regretted being cut out of the project. But at the time, he couldn't see how his own ethical decisions and priorities got in the way and prevented him from jump starting his own speaking and workshop career.

SUMMING UP

In sum, as we make decisions about who we are, determine our priorities, and make choices about what we want, ethical dilemmas often present themselves. They occur because of the pulls to do something other than what we ideally want—such as practical considerations of money in making choices about careers and business opportunities, and the conflict between putting our self-interest first or keeping our promises to others.

Ideally, the "moral" choice according to traditional morality is the one made for altruistic reasons, where we put self-interest and pragmatic pressures aside, go along with the rules, do what we should, and know strongly and intuitively this is the right thing to do.

But in the real world, as the dilemmas of the interviewees illustrate, when these basic identity and economic issues come up over career and work choices, one cannot always make that traditional, moral choice. Instead, pragmatic and personal interest considerations may become especially important; and often that's how people choose—sometimes because they want to follow a personal goal or ideal, other times just to survive.

CHAPTER 18

•

RESOLVING ETHICAL DILEMMAS
IN THE FAMILY

After the self, the next closest circle of relationships is the family—including one's parents, children, spouse or committed intimate other. For most of us, ties of blood or formal adoption forever bind us to each other, so though distance or disputes might sever connections, we still feel some emotional or psychic tie.

When family members live together, that gives rise to all sorts of intense, emotional ethical dilemmas that could be a book themselves—questions over life, death, raising children, discipline, rebellion against parents, and so forth. So I will not try to focus on these here.

Rather I will look at the major dilemmas that come up for people who are living independently of their parents or grown children. These problems center around two key themes—continued dependency and money. In fact, the two issues are closely related, raising questions like: "How much continued support—emotional or financial—do I owe my children?" or "How much continued support can I ask of my parents?"

As usual, in ethical issues, the answer is "it depends..."—on such factors as the strength of the tie, the need of the child or parent, the ability of either to provide the requested support, and beliefs about the appropriate thing to do. The interviewees expressed these different considerations and came to varying results, depending on how these factors affected them and their overall ethical approach. Here are some examples of the issues they faced and how they resolved them.

GETTING HELP FROM ONE'S PARENTS

Supposedly, grown children should be independent and self-supporting. But what if they aren't? Or what if they have some career goal they would like to realize but can't make it on their own?

That's when there can be an ethical dilemma over getting help from home. For the children, the question becomes—"Should I ask?" For the parents, it is—"Should I give?" Another question is whether the help given should be repaid, and what happens if it isn't?

These issues affected several interviewees. All of them truly wanted to be independent; they didn't like turning to their parents for support. But for various reasons, they hadn't fully realized their career or financial goals—though most of them were now in their late 30s and 40s. They ended up still needing and asking for their parents' help, as much as they didn't want to do it, and some later regretted they had asked.

In terms of the Ethical Choices Map, to get support for what they wanted to do, the interviewees were making a self-oriented pragmatic choice in asking for help, and they were breaking the customary rule that says one should be independent after a certain age.

GETTING HELP FOR A NEW VENTURE: FEELING DEPENDENCY AND OBLIGATION

For Janet, the nurse turned writer, a big source of conflict was getting help from her mother, since she had long been independent and didn't feel comfortable about getting this support. Yet she chose to accept it, since a priority was embarking on a new creative venture, and she couldn't do this herself. As she explained:

> I had a problem taking money from my parents, because I have been totally independent from the time I was a teenager. Even when I went to college, I had a little scholarship for my books and I worked too, so I never asked them for anything. My parents were never the type of people to provide financial support, though they encouraged me to go to college. As a result, I never expected their help, and I thought I would feel tremendous guilt if I had to ask.

But just recently, I asked my mother, who's divorced from my father, to lend me some money, because I was waiting for some financial things to get settled. She sounded like she was in shock at first.

She called me back several times to find out if I was okay, and I kept saying I was fine and to forget about giving me any money. But she was really concerned about me and finally insisted on giving me the money, though she told me: "I don't want you to think of this as a loan. I just want to give it to you and I don't want to hear anymore about it."

So finally I took the money. I really don't feel good about it, because I feel there's a price I will have to pay for it, since my mother normally does things with a condition attached. I don't think she does this consciously, but I think she has certain expectations that go along with her doing things.

GETTING HELP AND FEELING GOOD

Not everyone feels the same moral pangs of dependency in getting help, however. Joyce the entrepreneur, who launched several direct sales and mail order businesses when she was younger felt no such qualms about seeking assistance. Rather, she made something of a career of getting help from home. In her 20s, she initially felt some concern about the strings that might be attached to any family contributions. But after awhile, she got used to getting funds, and came to see both of her parents as a fall-back bank and security blanket. She felt no guilty or dependency—particularly since her parents lived hundreds of miles away in another state. As she commented:

It was hard asking at first, particularly since my parents had hoped I would get settled at having a regular job. Then I got into selling, marketing, and starting small businesses, and they appreciated my hard work and entrepreneurship. So they were willing to help out, although they didn't expect it to take so long for me to get established.

At first asking them for money bothered me a little, because I wanted to feel independent and know I could support myself. But I realized I couldn't try what I wanted to do without their help. So I finally asked, and they loaned me several thousand to get started, and from time to time after that, several thousand more. At first, I felt them checking up on me, and it bothered me a little to have to give up my privacy to get their advice and direction, because I needed their help.

After awhile, though, I didn't let that bother me. It was more important to me to make it on my own in business, and I found ways to answer their questions to reassure them and keep them from prying. Or I quietly let what they were saying slide past me, like water off a duck's back, so their questions didn't trigger my hot buttons anymore. I compromised so I could have the freedom and independence to do what I want in the business world, which I couldn't have without some financial help from my parents. And it came with some strings attached. But eventually, my parents came to feel helping me was for a good cause, as I started to become successful, and they stopped questioning what I was doing.

GETTING HELP AND RUNNING INTO FAMILY PROBLEMS

Even if feelings of dependency or guilt aren't an issue, getting financial support can bring other problems. It can trigger family jealousies, as one woman found. Or, there can be difficulties if the promised funds aren't paid back, as another discovered.

For Ari, the public health nurse, a problem developed when her sister challenged her mother's loan, claiming that Ari had taken advantage of their aging mother to get the money. As Ari described what happened:

In my family, I'm the eldest of three siblings, and I normally did everything on my own. I didn't have any financial help from my family, and I never expected it.

But a few years ago, when I was about 50 and bought my small house, I decided to go out on a limb emotionally and ask my mother for some help—basically a gift to help buy the house. I suggested that since she had helped my sisters in the past, maybe this one time, she could help me.

When I asked her, she really surprised me because she said: "Oh, I would *love* to." I was amazed she would be so supportive. Then, she asked: "How much do you want?" and I said, "Mom, it's a gift. Whatever you think would be wonderful." A few days later, she sent a check for $3000. So I was really pleased.

But then that check created some family problems about two years later when my mother was having trouble doing things for herself, shortly before she died. My sister back East was sorting through my mother's things and found this check my mother had written to me. My sister accused me of coercing my mother to give me the money by threatening her in some way. I tried to explain that it had been a gift, but my sister didn't believe me.

Then, based on what my sister said, the rest of the family accused me of coercing my mother for the gift, and my mother never spoke up to say: "No, it was a gift. I gave her the money because I wanted," since my mother has always been a person who doesn't speak up. So I was left out on this limb, feeling very frustrated and angry about the whole situation. I was angry at my sister for starting the conflict, and angry at my mother for not saying anything.

Connie, the art director's problem over money was even worse, because it led to a complete break with her father for many years when she didn't pay him back as she promised. As Connie explained:

I borrowed money from my father about 15 years ago when I was in my late 20s. It was a few thousand dollars. There was an open-ended agreement of when the money was due to be paid back, and I always intended to pay it back.

It was for a publishing project I was involved in, and I got the loan from my father on the assumption this money could generate certain cash revenues. But then this didn't happen in the time frame I expected. So I kept putting my father off, expecting the money would finally be there, but it wasn't.

I tried to explain, but my father is the kind of person who has a window in his mind about when things are supposed to happen. So finally, we agreed on a certain day when the money was supposed to be due. But I didn't have the money, so there was no further discussion. He simply cut me off and stopped speaking to me.

After that, there were plenty of opportunities for me to pay the money back. But for a long time, I held such resentment and so much hurt over what happened that I didn't return it. I felt my father punished me too much for that one mistake. So that cut off our relationship for over a decade, though it taught me to value the commitments and promises I make after that. And now I do what I say I will. It's a lesson I never forgot, though I felt it was unfair and hard at the time.

Thus, money can become a power fuel for ethical dilemmas between children and parents because it triggers conflicts over dependency, obligation, making and breaking promises, and other types of disputes, especially when other family members get involved.

TAKING ON OBLIGATIONS AS A PARENT OR CHILD

The opposite side of seeking help is giving it—and ethical dilemmas can arise around that, too, when a parent or child is asked to help out. Relatives can further complicate matters when they have their own ideas about the right or proper thing to do.

The major dimensions on the Ethical Choices Map that come into play are the Self-Other choices ("Should I help or think of myself?"), the Moral-Pragmatic pulls ("Should I follow traditional charitable ideals or favor practical considerations?"), and the Follower-Innovator dimension ("Should I give what's expected or might an alternative be better?"). Though there is pressure to help in some way, one may be uncertain how; and saying no may raise questions from others, too.

PUTTING OTHER'S INTEREST FIRST

For some of the interviewees with children, a common dilemma was over doing something they wanted versus what was better for their children—a classic self-other issue. Commonly, the rules of society urge doing what's best for the children, not oneself. And the interviewees did this. They chose what traditional morality would say is the right thing to do, despite disappointed aspirations.

That's what happened when Gaby the psychotherapist turned down an academic career for her daughter, while Janet the public health nurse, now trying to be a writer, stayed in her situation until her daughter was grown. Both put their children's needs first. As Gaby explained:

> I stayed in New York as long as I did for my daughter, so she wouldn't have to move. I gave up my academic career to work at home as a therapist, and I didn't particularly want to be a therapist. I really wanted to have a college teaching career, but I was divorced, and my daughter had only one parent, since my ex-husband was pretty much out of the picture. I felt an obligation to her.

And Janet commented:

> I made my daughter my first priority. Before her, I had never taken on any major responsibilities. I just wanted to live life, and didn't think about money much. I felt as long as I could make ends meet and get by, I was fine. I never even did any babysitting. Having my daughter was my turnaround point, and I became a serious mother. I had someone to take care of, and I turned things down that I would otherwise have wanted to do.

HELPING—BUT DOES HELP HELP?

While the decision to put their children first worked out well for some, others found that the decision to help raised questions about how much help to give. These were questions like: "When is enough enough?" "When is it too much?" and could they comfortably withdraw their help once given. Typically, questions of helping out became intertwined with questions of money, too.

Iris, the therapist, faced a helping dilemma as a parent, when her son kept asking her for help, though she felt he should be independent. He kept coming to her because of personal problems, but eventually she felt it was time to stop helping. It was a difficult decision, because she felt a sense of obligation to help if she could, though she felt her help was contributing to a cycle of continued dependency. As Iris explained:

My son has been a heroine addict and addicted to other drugs for many years. He's 32 and has been out of work for a number of months, as well as in a methadone treatment program. It's been a very difficult situation for the family, because he's needed a lot of money.

Finally I decided I had to stop giving. It was just continuing his dependency, as well as exhausting me. For example, he called collect Sunday, which is the way he usually calls, and he explained he had been abducted at gunpoint by two people on whom he had turned state's evidence several years before.

So what did he want now? He didn't phrase it as a request, since we had agreed in some previous therapy sessions that he wasn't going to ask me for anything else. But of course, he was asking again, though he didn't have to ask me in words. It was obvious. He had no money, nothing. He's on the street corner. He's beaten up. He's in pain. It's raining. He obviously wants me to come get him and take care of him.

But I decided to stay firm. So I told him again and again: "Joe, I can't help you. I cannot help you." It was an ethical or moral dilemma for me at the time, because I had to say no to him and yes to myself. It was also for his own good, so he would learn to stand on his own.

So I said no. But it was still very painful to do this. But I know I had to do it—for me, and perhaps also for him.

TURNING DOWN A REQUEST FOR HELP— AND FEELING GOOD

While Iris had to struggle with a request for help *as* a parent, Joyce the entrepreneur had to struggle with such a request *from* an aging parent. However, while Iris felt bad about continuing to help or turning down a request, Joyce had an easier time of saying no, deciding it was not only in her own interest, but her mother's, to refuse. Her self-interested response helped her mother, too, since it led her to overcome her problem by helping herself. Here's what happened, as Joyce described it:

When I was younger, my mother helped me get on my feet in running my own business. Then a few years ago, when she was around 75 and I was in my late 30s, she went through a crisis and turned to me for help. She wanted me to give up everything I was doing to move and live with her, so I could take care of her, but I said no.

It happened when I had finally gotten on my feet and had a fairly successful mail order company going. She had some health problems that come with age, became suicidal, and made a few suicide attempts with an overdose of pills. Each time she called a friend or the police to report what she had done and she ended up in the hospital. Meanwhile, she became very depressed and was not motivated to do anything. She couldn't even sign checks or drive a car.

After her second attempt, my mother called me a few times for help. The first time I flew down for a couple of days to visit her in the hospital. But when she asked me to stay for a week or more, I said I couldn't, because I had to get back to run my business and I was the only one who could do so.

After her next attempt, I said I couldn't come because I was busy making a deadline. Then, with her fourth attempt, she really put on the pressure, and her request became an ethical dilemma for me. The issue was basically: "Do I drop everything to put my mother first because she helped me in the past and says she needs me now? Or, do I do what I think makes the most sense, which is best for me and I think for her, too." What she wanted is for me to move in with her, take over her life as a conservator, and do all the things she now claimed she couldn't. She said I didn't have to worry about my business, because I could draw on her regular pension and stock dividends each month.

I didn't know what to do. When I told her I didn't think this was a good idea, because I'd have to drop everything in my own life to move and take care of her, she said I was being selfish and she recounted the many things she had done for me. Then, after I said I wasn't sure and had to think about it, she hung up on me saying she felt betrayed, didn't have a daughter anymore, and didn't want to live anymore. She said I was the only one who could save her. A few hours later, one of her good friends called me to urge me to do this, saying: "How can you not do this—your own mother?" Even my mother's doctor called urging me to relocate and be her conservator because of her depressed, suicidal state.

So now I felt all these people pressuring me to take on this unwanted family obligation, which would mean dropping my own life to take over my mother's life. But then, the more I thought about the situation, the more I felt my mother was playing the sick role to have power over me. I realized that even if I became her conservator, she would be paying the bills and asking me to do whatever she wanted, so in reality she would still be in charge. At the same time, I would have to give up everything I had been working towards for years to do this.

This choice didn't make sense for me personally. It also didn't seem to be good for my mother, despite what she and everyone else urged, since I would be helping her stay sick and dependent. Also, I felt she should decide to live because she wanted to for herself, not because she felt dependent on me. I felt the whole scenario was unhealthy for everyone involved, so I turned her down.

She and everyone else were very mad at me for a time, because I did. But as it turned out, my refusal was really the best thing. Soon after I told her "no," my mother pulled herself together enough to leave the hospital and started going to a regular therapy group. After a few months, she started volunteering for some community programs to help older people and became her old independent self again.

Afterwards, she never spoke of what happened, except to say she felt better. So in the long run, I felt I made the right decision, though it seemed like I was doing the selfish thing at the time. That's because by doing what I did, I forced my mother to become stronger and independent again, and that helped to restore her mental health. But if I did what she wanted and what seemed to be the moral, altruistic thing to do, that would have created an unhealthy mutual dependency and a lot of anger, I think.

HELPING TO HANDLE THE FAMILY ESTATE— AND CREATING CONFLICTS WITH THE RELATIVES

Being asked to help can also lead to other ethical dilemmas, when different people, such as other family members, have different visions of what kind of help should be given.

Bret the political consultant experienced this after his mother died, and he stepped in to help manage the estate. He thought he was doing the best, most "ethical" thing, using his usual rational, moral/pragmatic, and other-oriented approach in trying to maximize the earning potential of the money in the estate to benefit all the relatives. But other relatives objected, feeling he was being too controlling and manipulative. As he described what happened:

> When my mother died, she set up an educational trust fund for her grandchildren, and my brother and I were to be the executors. But we had a conflict because we have different ways of looking at things. I'm much more conservative in my investments and in my approach to how the money should be distributed.
>
> My brother's view was we should split up all the money between the heirs. After we argued about this for awhile, we split the money between us, and he gave his half to each person—about $5000 to each child. But I felt my mother's wishes were that the money should be kept collectively and used to make sure the children finished their education. The money my brother gave them was gone in a year. But I set up an educational trust fund and planned to parcel it out.
>
> My brother got angry about the fund, though. He said "You're being manipulative. You're trying to control. Mother is trying to control the family from the grave, and you're helping her along."
>
> But I believed she could choose where she wanted the money to go, and I wanted to obey the spirit of what she wanted, and what I think was for the best.
>
> Still, this decision created real emotional problems, because my brother bad-mouthed me before the nephews and nieces. I think if I had the choice about managing the estate again and my mother was still alive, I would say: "Get a third party to deal with this, and don't let either of us run the estate."
>
> But since it was the way it was, I tried to do the best I could under the circumstances, which was to think about the whole matter as logically as I could and do the most practical thing to carry out my mother's wishes. That's what I felt and still feel is the right thing to do—since it provides the most benefit for the kids, which is what my mother wanted after all.

SUMMING UP

In sum, seeking and giving help, often in the form of money, can be the source of many family ethical dilemmas, whether one is asking, giving, or trying to help sort out family finances. The issue is further intensified because of the closeness and emotional intensity common in family relationships. These make conflicts of interest in different situations even more difficult.

As you think about your own family relationships, consider the kinds of issues that come up for you and how you might respond, given your own priorities and how other family members might react. Where are they coming from ethically? And what kind of power do you or they have to put your differing ethical views into practice?

CHAPTER 19

•

ETHICAL DILEMMAS IN CLOSE RELATIONSHIPS: SPOUSES, LOVERS, AND CLOSE RELATIVES

The next zone around oneself is close relationships with spouses, lovers, and close relatives. Some of the bigger ethical conflicts, which have the subject of individual books, have involved monogamy, fidelity, adultery, and telling lies.

Aside from these big issues, based on basic premises about what the relationship should be, many conflicts in close relationships are not viewed as ethical dilemmas, because we often view personal relationships in our culture in terms of psychological dynamics. How do I feel about this? What does my inner child say to do? Is this choice helping me grow personally? Why am I having problems communicating my needs to my partner and making him understand? We also tend to downplay rules and obligations in close relationships in favor of focusing on feelings, communication, and understanding.

By contrast, ethical dilemmas are more in the realm of dealing with rules, obligations, and expectations that raise personal conflicts over carrying them out; they deal with adhering to the strictures of moral teachings versus doing what feels practical; they involve weighing whether to put the other person first or do what we want. When we try to eliminate notions of rules and traditional right and wrong principles from personal relationships and emphasize ideals of self-growth, that approach almost by definition eliminates the ethical component. (The major exception is in the few areas where notions about rules and right and wrong do arise, like having affairs, lying, and keeping secrets.) In turn, this focus on the self is related to our culture's emphasis on individualism and independence, which contributes to eliminating the ethical dilemma based on obligations and the expectations of others.

In other cultures, the ethical dimension comes into play much more in close relationships, because is there is more emphasis on the family and carrying out obligations associated with one's role in marriage. For example, in China and Japan, there are clear notions about being a dutiful son or daughter, and traditionally, the parents often picked out the marriage partner for their child. So an ethical dilemma might occur should a person feel some resistance to carrying out those rules or accepting a selected partner. By contrast, when the rules and expectations in a relationships are less important, opposing views turn into battles of wills, opposing feelings, misunderstandings, and betrayed hopes and dreams. But such conflicts are not really ethical dilemmas, because the expectations and rules are not there or are unclear.

That's a reason why, when I asked interviewees to talk about three or four major ethical dilemmas in their lives, few mentioned close relationships. Rather, they talked about the areas of their life where ethical rules and obligations are especially clear, such as in their work and professional lives. Those who did talk of ethical issues in close relationships raised only a few limited problems.

The most common dilemmas they raised were these: 1) getting in or out of the relationship; 2) dealing with money issues that raised ethical problems in the relationship; and 3) doing what's considered "wrong," such as having an affair or an abortion.

GETTING INTO OR OUT OF THE RELATIONSHIP

For Alan, the business manager, now in his late 20s, the big dilemma was over whether to get married or not. For him, it was an ethical issue because it meant having to give up his whole way of being in life—being independent, rational, and doing the practical thing in almost all he did—in order to share a commitment to someone else and allow emotion to guide many of his choices. Making his decision more difficult, he had to let emotional and other considerations affect his decision-making process, which he normally never did. At one point, he even questioned whether it would be ethical to change his mind and get out of his initial decision to get married. As Alan explained:

> About a month and a half before my wife, Jane, and I got married a couple of years ago, my mother passed away. Her death hit me hard, and I felt even more stressed because of the wedding coming up.
>
> Two days before the wedding my wife and I and some friends had a bachelor/bachelorette party. My wife knew even then about my negative feelings about drinking. I had gone through a period when I used drugs and alcohol a lot in my late teens and early twenties. But after I realized what I was doing was wrong and gave them up, I have been very much against them, except for perhaps a beer every once in a while.
>
> At the party Jane got really drunk. It drove me nuts that she was so drunk, and I was under such stress because of my mother's death. After the party, we went back to my mom's place in the country where we were staying, and I was literally one word away from saying: "Never mind, I don't want to get married."
>
> I was really upset that night. Getting married or not was one of the most critical decisions I've ever made. I sat in the car in the middle of the night, freezing, thinking over and over what to do.
>
> I realized that Jane had become my best friend, and we had a great deal of love for each other. She gave me something I always wanted that I thought I would never have, which is a partnership, because until then I had been a loner my whole life. I had a lot of anger and hatred, because my mother had cancer and was sick for so long while I was growing up, while my father was dead, and I hated my stepfather. So it had always been me against the world. Now I had to make a big decision—am I going to live by my anger and stay a loner, or am I going to live the way I've always felt I need to, which is being a part of the community.
>
> I think if Jane hadn't been drunk that night, this would still have been an issue for me. But since she was, I had to face these things about myself and decide what I wanted now. I realized that getting married was more than just exchanging

vows of love. It also was a decision that involved making a transition, and I felt if I could form a close partnership, it would be
making a transition to attaining what I had always idealized
but never had in my life—a close partnership with someone
else I really cared for. This decision also meant I would be in a
situation of give and take, no longer by myself. I would have to
think of someone else's desires, too. So finally I decided to go
ahead with the marriage after all.

Looking back, it's a decision I'm very glad I made. Jane and
I have become closer and closer, and I'm not so angry anymore.
I still believe all the same things, like about drugs being wrong.
But I'm more willing now to trust and work with other people
and deal with their flaws. I'm not so arrogant anymore, or at
least I'm attempting not to be.

In contrast to Alan's dilemma over whether to get into a marriage,
Francine, the freelance PR consultant, had to decide whether and
how to get out of one. Her approach to deciding differed, too.
Whereas Alan worked through the process mostly rationally, weighing one possibility or another, Francine responded much more emotionally and intuitively, doing what felt right. While Alan's focus
was more on what's "best for me," Francine, who tended to be very
other-oriented—maybe too much, she now feels—was strongly influenced by how her decision would affect her partner. As Francine
describes her story:

> The divorce changed my life a lot and it was a difficult deci-
> sion for me. I carry my emotions for a long time, and after 20
> years in my 40s, I'm still not fully over it, though I know you're
> supposed to move on.
> I have very strong feelings about principles and commit-
> ments, because I grew up in the 1960s and 70s, when these
> ideals were very important. That's why the divorce really both-
> ered me. It happened when I was young, just 23. We were
> only married for a year, and my boyfriend wanted very much
> to marry me. But as soon as we got married, he freaked out
> over making the commitment, because it was a time when
> people weren't getting married that much.
> As a result, about a year after we got married and moved to
> Florida, he decided to divorce me in a state where all he had to

206 • Making Ethical Choices, Resolving Ethical Dilemmas

do was serve the papers and I either had to fight it or I was divorced.

When I went to a lawyer, he said I could get everything—the house, the car, and alimony. Additionally, I had given up a good job in Washington, DC and completely changed my life to get married. So I had really committed myself to this man, and my lawyer urged me to go for it. But soon my ex-husband started threatening me. And then I started feeling sorry for him, because he had had a hard life in many ways.

It was an ethical dilemma for me. Should I go the high road and not get anything? Or should I try for everything I could get? But then, if I did, I was concerned about my ex-husband's threats and worried who would protect me if they were real. Mostly, they were verbal threats that if you fight me, you'll be sorry. However, when were married, a few times he pulled a knife on me, threw me down, and punched me in the arm. So now that he wanted to get divorced, I decided not to fight it, and I decided not to try to get anything.

In retrospect, I realize that my problem was I didn't take care of myself. I should have gotten what I could. Since then, I've never had a house again. I never had the security or material goods I had then. I thought at the time, I'm young. I can pick up and start again. I didn't realize how my self-esteem had been crushed by this, and that's what's so hard to get over.

Looking back, I realize how much I gave up to get married and be with my husband, including giving up a good job on Capitol Hill. I feel like my husband really did owe me something when he decided that he wanted out. But I didn't have the self-esteem at the time to try to get what I feel now he owed me. Instead, feeling sorry for him, and a little afraid of his threats, I let him keep everything, and I walked away with nothing. I was too concerned about him at the time and not concerned enough about myself.

Thus, for Francine, resolving the dilemma over her divorce was tied up with her feelings about herself and her husband, so any ethical decision-making was affected by psychological dynamics, too. In trying to do the "right" thing and being other-oriented (putting her husband's needs first), she was not paying enough attention to herself, in part because of her lowered feelings of self-esteem, as she later realized. As her case illustrates, ethical choices often cannot be separated from underlying psychological factors.

That close link occurs because issues of trust and previous difficulties and losses in relationships can influence subsequent ethical decisions about getting in or out of relationships. While the ethical imperative from traditional codes of ethics and morality is to keep commitments and tell the truth, many other psychological dynamics come into play in close relationships, so it's no longer purely an ethical dilemma.

DEALING WITH MONEY ISSUES THAT RAISE ETHICAL DILEMMAS

Money issues in a relationship may also have an ethical component, in that they raise questions about mutual sharing and obligations, responsibility, and promises about who will do and contribute what. There are also psychological meanings associated with contributing and taking money in a relationship, in that these actions raise issues around independence and dependency, self-esteem, and power. Such issues that are too complicated to get into here, given the focus on ethical choices and dilemmas.

But one money issue more closely tied to ethical considerations for several couples was what happens when the partners have different ethical ideas that affect how much money should be made or how it is spent. Who decides what to do? The couples I interviewed in marriages or close partnerships resolved this issue so that the person with higher "ethical" ideals could follow his or her occupational choices, while the more pragmatically-oriented partner provided the additional funds, if needed for financial support. These couples were able to do this, because the primary or more stable earning partner earned enough, so they could still manage financially, although one partner opted to earn less. But couples without such resources often have to make other decisions—such as choosing more prosaic, more practical alternatives, that include ethical compromises.

One person who was able to pursue this more ethical approach to work because of his partner's support was Dick, the architect, who explained his situation thus:

I don't make as much as my wife, because I'm on my own, and I've tried to be very selective in what I do. I only want to take on clients where I feel 100% behind their projects. I'm able to do this because my wife, who's also in architecture, has a pretty decent job and does well. She's been at the place for about five years, and she likes it and they like her, so it's pretty consistent.

She's the main breadwinner much of the time. We've talked about this and she feels comfortable with bringing in most of the money, and with the ups and downs I've experienced. She knows I'm really committed to the approach I have in the field, and she's been trying to support me, even though it's a little less secure.

Similarly, Karen, the ad agency owner, had the freedom to be selective to in the accounts she represented, because her more practical husband went along with her approach. As she explained:

I'm in a long-term marriage, almost 25 years. Sometimes I talk about business issues with my husband, and he has a slightly different take on things, because he's more concerned about money and the bottom line.

But while we need a certain amount of money to survive, he's pretty accepting about what I choose to do. Lately, I've been making more decisions on what personally is enriching and feels good, rather than choosing something because it could bring in a large dollar amount. My husband is more money-based than I am. I'm more based on getting excited about what the project is and whether it feels good and whether I'm going to learn from it.

But that doesn't create any conflicts for us. Even if he wouldn't make that choice himself, since he considers the bottom line more, he accepts what I do.

DOING WHAT'S CONSIDERED "WRONG"

A few interviewees also described crossing the line and doing something traditionally considered morally "wrong"—having an affair or an abortion. Such choices proved especially difficult, since they counter traditional key moral imperatives that support monogamy and oppose abortion. These include being other-oriented (i.e., considering the other married partner, the unborn child, or the larger community concerned with family stability and reproducing future generations), following the rules, and doing the "right" thing. By contrast, choosing to have an affair or an abortion involves breaking powerful norms to follow one's self-interest, do what seems practical, and cast aside the traditional teachings that these acts are wrong.

The big conflict, of course, is that if one does the "right" moral thing, it will be very damaging to oneself and have negative practical consequences. For example, having the affair provides passion, emotional fulfillment, excitement, and increased feelings of self-worth. The abortion means one can escape having to raise a child one doesn't want or can't afford, or one which may severely limit or bring shame in one's life; not having it means possibly facing these difficult consequences. Whatever the particular wrong act contemplated, one faces various negative consequences however one chooses. On the one hand, one may feel guilty about doing the wrong thing or being a bad person; on the other hand; one may experience practical consequences by doing the right thing.

In turn, priorities, circumstances, and other factors play a part in how one decides and deals with the resulting consequences, illustrated by two interviewees who faced such choices—Gaby, the therapist, who was attracted to a married man; and Francine, the PR consultant, who found herself unmarried and pregnant, and had to decide whether to have an abortion.

For Gaby, the decision was somewhat easier, since she already had a strong pragmatic orientation, was balanced on the self-other dimension, and was flexible in which rules she followed, though she generally followed the rules. Once she justified the affair on the grounds that the man was in an unsatisfying relationship with a woman who wouldn't divorce him and she was single, she found it easy to bend the rules. In addition, her own friends were understanding and forgiving. So she readily chose to begin and remain in the relationship, which turned into a long-term relationship, lasting over 20 years. As Gaby described what happened:

I don't normally see a relationship in terms of rules, but I felt a certain guilt when I met Jerry, because I knew I would be breaking an unspoken 'don't touch' rule when I started seeing him because he was married. I did feel an initial guilt, since I'm a feminist psychologist, and as a feminist, I know you're not supposed to do bad things to other woman.

So briefly I wondered, "Should I be having a relationship with a married man, which could do possibly destructive things to this other woman?" But I quickly stopped seeing our relationship in those terms, because I felt their relationship was so terrible. A good friend who knew them told me what was going on, which corroborated everything Jerry had told me. So I felt sure what Jerry told me was the truth—that their marriage was awful and she hated him. So after that I felt fine about seeing him and the relationship continued.

Marriage never became possible, because for practical reasons, Jerry never wanted to get divorced. But Gaby was willing to let the situation continue, again for practical reasons, although she made one decision to suit her own sense of rightness—not to be secretive or lie about the relationship. As Gaby explained:

> We met at a conference, and Jerry lived a few blocks away. When we first started seeing each other, he wanted to keep the relationship secret—and at that time, I said to him: "It's not my secret. It's your secret." Also, I told him, "I'm not a secretive person. I'm very open, and I think secrets are dangerous and bad for the person who's keeping the secret and bad for reality." "I mean, how can you know what's real when you go around telling secrets?"

Apparently this arrangement worked. Gaby felt comfortable to continue the relationship and talk about it with her close friends, who gave her the support she needed for breaking the rules and continuing to see Jerry. Their acceptance helped her feel she had created new acceptable rules she could follow. Meanwhile, Jerry was able to keep the secret from his own wife with whom he was already distant—or if she knew, she didn't interfere.

For a time, Gaby hoped for marriage, since their relationship was working so well, but since Jerry was committed to staying with his wife, Gaby let the relationship continue as it was rather than have nothing at all. Eventually, though, although finally, this unresolved situation contributed to her decision to move away, since she had no ties holding her back. As Gaby put it:

> I never made him choose, because I didn't think he would choose me. So our relationship continued the way it was.
>
> But eventually, since I didn't have any firm tie to him, that contributed to my leaving New York and moving to San Francisco. The city was deteriorating; my practice as a therapist wasn't that active anymore; my daughter from my first marriage was grown up and gone; life was very expensive. And as I got older, I felt more frustration and resentment that Jerry wasn't going to ever take care of me; instead he was taking care of this woman who he hated and she hated him.
>
> I started to feel more and more angry and resentful towards him. So finally I decided it was time to leave, though afterwards, we started to visit each other and became close friends, and there's none of the anger and resentment anymore.

In contrast to Gaby, Francine found making her abortion decision much more difficult, because it mean not only breaking the rules, but overcoming her strong feelings of right and wrong, implanted by her strong Catholic upbringing. Plus she lacked the peer support Gaby had, since she could not tell those close to her, such as her family, about her problem, because she knew they would disapprove. Thus, she felt a great deal of guilt as she considered having the abortion, and unlike Gaby, she was very other-oriented. So deciding to have an abortion meant contradicting three elements of traditional moral teachings which were very strong in her—following the rules, doing what's right, and doing for others. Instead, she would have to break the rules and do what was practical in her own self-interest. Also, making the decision process even more difficult, she was using a more rational, weigh the consequences approach foreign to her more natural intuitive style. As Francine told her story:

Though having the abortion happened twelve years ago, it's still an extremely emotional issue for me. I grew up Catholic, and all the members of my family were, and still are, very pro-life. Unfortunately, there was no way I could support a child, even if the father wanted to have the child. He wasn't offering marriage; even any money to help.

Had my boyfriend been able to take care of me at the time, it would have been a different situation, but there wasn't that choice then. So that's finally why I had the abortion—because I had to be realistic. But it was extremely difficult and painful to do.

And what made it even harder is I couldn't tell anyone in my family, because I knew how they would react. So it was my big secret for years and years. I didn't tell anyone anything for ten years, except for a few of my friends. And even twelve years later, I'm still extremely emotional about it.

Many years later though, Francine finally did tell some members of her family, which helped her feel better about what she had done. A key reason she spoke up is these family members had changed to become more accepting, after experiencing their own problems in relationships. And telling them relieved some of the burden she had long felt. Though she had broken the rules, done what wasn't right, and done something for herself and not others, their understanding helped her feel her actions were acceptable now. So she no longer felt she was such a bad person or felt so guilty. As Francine commented:

I grew up with a lot of Catholic guilt. Even though I try not to let that affect me now, it still does. I've felt bad over the years that I haven't had children, and I feel like I've had this secret from my family that I would have been a mother. Then, one Mother's Day a few years ago, when I was visiting my mother and sisters, wishing them a Happy Mother's Day, I ended up telling them. The reason I did is they had changed themselves. I couldn't tell them anything in the beginning because they were so judgmental. But then my mother and sisters went through divorces themselves. I was the first woman in the family to get divorced, so it was harder for me. But after two of my sisters decided they wanted to get divorced to and my older sister's husband divorced her, they were more accepting.

After that, I also told a few close friends who were understanding. Telling a few people has made it easier for me to accept what happened, since I find others are accepting—and particularly the members of my family. That's been a real load off my mind to feel accepted by them, too.

SUMMING UP

In sum, these ethical issues that occur in close relationships can be especially intense and difficult because of the high level of emotions sometimes involved. Also, this arena of life is influenced by some of the strongest traditional moral principles about what to do. These are further affected by various psychological influences shaping one's decision.

While some ethical dilemmas are less important or less complicated, and therefore easier to resolve—such as choices about whether one partner can earn less money and pursue more "ethical" work, other issues go much deeper and are more complicated. These require more hard thought or meditation, such as choices about whether to get married, divorced, or have an affair or an abortion. In such cases, while the traditional ethical admonitions might be very clear—get married, stay married, don't have an affair, and don't have an abortion—in practice, other influences have an effect, and they have a different impact on different people, depending on their own ethical makeup. For some people, breaking the rules or acting pragmatically out of self-interest to do what they want is much easier. By contrast, others feel more drawn to follow the rules, do what's right, or consider others—and they find it harder to break that mold when a major conflict occurs.

The interviewees illustrate the range of problems and approaches that might occur in close relationships. As you think about your own relationships, think about what has been important for you, where you fall on the Ethical Choices Map, and how this has influenced your past choices. Then you can apply these insights to help you deal with issues that come up in your own relationships.

CHAPTER 20

•

DEALING WITH FRIENDS, DATES, AND DISTANT RELATIVES

The third zone around oneself includes friends, dates, and more distant relationships—although at any time, any of these people can move into a closer zone. As long as they are further away, these relationships are less intense; less emotional. Sometimes the issues in these relationships involve philosophical or value considerations when people discover deep-seated value differences that set them apart. But often these dilemmas deal with attitudes and orientation issues, such as conflicting rules and expectations, or whether to put the other person's interests or one's own first.

These problems also tend to be simpler to resolve than those in closer relationships, since they are less complex. They don't have the long history of a deep, continuing relationship or the traditional moral imperatives associated with close relationships, which sometimes make closer relationships so much more difficult to deal with.

The type of ethical issues that arise is further affected by the fact that many of these relationships are transitional. They are in a zone between our more personal and professional life, and some of these relationships span both. Still others fall into a kind of limbo as we assess whether we want them to become closer.

An example of a relationship that spans the personal and professional is the close blood relative who has become very distant (like the parent who lives cross country and one hardly sees, or the friend or cousin with whom one also has a business relationship). Whether the relationship is more of a personal or professional one depends on which relationship is most influential—do we relate to the person more closely as an intimate family member or partner, or more distantly as a person with whom we primarily have a professional or business relationship. Or is the relationship somewhere in between?

Similarly, where a dating relationship falls may be uncertain, since a dating relationship is often transitional—as we decide whether we want to create a closer relationship with a partner, continue the relationship as a good friendship, or regard the date in the future as another casual social or professional acquaintance.

This more casual and sometimes transitional nature of these relationships can result in certain types of dilemmas, such as: 1) dealing with discoveries about the other person that affect the relationship; 2) deciding whether to continue the relationship and on what basis; and 3) determining how to most diplomatically break off or change the nature of a relationship. In turn, how one resolves one issue affects others—such as how one decides to continue the relationship affects how one later chooses to break it off.

To illustrate these patterns, following are examples of how the interviewees dealt with ethical dilemmas in these areas.

DISCOVERING AND DEALING WITH DIFFERENT VALUES AND MORAL PERSPECTIVES

When friendships or dating relationships are new or still in an early transitional stage, one issue that sometimes arises is what happens when one discovers differences in values or ideas that challenge one's views about what's right or appropriate. Some examples of this might be the fundamentalist who discovers a friend is an atheist, or homosexual; the ardent liberal Democrat who learns a friend is a conservative Republican; the person who holds up a person as an ideal only to find that a friend doesn't similarly value that person. For some people, it's easy to set aside such differences and decide to simply disagree. But for others, the differences in beliefs and values are so basic, that they experience an ethical dilemma over what to do. They don't know, for example, whether to suffer in silence, have a confrontation and try to persuade the other person to think or act differently, or end the relationship.

Connie, the art director, had such a values dilemma when she discovered a good friend with whom she was starting to develop a romantic relationship held views that discredited one of her long-held idols. The revelation triggered such strong feelings of antipathy that she couldn't continue the friendship. As Connie explained it:

> I was with a friend of mine, a computer engineer, and we were watching television, when Ralph Nader suddenly appeared on TV. I was thrilled to hear his name again in the news, because I feel so strongly and positively about him as an activist. To me, he's someone who really believes in something and fights for what he believes him.
>
> As we were watching, this guy said: "Oh, Ralph Nader. What a jerk." Then, he proceeded to put him down. I thought to myself: "My God. How could he say such things about Ralph Nader?" I had never seen this side of this man before, and I had such strong opinions opposing what he was saying.
>
> We had a real debate about our differences and different values. His views were so appalling to me, they made me not like him. I believe in allowing people to be who they are, but I had no idea that his politics were so off compared to mine. Though we shared so many other common interests and had so much fun being together, I suddenly realized our belief structures were so different. What he said was so offensive to everything that I believe in.
>
> So that was the end of our possibly romantic relationship, because I don't like that kind of mentality. I don't want to be around a person with that kind of mind set or energy.

Because Connie valued honesty and openness in a relationship, she directly told her friend that this was the end of possibly developing a close relationship, though she was still open to a casual one. As Connie explained:

> I told him: "I never saw you as such a conservative before. So this totally changes my opinions of you. To be honest with you, I'm less attracted to you. I don't like the way you think." We can still be friends. But it's over in a romantic way for me. It wasn't really serious yet, and now it won't be.

Alan the business manager similarly faced a value conflict when he discovered that two people he had considered friends were drug users. For Alan, a former drug user, being drug-free was a central moral conviction. So he was not willing to compromise or understand if someone used drugs, though he usually approached other issues in a pragmatic rational way. As he explained:

> I had some friends with whom my wife and I had socialized for about a year—a couple, David and Pam. One night they came over for dinner. Somehow the subject got around to drugs and they were talking positively about them. They were saying how they were cool and they liked to take them every once in a while.
>
> That was it for me. I don't want people like that in my life. It was easy for me to never see them again, and we haven't spoken to them for six or eight months.

In another case, Alan called the authorities on a man who had been a friend at a time when Alan was still involved with drugs. After Alan quit and this man didn't, he reported him as a user, because he felt the man's activities with drugs might negatively influence the man's child. Alan reacted in moral terms, since for him drugs had become a defining issue.

But unlike Connie who told her friend what changed their relationship, Alan did not say anything to his friend about his opinions or even warn him he was going to report him. He didn't think it would do any good. As he explained:

> I had already tried to tell my friend Peter over and over that it's not cool—doing drugs in general or doing it in front of his kid. But Peter wasn't getting the message, so I felt, screw him. That's why I tried to take the decision-making process out of his hands by calling child protective services. I didn't tell him I did, because God only knows what he would have done if I told him. He might have taken the kid and left town, maybe even gone to Tijuana. So, I didn't tell him.

DEFINING THE STRENGTH OR NATURE OF THE RELATIONSHIP

Another ethical dilemma in the relationships in this zone with friends, dates, and distant relatives centers around the bond of the relationship. How strong is it? How much can one depend on the other person? What can one ask or reveal? What should one offer or conceal?

When these problems are minor ones, they may be more like questions of social etiquette, diplomacy, or understanding the rules of appropriate behavior. But as they become more complex and serious, they can raise questions about obligations, responsibility, loyalty, commitment, and dependency that raise ethical questions.

TO TELL OR NOT TO TELL

Other issues revolve around revealing or concealing information and being open and honest versus being tactful or taciturn. These choices can range from simple matters of exercising discretion in everyday situations to more serious conflicts over sharing very critical and sensitive information.

At the low end of the scale is what happened to Sam, the writer, when he was trying to break in as a stand-up comic. He noticed that a friend of his had a flaw in his act that was undermining his performance. Should Sam tell him? Did he have an obligation to do so as a friend? Would his friend be hurt? Or would it be more diplomatic for the friendship if Sam didn't say anything? As Sam explained:

> I have a friend who's also a comedian, and I saw a defect in his work. I wanted to point it out to him because I felt he'd should know or might appreciate knowing, though it could be upsetting, because there's an ego involved in the work. So at first I hesitated to bring it up. But ultimately, I figured he could handle it and I told him.
>
> I explained that he presents himself in his act as a guy who finds it hard to get dates, because he's ineffectual with the opposite sex and is very insecure about that. But his manner on stage is very confident, and he's very good looking, so what he's

saying isn't believable. His image isn't consistent with the persona that he's presents. So I felt like I ought to tell him this, but I felt I could hurt him a lot.

Fortunately, when I told him, it had a happy ending. He agreed with me and so we talked about how to change it.

Sam's choice thus involved making a fairly simple other-oriented and moral choice. He decided to do what was best for his friend and the honest thing to do, rather than doing what felt initially more comfortable for himself, since he liked keeping relationships smooth by being "nice" to people.

By contrast, Kelly the speaker and PR consultant faced a much more difficult decision about what to conceal or reveal, when a friend asked her to share some confidential information about an ex-boyfriend the friend was now dating. After using her usual style of rationally weighing the matter and sensing intuitively what was right, Kelly decided not to say anything. Though sharing the information might help her feel closer to the woman, she felt sharing it would be a betrayal of her ex-boyfriend. As Kelly explained:

> I have an ex-boyfriend who is still a good friend. We're pals and we occasionally go to the theater together. We haven't dated in about five or six years, and he sometimes brings his new girlfriend along, sometimes just the three of us, or sometimes a foursome when I bring a date. I've known her for about a year and like her.
>
> On several occasions this woman said to me that "We must spend some time together. I'd love to have lunch and compare notes on the man we have in common." As much as I like her and share other things with her, I felt very awkward about this, because he's still a friend, and I didn't want to divulge all of his flaws that I saw and the things that didn't work between us that made me break up the relationship. For one thing, I didn't want to disillusion her, and secondly I didn't feel it would be very nice of me. He would be very upset if I talked to her about that. I like her and would like to develop a friendship with her, but I felt I couldn't be that intimate with her about issues relating to him.

Kelly also felt concerned that if she did say something, this could possibly damage the relationship the woman had with her friend, and she felt this wasn't a nice thing to do. As Kelly observed:

> I thought there was a danger that if I told her how I feel it could break up their relationship, because when I saw them together, I saw some of the problems that broke up my own relationship with him. For example, I noticed them arguing about some of the same things we argued about. She already has some mixed feelings about the relationship, and I felt what I might say would add fuel to the fire.
>
> But I decided not to say anything and possibly ruin the relationship, because she was getting something out of it. He's a very good person. He cares for her a lot and pays a lot of attention to her. I didn't want to spoil it for her. Also, while, I felt opening up might help me feel closer to this woman I like, I felt there was too much of a risk to my friendship with a man I have known for a long time as a friend.

Finally, having made this decision not to tell, primarily due to practical and moral considerations, the next question was what to do if the woman asked again. Kelly thought she would since the woman had already asked her several times, and Kelly decided to talk to the woman and explain her own feelings, rather than avoid the issue and hope things would slide. This time she used her intuition to help her imagine the best approach. As Kelly described her feelings:

> I have been feeling a little discomfort with her as a friend because she kept asking. I know she seriously wants to know, and I feel I have to say something.
>
> So sometime when we do something together, I will tell her something like: "I'm in a quandary about this. I'd like to talk to you and ordinarily I'd feel fine sharing my feelings about someone with you. But you're dating him right now and I feel a loyalty to him as a friend. So I don't want to tell you things about him that I had difficulty with, because he'll probably be hurt." Hopefully, she'll appreciate my honesty, and that feels like the most comfortable, honest way for me to deal with this issue.

Thus, by a combination of rationally weighing alternatives and finally intuiting what to do, Kelly was able to make a comfortable decision. It mixed moral and practical considerations, and it paid homage to the rules of friendship, which include notions of loyalty. Plus she showed a concern for others in her choice.

TO HELP OR NOT TO HELP

Kelly went through a similar process in determining whether to help a friend who needed money. The friend, woman in her mid-50s, was having trouble after a successful career, and she had already approached Kelly a few times for help and borrowed money each time. Now she needed help again, and she said she had no one else to turn to. But Kelly herself was finding financial conditions tight. Should she help again or not? Kelly went through some personal turmoil before deciding to help in a limited way, taking into consideration both the needs of her friend and her own. As Kelly explained:

> I had an awkward situation with a girlfriend about money. She's very well educated and has lots of talent. We both went through some hard times financially a few years ago, and after I came into a little money, I lent her some. This went on for about four years, and now she owes me about $10,000. She keeps promising that a break is going to happen with the various projects she is working on. But so far, she has never been able to pay me back. Then, she called a week ago and asked to borrow another couple of thousand dollars.
>
> She understands that I'm not rolling in money myself, and she has helped me in other ways since she hasn't been able to pay me back. For example, she'll make phone calls for me or run errands, and she always listens and understands when I'm in trouble. She's been a good friend and is a good person.
>
> But I don't know what to do about this money thing. She said she needs another couple of thousand and says she's tried everybody else and can't find it.

For Kelly, the key dimensions at issue were the other/self (help her friend or put her own tight financial situation first) and the moral/

practical dimension (support a friend versus consider the likelihood of continued financial losses). Again Kelly used rational considerations and intuition to decide. As she described what she finally did:

> My heart would like to help out. I feel that when somebody's in need and has been a good and loyal friend, I would like to help. But then, I have to look at myself. Until I get my next advance I'm barely making it from month to month myself, and I'm on a very tight budget. She has friends who have a lot more money than I do who have turned her down. I think that's cruel that they have said "no," when they have the money.
>
> So the ethics for me are how far do you go for a friend who's in need? How far do you put yourself in jeopardy for a friend?
>
> Finally, I told her I would look at my budget very carefully for the next three or four months, and I will squeeze out whatever I can. I told her "I am getting a check for a client I just worked with, and out of that check I will give you as much as I can without harming myself. But I don't think I can give you the full $2000 you want."
>
> So I decided to help as I can, because she really needs the help and tries to be helpful and understanding in return. But I can't help as much as she would like right now, because I can't put myself in jeopardy.

TO DEAL WITH NEGATIVE FEELINGS IN A RELATIONSHIP

Sometimes ethical conflicts can arise out of or contribute to psychological conflicts in the relationship. While the ethical component involves not following certain rules, taking on certain responsibilities, or carrying out certain promises, these other dynamics can make the conflict even more intense by provoking negative feelings like anger, jealousy, and revenge, that need to be dealt with, too.

This is what happened for June, the tax consultant, in a relationship with a friend. As June described what happened:

> I felt hurt several months before when my friend Annie gave away a handkerchief I had given her as a Christmas present, though I didn't say anything at the time. Then several months

later, when she did something that made me angry, I criticized her for this and she was angry I criticized her. So after that our relationship was on fairly fragile ground.

Then another incident made things worse. I told her I had put a poem to music for a mutual friend, and she felt jealous I had done this. So I said: "I can do it for your poems, too." But after I did one for her, she didn't like it at first, though her lover and therapist thought it was very good. I think their opinion bothered her, because it invalidated her own reactions, and I think she wanted not to like it, because she was angry at me because I had criticized her Christmas gift.

A couple of days later she sent me a letter, saying she wanted to cut off our friendship, accusing me of being insensitive in our relationship. And I suppose in a way I was, because I sometimes acted arrogant and superior, as if I know what's right, like telling her she was wrong about the Christmas gift. And then I think the music I wrote for her poem as a friendly gesture led her to feel put down.

So for me the ethical issue is knowing how to act towards her and treat her. Can I continue a friendship with someone I care for as a friend, but feel superior to, so she feels overshadowed. Can I really be me in the relationship, or do I have to compromise too much to consider her sensibilities, so it becomes a relationship on her terms?

At the time we spoke, June was still trying to work out the best thing to do in her own mind, though she was leaning towards being more sensitive and understanding and putting her friend's needs first, since she felt her friend was in a fragile psychological state because of problems with feelings of self-esteem. "But I'll know what to do when the time is right," June said, since she usually used her intuition to decide.

TO BE GENERALLY MORE OPEN AND HONEST OR MORE CONCEALING

How open or honest to be in a relationship are other key considerations for some. This was the case for Jerry, the lawyer, still single in his early 30s. At one time, he was more likely to conceal information and be evasive to protect himself and look better. But increasingly, he felt pushed into opening up and being more straightforward in relationships, because the women he dated wanted this, and he had difficulty keeping the relationships going otherwise. As a result, though he was usually very self-oriented, he was motivated to be more other-oriented, because this seemed the most practical, reasonable thing to do. As Jerry explained:

> In my personal relationships with women, I have had an ethical dilemma involving not doing or telling certain things my girlfriends thought I should do or say. Some of them got mad at me because I didn't tell them things they thought I should, whereas I felt it was okay not say things, as long as I didn't lie. For example, I didn't like to reveal personal weaknesses or things I felt were private, though my girlfriends felt not revealing them was a breach of trust in a relationship.
>
> In the past, I used to reveal as little as I have to, though if a date or girlfriend was insistent, then I would tell. So I usually resolved the ethical dilemma through inaction and stonewalling as much as possible, particularly over the issue of seeing other women. If we didn't have an agreement to be exclusive, I wouldn't volunteer the information I was seeing anyone else, and some women got very angry at me for not saying anything.
>
> I used to feel justified from a man's perspective in not revealing anymore. But now as I get a little older and more mature, I'm more open to other viewpoints and I can see the woman's view, too. I can see how different people have different ideas about what's right depending on how they grew up, their family, their community, and when they grew up. So they have different views about how open you should be, too.
>
> Anyway, after becoming aware of these differences, I've come to realize that the best way to resolve these issues is to talk about them and bring those differences and beliefs out in the open. That's because that's the only way two people can really communicate—by bringing things into the open and not assuming certain rules of behavior. I think I'm about 70% good at doing this now.

In turn, by becoming more open and receptive to the other person's point of view, Jerry had better relationships, so pragmatically, his shift to become more other-oriented, was of benefit to himself. As Jerry realized, his relationships became better when he changed because being more open contributed to improved understanding and led the women he dated to feel closer to him. Conversely, Jerry discovered what happened when he wasn't open, particularly in one vivid example, when one woman he dated dropped him because he didn't show her how he really felt. As Jerry described it:

> Unfortunately, I destroyed a couple of relationships because I wasn't more open in volunteering information, and in each case, it was because I thought I was doing something that would be in my self-interest. I thought by not revealing something, I wouldn't scare away the woman, but the exact opposite happened.
>
> The incident that really brought this home and made me realize I had to change occurred with a woman I really liked a lot. I tried for months to get her to go out with me, and finally after we did, she agreed to be my girlfriend.
>
> Then, one day she expressed her warm feelings to me outside of her place of work, and I really felt ecstatic. However, I didn't react very affectionately with my physical body language. I just hung back and acted really distant. Had I demonstrated how excited I really felt and given her a hug or done something to show my real feelings, I think that would have made all the difference. We would have continued going out and she would have stayed with me.
>
> Instead she reconsidered the relationship. She thought I was cold, so she broke up with me soon after that.

TO TELL THE TRUTH OR NOT

A related ethical issue to telling or not telling is whether to tell the truth or lie. The lie is one of the traditional ethical taboos, but in practice, it can be tempting to lie to cover up mistakes, embarrassments, or otherwise unacceptable behavior; to protect someone else; or for many other reasons.

Most commonly, the interviewees who used lying to help or protect others were most successful. If discovered, they experienced some embarrassment, but the revelation wasn't too serious. It was like they had told an acceptable social lie, so any discovery just caused some hurt feelings and after apologies, all was well. They also didn't experience much conflict in deciding to tell the social lie; it just seemed like the most practical thing to do at the time, to help themselves out of an undesirable situation or relationship (self-orientation), to help protect the other person's feelings (other orientation), or both. In this way, lying helped them follow the usual social rules about having comfortable, friendly social relationships; whereas saying what one really felt might be taken as an insult or be otherwise socially disruptive.

For example, Pam the single nurse, in her 30s, had this experience when she met men and wasn't interested in dating them, or when she wanted to break off the relationship with a man who still wanted to see her. Rather than telling the man what she felt, she created diplomatic excuses or explanations, such as being too busy with work or seeing another man, instead of saying honestly: "I'm not interested," or "I'm not attracted to you." As Pam explained:

> Usually, I try to say I'm busy, will be out of town, or something like that, so the man I don't want to date gets the picture and stops calling. That way the guy doesn't feel there's anything wrong with him. I don't like to hurt a guy's feelings.
>
> However, one time I met a guy at a dance and went out with him a few times, which led him to think I was more interested than I was. I should have been more explicit from the beginning, since he just wasn't getting the picture, and wanted to get a lot closer than I wanted.
>
> On the first date, we went to the movies, and he tried to get friendly with me. I didn't want to get that friendly, and I realized I had encouraged him that first night by the way I danced close, though I was just having fun. So I suppose I should have been more explicit on our date and say: "I really just like you as a friend." But I didn't.
>
> In the end, he did get angry, because after I put him off several times and he didn't go away, he started feeling I was playing with him. That happened when he called after I had given him a number of previous excuses and he asked: "Can you go out tonight?" I said "No, because I have to be somewhere," which was true. But I said what I did very abruptly, and he got

mad, saying: "Oh, well, now at least we know the truth." So he hung up mad.

I felt bad he was upset. I think it would have been better if I had given him a good excuse early on, like I often do to end a relationship without hurting a guy, such as saying there was another guy who came back into my life.

For Pam, these little dating lies were usually better than saying the truth because in most cases, the guys accepted them and felt better when the relationship didn't work, since they didn't feel they had done something wrong or were inadequate. It helped them maintain their illusion of competency and power. While the lie might not be right, Pam felt her reason for using it was a good one—looking out for the other person's feelings and finding a practical way to make him feel good and end the relationship with minimal recriminations.

Then, too, Pam had a self-interested reason for using this strategy—at the time, she was feeling lonely, so she wanted to keep the guy around as long as possible. She tried to have it both ways—having him as a friend and keeping him there by letting him think she might be interested romantically. Otherwise, if she told him the truth early on, he might have left. As she explained:

> I guess I wasn't doing the ethical thing. I wasn't being really honest with him by letting him think I was interested, because I saw him as a kind of filler. That's a person you go out with, thought it's not the right person for you. But they're satisfying certain needs that you have. In this case, this was my need for somebody that was interested in me, who I found halfway attractive, which I've done with a couple of other guys. Also, I found it flattering to have this young guy, maybe about 5 or 6 years younger than me, come after me.

Thus, though she didn't feel it was the most honest or "ethical" thing to do, generally Pam opted for social lies and game-playing to make a dating relationship go or end more smoothly. Still, she felt bad when this approach didn't work—and that's when she would be more direct and say what she really felt.

By contrast, Jerry found that many of his lies, as well as his tendency to conceal things, backfired, leading him to stop telling lies, too; because from a pragmatic perspective, lying got him in trouble. It was better to tell the truth. As he described one incident that contributed to this decision:

> I'm a songwriter on the side, and in one case, I wrote a song for one woman. Then I told a woman with whom I was supposed to be in an exclusive relationship that the song was for her. I lied. First, I lied to her about who the song was for; second, I didn't disclose that I was seeing someone else.
>
> When she found out the song was really for someone else, all hell broke loose. Worse, it was a love song. If I hadn't told this woman that this song was for her, it wouldn't have been a big deal, because you can always use different women's names in a song. But since I said it was for her but it was for another woman, she got justifiably upset.
>
> So my biggest ethical dilemma has been this issue of nondisclosure and not telling the truth. But now that I've been finding that my approach doesn't work very well and keeps getting me in hot water, I'm trying to change.

DECIDING WHETHER TO START, CONTINUE, OR END THE RELATIONSHIP

Since dating is a transitional relationship, many questions arise about whether to start, continue, or end it, resulting in various ethical considerations. Such issues often involve making choices in a situation where the rules for how to act aren't clear or relevant, since these are more matters of the heart. Though moral considerations about honesty and commitment are common, generally the interviewees did what worked, presenting themselves in the best possible light to promote the relationship.

Henry, the supervisor, now in his 50s, typified this pragmatic self-oriented approach as he tried various techniques to find a woman. He was direct, blunt, and not very solicitous of the women's feelings as he tried to find someone he liked as quickly as possible. As he explained:

In my time of life, I would choose self-interest over what's morally right 90% of the time. I don't have much time left to find the right person and settle down. So I don't want to waste time. When I talk to the women I meet on the phone through advertising, I talk to them about my interests, my likes, and theirs. I tell them some of the things I want and don't want; find out some of the things they want and don't want. And if the interest is not really there for me, I don't try to smooth things over or be polite. I just say, "Look, you're a nice person, but I don't want to see or date you." I'm very direct and decide quickly ,because I don't want to waste six months or so finding out the relationship's not going to work.

Similarly, Joyce, the government researcher in her 40s, put self-interest ahead of traditional moral ideals about truth-telling when she first met prospective dates and in the early stages of the relationship. As she explained:

Dating and creating relationships today is so much about packaging and image. You have to dress and look a certain way. I have found you can't always be straightforward, at least in the beginning, so I try to present myself a certain way.

For example, I look younger than I am, so I don't tell my real age. I say I'm about ten years younger, in my 30s, because if I said my real age, men wouldn't be interested. They have certain images associated with women in their 40s or women who are older than they are. So I've learned to lie about my age. Then if anything develops, maybe down the road I'll tell them the truth, because then they'll have a chance to know me, so age won't matter as much. But if I said anything earlier, their beliefs about age would be a barrier.

It's the same way with interests. I'm not particularly interested in sports, but I've learned to read the sports pages and talk about that, because I know guys are really interested in sports. This discussion makes them think I share their interest. But after the relationship is going for awhile, and I know they are interested in me, I start pulling them around to my own interests, say by taking them to art galleries or films, and they seem to respond.

I know it sounds manipulative, but once there's that emotional and sexual hook, you can start using it to get what you want in the relationship. So that's what I do. It may not be particularly ethical and moral to be a little devious this way. But I've found that works for me in getting a relationship going, and then getting it to go in the direction I want.

This tendency to put self-interest first also meant that friends might be pushed aside in a kind of survival of the fittest scenario. At times, this response might occur in a direct up-front way, such as when a man turned on the charm and wooed a woman away from his friend, as Henry sometimes did. Or it might be done more manipulatively and surreptitiously, as Joyce did when she set her sights on a man a friend was dating and found ways to see him when her friend wasn't around.

By being direct, though, Henry sometimes got his male friends mad when he took a woman they liked away, though he didn't do so enough to permanently damage the friendship. As he explained:

> I'm the kind of man that talks easily with women. I can easily go to a bar or anywhere and engross people in conversation. So many friends have wanted to come along with me, because it makes it easier for them to meet women when I open the door like this, particularly when the woman I start talking to has a friend. Then, they can slide right in and start talking to her.
>
> Sometimes, we agree that I'll get a woman the man likes talking, and then, I'll step back and he'll take over. However, sometimes when the woman and I have really hit it off, I won't back off or the woman won't switch. Though the guy makes a big effort, he won't get to first base, and then he'll be mad at me.
>
> A few times, I also got a friend mad when he started talking to someone, and I found her interesting myself. Then I turned on my charm and I usually got her interested in me. He'd be mad, then, too.
>
> I guess on balance, this hasn't happened enough that the guys stopped doing things with me, though they were mad for awhile. And I suppose it's not the right moral thing to do. Ideally, I should consider my friend's feelings. But the way I look on it, dating is like a game and may the best man win. I just happen to be the best man a lot of the time, so I win.

By contrast, Joyce's approach was more indirect, so normally her own friends wouldn't know, though she used this approach effectively. As she described it:

> One basic rule in friendship and dating relationships is you are not supposed to go after your friend's dates. In the beginning when it's not clear who a guy is interested in—say if you both meet at the same time at a party—the rule is that it's pretty much open season. So even if a friend says she'd really like to go out with someone, the situation is still pretty open. This means you can both do what you can to get the guy interested. Then, when it seems he has settled on one of you, the rule is that the one he isn't interested in should back off.
>
> Usually I do follow that rule, and it makes for good relationships with your friends. After all, they will stop trusting you, if they think you are going to go after the guys they like. But there have been a few times when I really liked someone, and I felt our relationship would work better than him having a relationship with my friend. In that case, I've tried to find an opening, such as a good time to contact and get to know the guy myself. But I've tried to do it quietly, behind the scenes, so my friend won't get mad.
>
> For example, I might turn up at some places he might be to get a relationship started. Or maybe I could find out some information from my friend to learn more about him and what he likes. Then I could be better able to talk to him when I run into him. So in various ways I would try to create a natural opening. That way it doesn't look like I'm doing anything to interfere, so my friend won't be upset with me, and I can eventually get what I want—him.

Finally, leaving and breaking off a dating/friendship relationship can bring up ethical issues, such as when leaving triggers feelings of betrayal, broken promises, and failed commitments. Often the self-other dimension is involved when staying means putting the other's needs first, while leaving means following one's own desires. The interviewees who confronted this decision to leave or not generally felt some guilt or sad feelings that others might be hurt if they left.

Even so, they ultimately decided to act in their own best interest—often because it seemed the most practical and sensible thing to do.

Gaby the therapist had this experience when she decided to leave the East Coast and her lover to come to California. As she explained:

> I began to think of all the benefits of leaving. I thought to myself: "I could move away and I wouldn't have to think of my lover and why he didn't leave his wife anymore."
>
> On the other hand, I had a lot of friends and members of my profession who didn't support the move. One therapist friend said, "You know, as a therapist you can't move away from your problems. They will follow you wherever you go." Also, all my therapist friends felt betrayed by my leaving, since we were a cohesive group—when one member leaves, they feel that person is abandoning them.
>
> I did it anyway, though. I said to myself, "There's no way my life is going to be worse if I move." I knew I would be leaving my close friends, and my lover, who depended on me, even though he wouldn't leave his wife and marry me. But I felt ready to make the break for a new life.
>
> After I left, it was so much better. Now I go back two or three times a year, and still see my lover from time to time both in California and New York. I speak to some of my old friends on the phone about once a week, too. So moving was the best thing to do. I was tempted not to go for awhile, because I was thinking of what other people wanted. But then I started thinking about me, and the move seemed clearly the best thing to do.

SUMMING UP

In sum, in the early phases of a dating/friendship relationship, the influence of self-interest is especially strong, and that helps one decide whether to enter or stay in the relationship. In turn, one is relatively free to consider the benefits and ask, "What's in it for me?" since there are few rules governing informal, personal relationships. In fact, the dating process often seems like a competitive "survival of the fittest" struggle as friends become rivals and each seeks to be the one in the relationship, though this means pushing a competing friend aside. Paradoxically, this action overrides an ethical guideline about friendship—that friends are supposed to be mutually supportive and loyal. Here, though, self-interest often wins the day.

However, as the relationship develops, one increasingly is drawn to consider the feelings of the other person and to be more honest and open, because this mutual giving and sharing helps build and strengthen the relationship. In turn, while lying and not telling may work at times, deception can often undermine the relationship, leading to the opposite of the desired result. Thus, commonly, as the relationship continues, so does the pressure to put the other first and be more ethical, because whether moral or not, that's what seems to work.

CHAPTER 21

•

DEALING WITH ETHICAL DILEMMAS IN WORK AND BUSINESS: INDIVIDUAL AND ORGANIZATIONAL RULES AND GOALS

THE FACTORS INFLUENCING THE TYPE OF DILEMMA AND HOW WE DEAL WITH IT

In the workplace ethical dilemmas are influenced by the type of setting, as well as by the approach we use. The key factors which play a role include the following:

1. The industry or corporate culture—different groups have different values and norms; some even have formalized codes of ethics (such as lawyers, therapists, and many professional associations);

2. The type and size of the organization—people in sole proprietorships and small partnerships or companies face a very different environment than those in large organizations;

3. One's own profession or role—even in the same field or company, there are vast differences between those in sales, research, management, production, and creative development;

4. One's power or status—some key distinctions are whether one is free lancing or part of a company; and whether one is in charge of others, working for others, or a free agent;

5. Local influences from one's own company or professional group.

Besides all these influences, one brings one's own background and propensity to respond to ethical issues in a certain way. Each person's response will be unique—although the work environment plays a major role in shaping the issues and one's response, as illustrated by the interviewees' accounts. To a great extent, they reported different types of dilemmas and different ways of responding based on their type of work setting.

Accordingly, I'll deal with the dilemmas by type of setting here and in the next few chapters. These provide a sampling of the types of workplace dilemmas that arise and how the environment influences how we respond.

BEING IN A LOW POWER POSITION AND FEELING OPPRESSED

For those working in an organization, power and status are key influences—and for those who feel oppressed and exploited in their position, the recurring dilemma is "What to do?" Should one take it? Play along to survive? Quit? Or do something to clearly show one's feelings—the "I won't take it anymore" response? The ethical dimension comes into play when one acts or considers acting to break the rules, and in some cases, seeks revenge for a perceived mistreatment.

The two academics had this experience of feeling oppressed while in graduate school working on their dissertations, when professors on their committees wanted them to take an approach they didn't believe in. After a big personal struggle, Lars, who had a very self-oriented, utilitarian approach, finally caved in to get his degree. By contrast, Terry, coming from an other-oriented, moral perspective, was more determined to stick to his ethical guns. As a result, he didn't graduate, tried to sue, and failed. As the two described their situation:

Lars (who succeeded by giving up his ethical principles to do what was practical at the time):

> When I was working on my thesis on the philosophy of religion, I had people on my committee with points of view different from my own. We argued and the more we did, the more time it took to get ahead. It took me six months longer than it should.

Finally, I capitulated. I told my adviser things I didn't believe, but things he wanted to hear, so I could get my degree. I felt bad, but I felt it was better to fake it. After months of fighting, I sold my intellectual integrity to get my degree, and I put things in my thesis that I didn't believe. I feel my professors weren't qualified to pass judgment, since they didn't really know the topic I had chosen. But I had to let that slide by, I finally concluded, so I could get out and move on.

Terry (who failed by sticking to his ethical principles, when opposed by those in power to make the final decision):

I feel very oppressed in my work situation now. It's because my professors prevented me from getting my doctorate. They made my research as difficult as possible.

For one thing, I was doing a Marxist analysis of oppression, and they didn't like that. Secondly, I believe they went back on their word to accommodate some disabilities I have because they didn't like what I was doing. So they took advantage of the situation. It's not obvious I'm a disabled person, but I have a form of temple lobe epilepsy, and along with it some learning disabilities and frequent pain. The committee had agreed to accommodate me, but the committee chair continually blocked the accommodation. I think he did this because he didn't like my research which was sympathetic to the victims of oppression. As an oppressor himself he couldn't see this point of view.

That was my basic premise, so I wouldn't put it aside. However, my chairman continued to fight me on accommodations grounds rather than on an intellectual front. I couldn't get the necessary help to obtain and read the materials I needed, and since I wouldn't change my focus or suck up to this guy, he kept blocking me. Eventually, I was unable to complete my thesis and had to drop out of school. At one point, I tried suing the school and my professors, but it was too expensive, so I dropped that, too.

Like Terry, those employed in low power positions who confronted authority also tended to have problems at work. So did those who tended to be rule-breakers, often for altruistic or moralistic reasons. By standing up for principles, sometimes being whistle-blowers, rather than being team players and going along with the organizations cultural rules, they were perceived as troublemakers. This was the usual response, even when the rule they protested violated ethical or moral principles, since they were challenging authority and custom; they were considered a threat to the order of the organization. As a result, they often had their way blocked to getting ahead or sometimes found themselves out of a job.

This was the experience of Ari, the nurse who worked in a jail, and Francine, the free-lance PR consultant. As Ari explained what happened to her:

> There were many times I stood up for what I believed, or I reported people if I saw them goofing off. So I feel a lot of people at work didn't like me. I also think they saw me as different because I'm from New York and one of only two Jewish nurses there. Thus, I think there was that redneck mentality operating. The other people at the jail wanted to throw me out of the circle, because they saw me as different and a troublemaker. I would stand up and say what I thought, like when I saw people doing something I thought was wrong, like coming down on prisoners for no reason or drinking on work time. Then, too, I think my being a "stand-up-for-myself" woman in a macho environment helped turn many of my co-workers and supervisors against me.
>
> They did various things to get back to me, such as saying I did certain things incorrectly, trying to get me fired. I'm still on the job, though I know my attitude has contributed to a lot of problems there, because I antagonize people; they resent me. But that's how I am; I want to do what's right. So I say: "Screw them. I'll just fight them even harder for what I think is true."

While Ari's response was to dig into the trenches and fight harder, Francine struggled at first. But finally, feeling she couldn't do much to change anything and feeling oppressed by the harassment, she decided to leave. As Francine described her situation:

> When I worked in the international travel field, I was always sticking my neck out to complain if I saw something unfair. What finally led me to leave was I had a boss who manipulated

his way into his current top dog position. I let people know that he was doing this as he fought his way up. When he did get ahead, he did things to block my own advancement in the company, like assigning me to less interesting, less important projects.

I could have stayed, but I found his actions made my work unpleasant. The final straw was harassment. The company I was working for was not an American company, and they had different ideas about women. They felt women couldn't do as much and were more critical of their work. They insulted them for being women, calling them emotional, not serious, that sort of thing.

Eventually, I didn't want to be in that environment anymore. I felt I couldn't be myself and stand up for what I felt was right and thrive. I finally just quit, though it was very hard for me financially, and I started doing the freelance PR work I'm doing today.

Still another approach is to endure the oppressive situation and make the best of it, until there is an opportunity to do something better—a more pragmatic approach. It's what Iris, the therapist, did until she found an optimal time to quit. As Iris described her own strategy:

I was hired to be a provider relationships specialist, which involved finding therapists to provide services for the organization's clients. I thought I was going to be part of a team, but I soon discovered there was really no team—just a lot of infighting and turnover, along with other problems which made it hard to do my job properly. For example, my office was located very far from everyone else and my supervisor was often inaccessible, so I didn't know who to talk to or go to.

Early on I knew I was going to quit as soon as I could. But I didn't want to leave with bad feelings and hurt my reputation in the future. So I acted like everything was fine, and I tried to do the best I could to make the best of a bad situation, until I felt ready to leave.

This way, besides getting a good salary, I could build up credentials I could use to get a better job somewhere else. I didn't see any point in making a big issue of things at work by standing up and rocking the boat. It was easier to go along and try to deal with my feelings of stress off the job.

INDIVIDUAL VERSUS ORGANIZATIONAL CONFLICTS

Related to the dilemmas for the low-power individual who feels oppressed are the more general individual versus organizational conflicts. These involve the conflict between doing what benefits the individual or what seems right from an altruistic point of view versus doing what is considered more practical and efficient to benefit the organization. The problem for the individual in the organization is whether to go along with the organizational's rules and policies to do the practical thing the organization wants—the team player approach—or whether to do what he or she personally prefers or thinks is right. Using categories from the Ethical Choices Map, the dilemma looks like this:

	Individual's Goal	Organization's Goal
Orientation	Personal Self Others in Community	Organization's Interests
Philosophy	Moralist: Do what's right	Pragmatic: Do what's most practical, efficient, and effective
Approach to Rules	Innovator: Do what's right and follow one's own orientation	Follower: Be a team player, and go along with the group

Individuals can use whatever style they prefer—rational, intuitive or a combination—to decide whether to put individual or organizational goals first. Then the decision depends on various factors, including: one's overall ethical approach, financial considerations, the importance of keeping one's position in the organization, the importance of the issue, the degree to which the organization's goal seems morally right or wrong, and the support of others in the organization for one's view.

Generally, most people do go along with the organization, as did most interviewees, since they feel the organization's is power over them. In turn, it's realistic that most people do this, even if it means putting aside personal goals and views of what's right, since this greater power is how organizations and society as a whole survive. Generally, people do put aside their personal agendas when they conflict with the organization and submit to its demands, because the organization has more power and they need to continue to belong to it to make money and survive.

Thus, in general, the practical imperative wins out over moral concerns, although at times, the moral imperative feels so strong that the individual—or many individuals—stand up for that. When this happens, their response can act as a catalyst for change in the organization, either voluntarily from within or imposed from without. Or if the organization resists change, the protestors may end up leaving, perhaps to join a new organization with a more acceptable moral vision.

In turn, because of this potential conflict when individual and organizational goals collide, many companies today use visioning to create mission and vision statements to produce a greater alignment between individual and organizational goals, and to express a renewed commitment to a moral vision. This way company officials hope to gain a renewed commitment to the organization and its goals from members of the organization, so they become more enthusiastic, motivated, and increases productive. In other words, many companies now find it makes practical business sense to become more morally-driven, since this approach results in a more productive, committed workforce, although individual and organizational goals can never be completely aligned; there will always be some tensions between self-interest and what an organization aims to do.

This individual/organization, self/other, and moral/practical split recurs again and again in different settings. Three major contexts are 1) the individual in a large institution or corporation; 2) the individual in private practice who is affected by professional codes and customary practices; and 3) the individual involved in sales and promotion, a field with its own special codes and practices. Following are some of the major issues that occur in these different settings and the factors influencing how people choose what to do.

DEALING WITH DILEMMAS IN A LARGE INSTITUTION OR CORPORATION

These individual versus organizational dilemmas are especially writ large for anyone who works in a big institution or company, since the organization is so powerful relative to the individual. The interviewees who experienced such dilemmas included the three nurses who worked in a jail, private hospital, and in public health; the educational specialist who worked with schools; and the radio talk show host at a large station. The major problems and responses they described included: 1) fighting the system and finally accepting the way things were; 2) fighting the system, giving in, feeling resentful, and finally quitting; 3) going as far as possible in some situations and backing down at other times; 4) quietly doing what one thinks right when possible and otherwise going along with the system; and 5) going along but feeling resentful.

The chart on the following page illustrates the range of possibilities for action in an individual versus organization confrontation and how one responds and feels about the outcome. The responses of the interviewees in the following examples are indicated on the chart to illustrate how this chart can be applied.

If you work in an organization and have experienced any dilemmas yourself, you will fall somewhere on this chart in your response and your feelings about your actions and the outcome. Here's how the interviewees responded:

Fighting and Giving In

Ari chose to fight and finally go along with the system, when she worked at the county jail, because she felt it the most practical thing to do under the circumstances. She was getting close to retirement and had previously taken a job at the jail for practical purposes because of the benefits. She didn't want to give up her security, though she found herself in an environment full of conflict, where many people engaged in activities that weren't quite legal or were against the stated rules. Initially she tried speaking up against some of the

WAYS OF RESOLVING AN INDIVIDUAL/ORGANIZATION ETHICAL DILEMMA

Feelings About One's Actions or Outcome	Actions Taken					
	Fighting the System				Going Along With the System	
	Winning	Winning/Giving-In Based on Circumstances	Giving-In	Leaving	Playing Along But Quietly Doing What One Wants	Going Along With the Organization
Feeling Good About Winning or Accepting Losing		Don	Ari		Pam	
Feeling Bad About Losing or Not Taking Action (i.e., Feeling Resentful, Frustrated, or Guilty)				Janet		Lori

practices she observed, but after she found herself the target of anger from others in the jail, she decided to stop fighting and be more of a team player. She felt it wasn't worth the effort and hassle to keep struggling, particularly since she wanted to stay to get her benefits when she retired. As a result, she shifted into an "I'll do what they want" mode of acceptance, which she described as "a neutral resigned state," where she didn't feel really good, but didn't feel bad either. As Ari described her situation:

> I found being a nurse at the jail a conflictual situation to start with, when I began working there eight years ago. It was like being in the "enemy camp." The physical environment is dirty. There's noise and bars and big clanging gates all over the place. The sheriff's deputies are like the police, and like many people, I have a bad reaction to authority figures.
>
> So I felt a sense of initial resistance. I also was bothered by the guards' macho attitude, which was common, since most of the deputies are men, and many women who work as guards are very macho and tough-acting, too. Meanwhile, the attitude of the guards towards those of us on the small medical team wasn't too complimentary either, since we were there as caregivers, and they saw our role in a disparaging way.
>
> Soon I began to notice a number of things going on that bring out the negative in human qualities. For example, I saw the inmates get illegal substances on many occasions. I observed bribery among the inmates where they trade one thing for another—say some Motrin from the pharmacy for an extra piece of bread.
>
> I also discovered that sometimes the guards let this stuff go on, because they were getting something on the side. Or they didn't want the hassle of saying anything for a minor violation, so they looked the other way. Or I'd run into someone on a shift goofing off, say playing cards.
>
> Some of these activities bothered me, and I mentioned them to my supervisor. But soon I found my comments weren't particularly welcome. They were making me seem like even more of an outsider than I was in the first place. So soon I started shutting up and looking the way, too. I wanted to stay; I didn't want to jeopardize my chances for having a good job when I retired. So I didn't want to rock the boat. After that things

calmed down. I just did my job, and didn't try to worry about things if I saw things that I felt were wrong.

Playing the Game of Giving In and Getting What You Can

In contrast to Ari's give in and accept with resignation approach, Don the broadcaster turned his conflicts with his radio station into a kind of a game. He spoke up when he could and pulled back when he couldn't. While the radio station was most interested in infotainment to appeal to the broadest number of listeners for bottom-line profits, Don wanted to express his own more humanistic point of view as much as possible. He was like the perennial gadfly at the station—prodding and biting, but only going so far, so he could speak as freely as he could, yet stay at the station. As Don explained this relationship:

> There's a high contrast between my own ethics and the station's and industry ethics. I try to use the radio medium to let people share ideas, and I'm not agenda driven. Most of the popular talk programs on radio now are confrontational theater. My driving interest is in getting ideas to be exchanged in one form or another, though the station doesn't see it that way. Their whole premise is to attract the biggest possible audience and the management has no interest in the issues, the personalities, or the methods you use to do that.
>
> What they really want are the phone lines to be lit up and they like the hear entertaining or dramatic conversations. So if I have an argument with somebody on the air, they think that's great. Well, I don't like to do that everyday. I try to approach my listeners with the assumption that many of them want intelligent conversation and they're tired of being assaulted and insulted, although the industry is more driven now by economics and increasing pressure for a Howard Stern or Rush Limbaugh approach, instead of having a dialogue with a local audience.

While Don did manage to maintain a certain amount of freedom in his topics and presentation, at times he still had to back down to management pressures, and he accepted this as one of the costs of being on air. It was his way of balancing the various ethical considerations—in terms of his philosophy, approach to the rules, and orientation to self and others. As he explained:

> In my line of work, I have to make constant choices about how to present things and shade them. All broadcasters have to balance the desire to blurt out what we believe or think to be true with the impact on our employment. You have to juggle the interests of the advertisers and the pressure you get from your boss with what you feel yourself. There are many times I may soft peddle things or pass on a given story which I might like to cover otherwise. Still I have sometimes found a way to express my own opinion informally on the air, although I may not do a story on the subject. That's my way of bowing to the station's pressure, yet expressing my feelings about what concerns me.

Yet, at times, Don pushed a little too hard, which led to his finally leaving the station and moving to another station where he was headed at the time of our interview. Ultimately, there was too much pressure for him to continue to live with the uneasy balance between his sense of what was morally right and what the station wanted. A key blowup occurred when Don had some union organizers on to talk against the plans of a big supermarket giant, which was a station advertiser. As Don explained:

> The station got a very strong advertiser reaction, when I had members of the Teamsters' union on to talk about Safeway's plans to move their distribution center to a nonunion operation in Northern California. Though I invited a spokesman from Safeway to come on the program, he didn't respond. After the program, the Safeway people called the station manager and complained about their treatment.
>
> So that was one factor that led to my finally leaving the station for a station where I felt I would have more freedom to do the kind of programming I want, though there are still limits.

Yet, while Don had to accept some limits, at least he could often express his point of view and work out a compromise between his higher moral ideals and the station's bottom line thinking. As he described the process:

I give full expression to my point of view. I try to do it in a way that invites people to discuss it, as opposed to a sermon where I tell them what they ought to think. I'm very clear about my position, but I sometimes change a position or modify part of it, based on discussion with people, so there's a real exchange.

I'm kind of an inside agitator. Even though there are limits, I try to find creative ways to both present my own viewpoint and moral priorities and make it entertaining, too.

I know I'm different from many other people in the business, who consider being a talk show host a kind of acting, in which they project a certain persona on the air. But I care. I have a point of view. I try to get it across where I can.

Fighting the System, Giving Up, and Getting Out

While Don was able to achieve a good balance in expressing his own ideals, while compromising at times to remain in his field, Janet, the nurse, who was similarly other-oriented and concerned about doing what was right, was not able to do so when she worked in a hospital. Why? Primarily, because seeing herself as more of a rule breaker than a follower, she found it hard to make the necessary compromises to survive in the system. As a result, after years of stormy battles and feelings of resentment that people weren't listening to her and were holding her back, she dropped out to pursue a more ethically comfortable, though less financially secure route as a writer.

The conflicts with the organization Janet experienced were the same kinds of bottom-line considerations Don reported at his radio stations. In her case, what especially disturbed her is that these "bottom line" concerns were putting patients at risk. Additionally, she found that political infighting and personal agendas for achievement in the hospital sometimes got in the way of putting patient care first, and this deeply disturbed her. As Janet described what happened:

I'm happy to have left behind working with the health care system, because I felt it kept compromising all I believed in. A major reason I went into health care was because I felt health care is supposed to be idealistic. You are ideally doing what you are doing for the good of other people. But I found I could never really do that. The hospital always had its other agenda of taking care of the rules and regulations, and the administrators did this in the most basic way possible. They gave a lot of lip service to having a higher level of care. But that wasn't really what was happening. Instead, the real philosophy was "Let's get the patients in. Let's get as many as we can. Let's get the money."

I always felt I was compromised, and I fought the system a lot in the last five years I was there. For example, I would say that "We have a dangerous disease we're dealing with, and I need some help and certain things need to be done." Then I didn't get the help and these things weren't done.

I knew when I complained I would be very unpopular with the other nurses and administrators, because they didn't want to hear these things. The preferred approach was to take care of what you can and do it quietly. So my relationship with everyone was very tense and draining.

Janet felt the hospital even compromised on cases of people suffering and dying, because of the emphasis on going by the rules and watching the bottom line. As Janet explained:

One of the worst things I had to deal with as a public health nurse was the sudden appearance of measles out of nowhere, killing people. There were 30 deaths in the Los Angeles area where I was at the time.

When I realized that kids with a highly contagious disease that could be fatal were being put on a ward with many other people, I went to my nurse supervisor and the administrator, and said we had to start isolating these kids. But that was difficult to do because of room assignment problems, airflow problems, and other cost factors.

So my supervisor and the administrator didn't want to do anything. They told me they needed more documentation to do anything, and there wasn't much because this was a new problem. Instead of trying to recognize this problem which I pointed out, they were questioning me, putting me under fire, to try to get out of doing anything to deal with the problem, because of the high costs involved.

Others might have backed down at this point, but Janet's reaction was to fight. Like the classic whistle-blower, she kept pushing and prodding, which upped the tension between her and her supervisors without resolving the problem, since Janet lacked the power to make any changes herself. Instead, her resentment continued to build, and she felt increasingly angry and tense.

In the last six months that Janet was there, problems intensified, since the hospital got a new administrator, who increased the power of the nursing director with whom Janet was already having problems. So Janet felt even more squelched and powerless. She not only found it more difficult to achieve the ethical goals she wanted, but she was demeaned and humiliated by those blocking her, leading her to finally leave. As Janet described the situation:

> After years of fighting, I was finally getting some things through here and there. Then, one day, a new president, a businessman, came in and reorganized the whole hospital. As a result, the woman I had been working for became the new director in charge of management, and she really put the squeeze on me.
>
> One day, shortly before I was to leave for a conference, she called me in and said I had to take care of an emergency outside of my field. Although I was an infection control nurse and I was going to an important conference in my field, she wanted me to take care of a routine problem involving insects in the hospital and sterilizing some rooms. Since this was something anyone could do, I felt this was her way of getting back at me for all the speaking up I had been doing—by preventing me from going to this conference. She told me: "You're not going anywhere until this problem is completely resolved."
>
> Eventually I went after making sure the bug problem was totally handled, but when I returned the next day, she gave me a memo reprimanding me for unprofessional behavior, since I had complained about dealing with the bug problem. For me that was the last straw. I felt like my job was to deal with serious life-threatening diseases, and my going to the conference was to help me do it. But she kept putting blocks in my way and putting me down, keeping me from really doing my job properly.
>
> When I went to the director of the hospital to explain this, he didn't support me at all. He just told me I would have to work it out with the nursing director, though I said I had tried

but couldn't. Then when I went to personnel, that didn't help either.

I felt really terrible. I went into the hospital that week feeling a constant sense of anxiety and pressure. So finally, I left and never went back. I felt I had to move on and do something else that would be more satisfying.

Going Along—and Quietly Doing It My Way Sometimes

In contrast to Janet, Pam, also a nurse, used a very different approach to deal with similar frustrations in a hospital with a priority on containing costs. Whereas Janet, very much the other-oriented rule breaking moralist spoke up, felt resentful, and left when the conflict became too great, Pam, who was more of a balancer in all ways, played the organizational game—and when she could, quietly did what she wanted. Pam found this more low-key surreptitious approach worked well, since it enabled her to fit in, and behind the scenes, do what she could to help without rocking the organizational boat or hurting her self-interest. For instance, she used this approach a number of times in giving out pain medications without authorization to help a patient. As she explained:

> You are supposed to follow the orders of the doctor, but I've sometimes gone against them to help a patient feel better. This kind of situation happens when the person doesn't want to be kept alive and they're in pain. But the hospital won't give them enough medicine for the pain. Then, I have sometimes given them more on my own, and other nurses do it sometimes, too.
>
> The reason a doctor might hold back on medication is the doctors are afraid the patients might kill themselves on the medicine, and the doctors are afraid of the lawyers. They're afraid the family might sue if they gave a patient too much medication. So the patients often end up suffering needlessly as a result.
>
> That's why sometimes, we get more medication from someone else and give it anyway. It's not something people talk about much, but most nurses I know have done it. You can do it very easily without getting caught. And I do it when I feel I can, because I want to prevent as much harm and help as much as I can.

The risk, of course, is getting caught and being penalized. But it was a risk Pam, like many other nurses, was willing to take, because she felt being caught was unlikely and she wanted to help.

Conversely, when Pam faced the opposite problem of the doctors in the psych ward prescribing too much medication, such as tranquillizers to keep the patients quiet, she knew she couldn't do anything, so she didn't and she didn't complain. Once again, she used the rational/pragmatic approach to decide what to do—doing something quietly if she could and living with the system if she couldn't. As Pam put it:

> There are some patients in the psychiatric department who need the medication they get, because they are really wacky without it. So sometimes if I think they need it, I will ask the doctors to order extra medication or find some way to give the patients more medication on my own.
>
> Often, though, when the doctors prescribe a lot of medication with tranquillizers, so that the patients become confused, you can't do much. The psychiatrists are making them worse, but it doesn't do any good to say something. The doctors are not going to listen to a nurse. That's when I find it very frustrating, because I have to keep giving people pills all night that they shouldn't have. It annoys me. The people don't need the pills. If they have something bothering them, they need to talk about the problem, not take pills to calm them down. But in this case, I don't have the ability to do anything like with the pain patients. So I have learned to go along with what the doctors want, since that's what works in this situation.

Going Along—But Not Feeling Good About It

Like Pam, Lori the educational specialist learned to go along with the system, even when she felt it was wrong. But unlike Pam, she didn't look for under the table strategies to do what she could. Rather, she went along with the rules, though she resented the problems and inefficiencies in the system. Knowing she had to conform or leave, she decided to stay and learned to live with her bad feelings for going along with policies she didn't like to keep her job. As Lori explained:

There are certain things I have to do by law, such as report all incidences or even whispers of child abuse. I've done that and have felt good about it, because I feel like I'm all that kid has to protect him, such as when he says someone in his family is hitting on him.

But when I see other problems in the teaching system, say bad teaching, I don't say anything, because there's really little I can do without bringing trouble on myself. That's because teachers are not supposed to evaluate other teachers. Just administrators are supposed to evaluate teachers, although I don't see how administrators can really do this effectively. They don't see what's going on in the classroom on a day to day basis.

Sometimes I have been in a position to clearly see that another teacher is not doing a good job, such as when teachers aren't helping the handicapped kids in their classes as they should or haven't kept up on the latest methods of teaching reading comprehension. Then, too, the system might assign the wrong teachers to teach something.

But, I have learned not to say anything. Not to the administration or to the teachers themselves. Nobody wants to hear any criticism directly. So I've learned to be very indirect or just hint, but if the teacher or administrator doesn't pick up on this hint, there's nothing I can do. It's frustrating, but I've learned to shut up about these things, so I don't get into trouble myself.

Similarly, when Lori had her own classroom, before working as an educational consultant, she quietly went along with teacher policies that had developed to respond to problems in the system, rather than speaking out to try to change the system. As she explained:

Teachers often don't have enough books, and day class teachers aren't given any materials for science. So if a teacher wants to do anything besides textbook learning, you have to spend your own money and get what you can for hands-on science, so you can teach it properly.

There's a pressure to do that. Many teachers feel if you don't spend your own money, you're not doing the best job you can. So, I felt a pressure to do a good job and got some kits I could use year after year. But I didn't do anything to protest the lack of a decent budget. I didn't complain that I had to spend my own money, though I thought the school should have been paying for this.

DEALING WITH DILEMMAS IN THE PROFESSIONS

Just like employees in big organizations, professionals can face individual/organizational dilemmas when their personal views differ from those of their profession. This conflict may be with the professional organization, its codes of ethics, or with customary practices.

In some cases, professionals have these conflicts because they feel the customary practices are dubious—say because of the cutthroat competition or incentive to increase profits in their field. Then, they are much like the employees who feel their organizations are too bottom-line oriented.

Conversely, some professionals have the opposite problem—they are tempted to break professional rules, even the law, for their own advantage. Still another conflict is when professionals conform to the norms and values of a peer culture of colleagues which opposes certain formally accepted rules of conduct. Instead, the group creates its own rules of everyday practice, which differ from what the profession formally requires.

In all of these situations, the individual may feel some tension, because he or she is not following the usual rules, though not all do.

The following chart illustrates the possible ways of resolving these conflicts between the individual and the profession. The responses of the interviewees in each category are included to show how this chart might be applied to help you apply it yourself.

Trying to Avoid Participating in the "Unethical" Practices in One's Field

Trying to take the moral high road can sometimes be difficult when they conflict with common practices in the field, as Dick the architect found. He encountered this problem because the architect is in the middle between the customer and the contractor who have different interests creating contradictory pressures. While the architect is theoretically supposed to represent the customer's best interests, in reality, to be successful, the architect needs to have a continuing working relationship with the contractor, who often seeks ways to save money. Dick's way of dealing with this conflict of inter-

WAYS OF RESOLVING AN INDIVIDUAL/ORGANIZATION ETHICAL DILEMMA

Feelings About One's Actions or Outcome	Actions Taken					
	Breaking the Rules				Following the Rules	
	Objecting to Unethical Practices	Giving in to Temptation	Creating New Rules	Leaving	Going Along to Avoid Getting Caught	Going Along Since One Agrees
Feeling Good About One's Approach	Dick		Gaby		Jerry	Paul
Feeling Bad About One's Approach (i.e., Feeling Resentful, Anxious, or Guilty)		June		Janet		

ests was to do the "right" thing as much as he could, although at times he had to make compromises. As Dick explained:

> The architect is there to represent the owner's best interest and has a contract with the owner, while the owner has a contract with the contractor. The architect and contractor are not linked at all. But on certain projects where you know you may be getting more projects from this contractor or vice versa, some of these contractual obligations become a little grayer and can create ethical issues.
>
> Say the contractor makes a big mistake, but he tells the owner "It's a change." So the owner thinks, "Maybe I do owe more money." The problem for the architect is that if he hopes to get any more work from this contractor, there's a temptation to not say anything to the owner, though he values the mistake is the contractor's fault. And many architects don't speak up, though their obligation is supposed to be to the owner.
>
> It's a difficult problem, because many architects depend on work from contractors to sustain their practice, especially in areas where contractors own much or all of the buildable land. Then, an owner who wants to build a house has to buy the land from the contractor and the contractor finds the architect. This is the reverse of the traditional way where the owner finds the land, hires an architect, and the architect or owner finds the contractor. I've faced this problem in many of my projects, since I work in an area where the contractors have a great deal of power. So there's an incentive to cut corners at the expense of the owner when the contractor runs into problems.

This situation, as Dick explained, contributed to other temptations for many architects, such as not looking at plans too critically and not pointing out the owner's bad judgment to keep relations between the owner, contractor, and himself running smoothly. As Dick noted:

> Supposedly, the major reason the architect is on a job to find mistakes and make sure the building is being built the way the owner wanted it. Meanwhile, the contractor is under a great deal of pressure, because he can make tremendous profits or lose a great deal of money if he doesn't do it right. So the con-

tractor may be tempted to take shortcuts or use less expensive materials in places where no one will notice the difference, though the shorting can lead to problems later.

Unfortunately, the architect is in a weak position under the best conditions to point these problems out to the customer. That's because once construction starts, the contractor is there everyday, perhaps 60 hours a week, while the architect might stop by for an hour each week or two to check things over. So when the architect has a complaint, the owner may be less likely to take it that seriously.

Thus, it's a difficult three-way relationship. At one time, people had a strong commitment to the trade and to quality, so the system worked well. But today, the whole system is undermined by bottom line and profit considerations, and many people don't build with any degree of quality assurance. As a result, the architect who wants to be ethical is in the middle of this very difficult situation.

So how did Dick reconcile what he felt was the right thing to do with the way things worked? He used a kind of compromising approach, as he explained:

> Typically, I engage in a kind of conspiracy of compromise, as do many architects with contractors. You each make concessions to the other. For example, you might say something like: '"Maybe I got this angle a little wrong, but you messed up on some nailing. So we'll trade. You work a little harder to clean up the problem, and we won't mention what happened to the owner.'"
>
> This way, you each work a little harder to help out the other if necessary. It's a way of balancing out the mistakes both the contractor and architect might make.

Besides applying this balancing approach, Dick tried to avoid these problems as much as possible by cutting down on expenses in his personal life, so he could be choosier about the projects he did take. He preferred making more ethically-driven decisions in his work, and could do so, since his wife had a steady job she liked.

Breaking the Rules—And Drawing the Line

June the tax accountant's story illustrates the opposite situation—giving in to pressure to evade the rules of her profession, as well as the law, to help a client. June was drawn in this direction because of her own ethical mind-set. She was very much an other-oriented rule-breaker, though she still saw herself as a moral person who did what was right and felt some guilt if rule-breaking went too far. In this case, she didn't feel that breaking the rules were right, but was pulled into doing so because of her strong desire to assist her client. But when the client wanted her to break more rules and do something that was clearly fraud, her sense of morality overcame her other-oriented desire to help out—and she said no. As June explained her situation:

> I have had to face a number of professional ethics conflicts as a tax consultant. The big conflicts are over: Does the client want to cheat to save money? Do they want me to help them do that? Am I willing to lose sleep for the next three years if I help them? And how do I reconcile helping people cheat on their taxes with wanting to see myself as a moral person? For me that's the paradox.
>
> People bring up these questions when I tell them what they owe. They make painful, squeaking noises, or they say: "Isn't there something we can do?" At that point, I know things they can get away with that won't be a big risk. So I might suggest that. But a few times I have done something I think is very wrong, mainly because I was not assertive enough with the client.
>
> That happened one time when I had a client who over-reported the amount he spent on a stock, so he underreported how much he had gained. I became aware of this when I finished his taxes and looked at the figures. It was very hard for me to go along with this, because it was a lot of money—about $100,000 in taxes, on which he saved about $40,000. I had never done anything before that was this big.
>
> I tried to tell him not to do this, but he was someone I had known socially for ten or so years, and I had done many things with him. We once had an intimate dating relationship and still had mutual friends. So I felt a certain pressure to help him cheat, though I didn't feel good about it afterwards. In fact,

after that, I didn't do his taxes anymore and severed our social relationship. I just didn't want to talk to him anymore, and I'm mad at myself that I let it go that far. I only made $1000 on the whole deal myself, and it wasn't worth all the pain and suffering, because it was clearly fraud. It wasn't just pushing a client through a loophole.

By contrast, on a smaller scale, June was much more likely to help her clients break the rules, without feeling any qualms about doing so. For her, this was ethically acceptable. As June described it:

In a few situations, I worked with a client for many years, and they got a big tax bill that was hard for them to pay. So if I could do something small to help, like increase their charitable contribution, I would try to do that. And I feel good about that, because it's a "tug at the heartstrings" situation, where I feel I want to help.

Also, in this kind of situation, I don't feel anxious as I do when someone wants me to help them commit a fraud, because it's a small amount. So it's probably safe and won't come up in an audit. Or if it did, I could easily say: "Oh, I just made a mistake." It wouldn't look like I was trying to cheat the government. Then, too, if the amount is small, a part of me gets a thrill out of getting away with things, like a mischief maker. Plus, I like knowing I can help someone.

But if the amount is very big, it's obviously an attempt to commit fraud, and I find that difficult to do. It's too risky.

Yet, while June liked pushing the edges of what was legal without going too far, she felt uncomfortable when she encountered a "straight-shooter" client who was strict in following the rules. He was so honest, he undermined her own feeling of wanting to do the right thing, while breaking the rules. So she felt somehow "sleazy," as she explained:

This one client makes me feel uncomfortable because he's so "good." He's a lawyer, and he loves to live by the book and interpret the rules in the most conservative way. He has almost a fear of authority. For example, one time when I urged him to take an "office in the home" deduction, since he works out of

his home, he didn't want to do it, saying: "I do most of my
work at my office, not at home." Then, when I told him there
was no way for the IRS to know this, he told me: "Oh, but I
will know." So, I backed down, and followed the letter of the
law on his return. But at the same time, when he said this, a
part of me felt almost sleazy, because he was such a purist.

Thus, like Dick, June tried to find a balance in what she did—
rejecting the pressure to engage in major fraud, while not following
all the legal and ethical principles of her profession if she could
quietly get away with minor transgressions. Still, the compromises
increasingly upset her, and eventually, like Dick, she pulled back
from the amount of work she did, due to the continuing stress from
the push to be unethical. As she explained:

> The ethical issues have been a continuing stress, because year
> after year it's been the same thing—trying to help people save
> money on taxes, and many of them seem desperate. They start
> freaking out when I tell them they owe money. This has hap-
> pened because most of my clients have been struggling entre-
> preneurs trying to make it. So there's been this continuing pres-
> sure to help.
>
> That's why I finally decided to stop doing tax returns for the
> most part, because I had to take a break. It's been such a heavy
> burden with about three hundred clients each year. I finally felt
> I didn't want all that stress and wanted to lighten up my life to
> focus more on being creative and doing what I want. So now I
> just do a few returns a year for old customers. But otherwise,
> I've pretty much put it aside. It has been just too much.

Breaking the Rules and Creating One's Own

Another approach to dealing with professional rules or ethics are
creating a parallel universe of accepted codes of behavior, which
become the usual practice in one's peer group, though wrong by
official standards. That's the approach used by Gaby the therapist,
who described herself as "a follow the rules" person, and defined
ethics as following the rules. But the rules she followed were those
of her colleagues, not the official rules for therapists. As Gaby de-

scribed it:

> My colleagues and I have developed our own ethical rules, such
> as we can have certain kinds of dual relationships, can lend pa-
> tients money at times, and can freely gossip about patients
> within our peer group circle. These rules may not be accepted
> by therapists officially, but they have acquired their own valid-
> ity as a separate ethical basis for judging what's acceptable and
> what's not.
>
> Even though it's not supposed to be done, a lot of people do
> it. Then people do what they can to protect themselves against
> official sanction, because these alternate rules don't always work,
> so sometimes people get caught. These official rules are violated
> all the time, not just the ones against sexual relationships with
> patients. However, people try to violate any rules quietly, so
> they don't attract attention. Generally that's the accepted way
> things are done.

Given this split, Gaby used the rules of her colleagues, not the official rules, in dealing with any ethical dilemmas she faced. As she
explained:

> I Identify with therapists who believe in using a culturally sen-
> sitive approach in judging family problems, which may differ
> from the mainstream view. One time I took this position when
> I was asked to give my opinion about a social worker handling a
> case where an elderly Hispanic mother begged her middle-aged
> daughter not to put her in an old-aged residence. The daughter
> said she couldn't stay home to take care of her mother, because
> she had to work. The social worker sided with the daughter and
> was not sensitive to the mother's anguish that her daughter
> couldn't take care of her. That's because the mainstream view
> puts the interests of the individual first, but the Hispanic value
> is that you should take care of your elderly parents. So, I sided
> with the ethical standards of the therapists who would support
> the mother, not the mainstream standards.

Gaby similarly used peer guidelines to shape her own actions when
she encountered ethical conflicts due to differences between common peer practices and official guidelines. As Gaby explained:

There are many situations when you are tempted to engage in behavior which is unethical according to the rules of the profession, though it's not unethical according to what you believe and what your friends and associates do. It's unethical because somebody has written down that it is for your profession, so technically your client can sue you if you break these rules and he or she finds out. Many of these rules developed because certain problems became apparent in patient-therapist relationships, and therapists needed guidelines on what to do—especially to avoid liability in lawsuits—although that's not necessarily what people do in practice.

Take the case of dual relationships, which was much more common in the past, though it still happens today. This occurs when the therapist, who has a therapeutic relationship with the client, has another type of relationship, such as the client babysits for the agent or makes a business referral. I actually got my first agent through a patient who was a writer, and I said to her: "Do you mind if I called your agent?" That's considered unethical, but people still do it.

Dual relationships are considered unethical because the therapist is in a position of power and could presumably exploit the patient. Say a patient really didn't want to babysit or you could pay her less. Or you could even pay nothing and say it's for her own therapy. She might be afraid to challenge you as her therapist.

Even worse are relationships where you go into business with a client, borrow money, or begin an intimate relationship. Any relationship where you exploit your power as a therapist for your own gain is unethical, because the patient isn't equally able to say no or make demands.

In some cases, though, I admit I have engaged in these dual relationships, and I know other therapists who have, too. Technically, they are unethical, but those dual relationships aren't very serious violations, so they are commonly done, and people feel okay about doing them. I have done this as a writer who writes about patients. But the way I have resolved this problem for myself is to get the client's permission and disguise their name and identity. Also, I show the client a copy of what I write, so he or she has total control in suggesting corrections or deletions. Then, to protect myself legally, I've always gotten a release from the client.

Yet, even though I have the client's cooperation, there's still the subtle pressure on the client to agree since I am the therapist. Maybe the client agrees to please me. So is the client really agreeing freely, since this is still a dual relationship? But even so, I've done it, since I want to write about what I'm doing, and I don't feel I'm hurting the patient, since it's completely anonymous. It's technically not right, but I do it anyway—like many others I know.

Finally, Gaby described one other major ethical conflict between her peer group and official rules—talking about patients. She and her colleagues weren't supposed to do this, though everyone did, usually without any problems, though one colleague experienced repercussions, when he admitted what he did to a patient, who dropped out of therapy as a result. As Gaby reported:

> The rule is you're not supposed to talk or gossip about patients with other therapists—but everyone does. For example, a friend Sharon sent me a few patients, and sometimes when she tells me about her experiences with another patient, she mentions their name. In one case, I knew the person socially, and though it was unethical for me to talk to her about what was going on in this patient's life, I did. But then, I'm a very open person, so I like to say what I think.
>
> Everyone usually feels fine about talking to one another this way, though we shouldn't. However, one therapist did get in trouble with a former patient. This happened when the therapist, Randy, was seeing a gay patient, Jack, who rented a room in my apartment. Randy told me that Jack was HIV positive, which I already knew, since Jack had told me himself. However, Randy made the mistake of telling Jack that he had told me, and Jack was furious and left therapy with him. Of course, Jack was right to leave, because Randy had no right to tell me, and he was stupid to tell his patient he had done so.

What Gaby was most critical of, however, was not Randy's telling (which violated the official ethical code), but of telling the patient (which violated the common practice of her colleagues).

Thus, in numerous ways, Gaby put aside the official code of rules to follow those of other practitioners. In turn, these peer group rules better supported the therapists' personal interests, including their delight in gossiping about patients, whereas the official rules had been designed in part to further patient needs. In effect, the peer group rules had arisen to support the therapists' self-interest in contrast to the other-orientation of the official rules.

Paradoxically, though, in a few areas Gaby's approach was more other-oriented or "moral" than the official therapist position. This occurred when she acted as a whistleblower on the profession or sent clients to other therapists when she felt there wasn't a good fit. As Gaby explained:

> Although my openness gets me in trouble at times when I break confidentiality, I think my openness is highly moral, since it's motivated by the ideal that people should know the truth. Sometimes I've used it to reveal the secrets of the profession, which I think people should know. For example, research has shown that group therapy and self-help groups are as good for you as individual therapy, but it's far less expensive. Also, research has shown it doesn't matter what orientation a therapist has. No approach is better than another. The only thing that seems to matter in helping the client get better is the relationship with their therapist, whether a professional or not—and some therapy by paraprofessionals is even more effective.
>
> Of course, for professional and economic reasons, therapists don't like this information getting out. But I feel a strong desire to reveal it to help the patients, which is, after all, what therapy is supposed to do.
>
> A couple of times I've put my patient's interest first, even though it lost me that patient as a client. I didn't feel there was a very good fit between us, and so I told my clients to seek other therapy. I thought doing so was the more moral thing to do.

Other Alternatives: Leaving or Going Along with the Rules

Other outcomes that might occur in a conflict with the ethical codes of a professional organization include: 1) leaving because one disagrees so strongly, 2) getting thrown out by the group, or 3) going along with the rules to avoid the problems that might result if one is caught breaking them.

Only a few interviewees left a profession because they objected to the group's ethical codes, since they had already invested so much of themselves in their profession—a common situation for professionals generally. As a result, they continued using another approach. Besides quietly evading the rules they didn't like, as did June, or pursuing alternate peer group rules like Gaby, they generally followed the rules, even when they didn't want to do so.

That was Jerry the lawyer's way—going along, out of fear of what might happen if he didn't follow the rules and got caught. As he commented:

> I always go along with the professional codes of being a lawyer. Why? Because frankly I'm scared of getting caught and the consequences of that. In general, I think most of the rules and regulations are intended to protect the integrity of the profession and to make sure the clients don't get ripped off, so that's one reason I follow them. There are some I might not agree with, but I go along with those, because I don't want to bring any unnecessary trouble on myself.

Finally, some go along with the rules because they agree with them, and then there's no ethical dilemma. That's what Sam, the writer, experienced when he encountered ethical codes as he tried to break into the comedy scene.

> One important ethical code for comics is how you deal with each other's material. The basic rule is not to steal somebody's material and I don't. The rule sometimes gets a little ambiguous over what's stealing, say when somebody develops a topic and other people later develop jokes on that topic. That's not really stealing. But if the jokes are very similar, that's a problem. You're not supposed to use them if someone else developed the same joke first—and there's no way to use a joke and give someone else credit. It's not like using an academic footnote, because you're performing before an audience.
>
> Thus, the issue is whether to use the joke or not if someone else came up with it first. I happen to agree with the general rule that you shouldn't, and so there's no ethical conflict for me. I just don't use it.

264 BULLET MAKING ETHICAL CHOICES, RESOLVING ETHICAL DILEMMAS

SUMMING UP

In sum, for those who work in organizations or in certain professions, a common ethical dilemma occurs when individual interests or values differ from those of the organization or professional community. One alternative many follow is to go along with the system and follow the rules, sometimes due to a fear of the penalties for not doing so. Then those who do and sometimes feel frustrated and resentful for having to go along with these rules. Alternatively, some individuals quietly pursue their own interests or participate in an accepted but unofficial series of practices embraced by their peers, feeling these rules make more sense for them than the official ones.

While some feel guilty when they break certain rules out of self-interest, others feel this is just the way things are. And still others try to be even more ethical than their organization or profession, though in general, individuals feel they can do little to change the system. As a result, those who feel most strongly about the conflict may eventually leave the organization or profession in frustration. But most seem to go along to get along. They find their work and professional life runs more smoothly that way.

CHAPTER 22

•

DEALING WITH ETHICAL DILEMMAS IN EVERYDAY WORK AND BUSINESS CONFLICTS

Another type of ethical conflict is triggered by the disparate interests of people in different roles at work. Here one's power relative to others influences how one acts. As a general rule, the more power one has, like the more money one has, the more one can put high-minded, moral, and other-oriented considerations first. By contrast, the less power or money one has, the more one is apt to be guided by more pragmatic self-interest concerns to survive in a competitive workplace.

To illustrate, I'll focus on the five workplace environments experienced by the interviewees—being a supervisor in an organization, dealing with clients as a professional, engaging in business negotiations and sales, working with a partner, and participating in politics.

ACTING AS A SUPERVISOR

For supervisors, two common ethical issues are how to fairly handle discipline and how open and honest to be in dealing with problems. Supervisors use varying ethical approaches to resolve these issues as the interviewees who worked as supervisors—Henry, the supervisor in a government agency, and Tom, a manager at a scientific lab—described what they did.

Henry, who tended to be very pragmatic and self-oriented, drew his supervisory approach from his military training. He gave the people under him as much power as he could, as long as they performed. But if they didn't, he switched into a "take no prisoners" mode, firmly disciplining those who didn't make the grade. As Henry described his approach:

> I was trained as a leader in the Army. One thing that was hammered into me was to accomplish your mission, which I think any supervisor knows. The second thing is to take care of your troops, so I'm an empowering supervisor and I encourage people to do what they can.
>
> But I'll use fear if somebody consistently does something wrong. Then, I have no qualms about punishing or disciplining them. For example, I suspended one woman for two weeks without pay, and I took another woman off flex time and overtime, because I felt they were taking advantage of the situation, and I needed to do something to pull them back into line.
>
> At other times, I like to be able to walk up to any member of my staff and have them feel free to talk about problems, when I ask: "What went wrong? Why didn't this work?" I want them to feel they can contribute to solving the problem. Also, I try to accept each person as an individual, since I have a half-dozen people with very unique personalities in my department.

Henry felt this approach of combining firm, evenhanded discipline with support and open communication was fair and ethical, as long as he exercised any discipline fairly, didn't go too far, and didn't let anger or personalities get in the way. As Henry put it:

> I don't have any ethical problems with disciplining or punishing someone who hasn't done the work, because I give everyone a chance. I believe everyone should have a chance and everybody can make mistakes. I allow for this. But when somebody continues to make a mistake, keeps getting in my face, or causes a problem in the unit, this needs to be corrected.
>
> I start by going through the usual procedures for dealing with problems in my agency. I talk to the person first. If that doesn't work, I eventually take disciplinary action, such as suspending the person. And I don't feel badly or have any ethical problem with doing this, since I don't take action against somebody to satisfy myself. I don't think revenge is a good idea, though I don't see any value in putting myself out to help someone who hasn't helped me and has given me trouble in the past.

For me the ethical ideal is finding that balance, and that helps to avoid ethical problems. I believe that ideal involves guiding people, encouraging them, and understanding them, but then discipline them fairly when things aren't working to get them to do better.

Similarly, Tom the scientist now running for political office, tried to keep things running smoothly whether in charge of a lab or a political campaign. But whereas Henry tended to be more direct and unforgiving, Tom had a more diplomatic, political style, in which he sometimes use subterfuge in not telling the real reason for doing something to smooth over relationships.

For example, he used this indirect approach to keep things running smoothly when he had to deal with a computer programmer who he felt wasn't pulling her weight. As Tom explained:

I had a computer programmer working for me, and she was a good programmer. But I got the impression she wasn't working eight hours a day when she worked for both me and another supervisor in the computer department.

I had a discussion with her other boss about whether she was putting in a full day or not. But I never confronted her and let it drop. To be ethical, maybe I should have been up front with her and told her I was going to talk about the situation with her other boss. But since I decided not to make an issue about it, I feel what I did was appropriate in handling the matter quietly and smoothly. After I talked to the other supervisor, we both agreed that her work was so superior that even if she was working 7 1/4 hours rather than 8, we shouldn't make an issue out of it. So I let the matter drop.

Tom also found this indirect strategy worked well, when he felt a campaign manager working on his election was behaving inappropriately, even irrationally. But rather than fire her, he found a way with the aid of an associate to discourage her participation. This way, rather than confronting her directly, he could ease her out more smoothly. It wasn't the most honest approach, Tom admitted, but he felt it worked the best in this situation to help defuse the woman's anger. As Tom described what happened:

> The last time I ran for office, I had a woman who volunteered to help my campaign, and she was extremely energetic. She was doing very well for awhile, so I told her she could call herself my campaign manager, though I couldn't pay her.
>
> Then, I discovered she was doing things that were detrimental to the campaign, and the question came up of how to discharge her. She was a very emotional and reactive person, and I was afraid of what might happen. So I had a discussion with others on the campaign committee on how to handle her. I guess it was an ethical dilemma whether to tell her the truth up front or to try some other diplomatic way to ease her out of the effort. At the time, we decided that an up-front challenge, where we explained what we didn't like about what she was doing and said we didn't want her to participate anymore, might be more than she could handle psychologically.
>
> So I took the advice of my treasurer who is also a lawyer. He suggested that the way to handle this problem was for him to call her up, act very buddy-buddy, and dissuade her from further participation. So that's what he did. He tried to be very sympathetic with her concerns, spoke about her personality differences with me as the candidate, and gradually intimated that maybe she might consider not participating in the campaign. She was still very angry, but at least she dropped out.

Thus, in the interest of making things go more smoothly, protecting others' feelings, or protecting their own job, supervisors often choose to do what's pragmatic to resolve the problem. They may not be fully open, honest, clear, and direct in communicating with the other person. But very often this approach works, as Henry and Tom, the two supervisors, reported.

DEALING WITH CLIENTS

In dealing with clients, some common ethical issues are how open and honest to be marketing oneself to get clients, what to do when personal and client interests diverge, and how to respond when a client asks one to do something dishonest or illegal. In some cases, the individual's professional may have established ethical guidelines to deal with recurring problems in that profession; but then the existence of guidelines can raise another question—should one follow those guidelines or not? Again one's own ethical perspective affects how one decides what to do. Here's how some of the interviewees who worked with clients dealt with these issues.

Getting Clients

One basic ethical issue in getting clients is whether to work with a client who has a different ethical perspective or who engages in activities one considers wrong or unethical. Another issue is how direct and honest one will be—the basic truth in advertising or packaging question. What can one say or not? How much can one shape the truth to present oneself in the best possible light, yet still be ethical?

Karen, the ad agency owner, faced the client choice dilemma. But due to her strong right and wrong perspective and concern for others, coupled with support from her husband, she was able to turn down clients when she didn't like their perspective or politics. As Karen explained:

> I had a professional ethical dilemma when I met a graphic designer whose work I really admire, and I wanted to work with him as a copywriter. I sent him some materials and after six months, he called, saying he had a project I could work on writing copy for a video war game for boys.
>
> I was torn, because I really wanted to work with the company. But I didn't want to write copy for a game that encouraged boys to go to war. So I asked if I could think about it, because I had to examine my soul to see what to do. I finally did decide not to work on the assignment, and it was difficult to word my explanation so as not to offend him. I didn't want to accuse him of being unethical, because he was doing the design. I started off by saying I was not trying to make a value judgment about the work he did and that I wanted to work with him very much, but personally I didn't want to write copy that encouraged children to play war games. Then, he did get a

bit huffy, and I haven't received any other calls to work for him, though I would like to. But I still feel I made the right decision to follow my conscience.

It was a very hard decision, but ultimately I felt I had to do it, because I'm very committed to being nonviolent.

The experience made Karen even more committed to her ethical view, since after this situation occurred, she rewrote her business listing in several business directories to clearly state she was only seeking clients with certain types of products and services. They had to be nonviolent, beneficial, educational, and not harmful to the environment.

For Jerry the lawyer the ethical issue was not so much what kinds of clients to seek or reject but how to best approach prospective clients—and in particular what to conceal or reveal. It was the same sort of disclosure and concealment question he faced in his relationships with women, described earlier. As in the social context, he used a mix of reason and intuition, combined with self-interest and pragmatism, to decide what to do. As he described the problem and his approach:

I've only been doing my specialty, entertainment law, for about a year. So I still have to work hard to get clients. If a prospective client comes to me and asks if I have done a certain thing, say draft a certain kind of contract, I'll say no if the answer is clearly no. But if I've done the task once, even if it was for a very small matter, didn't get paid for it, or did the job on a contingency basis, I'll say "yes." I act confident and say "Yes, I've done that," if I can find the slightest way to claim I have.

Thus, admittedly, I'm repackaging myself, and it could be unethical if I stretch it too far. It's a matter of degree. I think it's okay to repackage and put a good spin on things, if you are able to do things. It's not ethical if you are actually lying or if you can't do something but lead a prospective client to think you can. Then, too, it depends on whether the other person is directly asking me to disclose something or not. Many times if they haven't asked, I won't say. It all depends on how relevant or important the information they haven't asked about is, and how disadvantageous or advantageous it would be to disclose it.

I use a mixture of logic and intuition in deciding what to do in a particular situation. The logical part is knowing that putting a spin on something is okay but lying isn't, and knowing if someone is directly asking me to disclose something or not. Then the intuitive part, which influences me the most, is what feels like the best thing to do in my self interest in the circumstances.

Dick the architect sometimes had the same kind of problem, since he was fairly new in his field, as well. And he, too, tended to downplay his lack of experience and act like he could do things he hadn't done before to get the client. As Dick described his situation:

My basic approach to new clients is to do what I can to show I can do something if I think I can, even if I haven't done it before or know someone else who could do it better. For example, this morning a guy called and wanted me to help him design part of a marina, which I never did before. But I didn't tell him that. Nor did I tell him I knew another person who might be better qualified, since he had done similar work. I just said: 'I'll come and talk to you and see what we can do.'

That's the kind of approach I use in general when people call me about any project. That's because I use a problem-solving approach and try to show how I can help them solve their problem, rather than having them judge me based only expertise.

It's a gray area, because you're supposed to be looking out for the client's best interest. And if you are, maybe the person who knows more about the subject than you could be better. But if I don't have much work, I'd rather try to get the project if I can. And that's generally how most people in the profession do it. Even if they know somebody is the better person for the job, they try to get the job and take it if they can get it.

Getting and Keeping Clients

A related issue to getting clients is keeping them, and a similar ethical issue can arise over how open and honest to be. Sometimes there is a temptation to hold back, shade things a little, or tell the client what he or she wants to hear to become or stay a client.

For example, June, the tax accountant, who helped clients keep their taxes down, sometimes shaded the truth a little with clients, to both get them and "keep them happy" as she put it. As she described it:

> Sometimes potential clients will call me and ask how long it will be for a tax return to be ready, and I'll tell them a little sooner than it actually will be. I'll say 'I'll try'. I won't promise exactly, since that would be a lie; but I let them think I can do it, and later I'll explain why it's taking a little longer. I do this because I want to get the client—and I know I can make the IRS deadline, though it might be a little later than they hope when they call me.
>
> Also, after clients have given me their returns, I sometimes ease them along, telling them something will be ready sooner than it actually is. I sometimes do this when a client calls asking when his return will be ready and I feel he is very anxious and wants to be reassured. So I'll tell him a lie so he will feel better. Say I'll tell him: "The return will be ready in two weeks." Then, when he calls and it isn't ready, I give him another date a few days or a week away.
>
> This way of lying is like a marketing tactic to snare and keep the client. It does cause some uncomfortableness for me and the client later on, because the client has expectations I've led them to believe that won't happen. But usually, I'm able to smooth it over, and most of these clients have stayed with me year after year.

Similarly, in getting and keeping clients, Iris, the therapist, sometimes had to decide how open to be in expressing an opinion about whether she could effectively help or whether her own issues might interfere with her being effective. Generally, she found a way to reconcile the interests of the client seeking help with her self-interest. As Iris explained:

> As a therapist there's always the ethical consideration of what to do when your client has the same dilemma as the therapist. The question is can you really help or not, and what should you tell the client.
>
> For example, I now have three clients with the same problem I haven't solved in my own life—which is dealing with an eld-

erly parent. I feel a little like a hypocrite and wonder if it's really ethical for me to try to help this person, when I haven't solved my own issues about being an abused child. But I'm still working with these clients, and I feel I have helped them by working on better resolving these issues in myself.

However, I generally don't tell the client that I have the same dilemma or that I'm working on the issue if that's the main issue they are working on. I might share some insights I have learned about it, but I don't tell, because it puts the client in a difficult position. Though it may contribute to better rapport by showing I can empathize with them, the risk is I am sharing this because I want to get this problem off my chest and so it's in my own self-interest, not my client's. So I don't say anything.

Instead, if I find that my having the same experience as the client is getting in the way, I try to work more on myself to resolve my own feelings. But if the issue is too difficult for me to deal with, the ethical thing is to let the client know that somebody else might be more useful to them. Then, I refer them to another therapist or explain the problem and give them the choice of what to do.

Dealing with Client Requests to Do Something Unethical or Illegal

Another issue in some fields is the client who wants to do something unethical or illegal. This raises several questions: should one participate or help to keep the client, and if not, should one still continue to work with that person? And how can one tell the person one won't do it, but still, if possible, keep the client?

Both the situation and one's ethical approach affect the way people decide. As already described, Marie, the tax accountant, who tended to be a rule breaker tried to help in borderline cases, while Karen, the ad agency owner, with a highly moral "follow the rules" approach, turned questionable requests down, preferring to only work with people and causes consistent with her code of integrity.

Perhaps most of all, Bill, the lawyer, had to frequently deal with such questions, because of his general law practice. Clients often came to him wanting to shape or ignore the law to their own advantage. But early on in his practice, he decided to take the high moral ground, though he did so for pragmatic reasons of self-interest. He was afraid of the risks of doing something wrong and getting caught, resulting in serious penalties, as well as looking foolish. Thus, depending on the circumstances, Bill turned down some clients who proposed doing something unethical or illegal, or he tried to help other clients see why their approach wouldn't work or why they shouldn't do it. Then, if he couldn't convince them, he declined to help.

Bill described some common situations he faced. Generally, when clients came to him trying to figure out what to say or not to win their case, his approach, practiced by many lawyers, was to give them a general overview of how the law would affect their case, while emphasizing that they had to tell the truth. As Bill described his approach:

> Often when a client comes to me, they start telling me their story about what happened, and usually it's spotty to begin with. So I start asking questions about did this happen before that or were you told "y" before you said "z". Then, when they get the drift of what I'm asking about to determine if they are liable or responsible for something or if they were truly victimized by someone, they sometimes start to adapt the story. For example, they'll say: "Oh, yeah, I think that's the way they happened." Or they try to shade the story. And sometimes they go past the line of what's acceptable by asking me: "Well, what do I have to say to make it come out right?"
>
> At that point, I tell them, "You've got to say the truth." Life is rarely that black and white, because people do try to put the best face they can on their position, and as an advocate, you have the duty to put the best face on their position, too. But you can't lie either. Thus, when somebody starts saying something happened that didn't or something didn't happen that did, there's no dispute about the ethics of the situation. You can't go forward on that basis—and I don't.
>
> Ethical questions aside, it isn't practical. If you manufacture something or you allow your client to do so, it is likely to hurt them in the long-run. Few people are practiced enough at lying to sustain a lie through all the testing that litigation usually

requires. Sooner or later it will come out. Then, too, if the client is dishonest, you don't want to condone it or make it seem like you're participating in their dishonesty, because then they have something they can hold over your head later on, say if you end up negotiating with your client about something, such as getting paid. It's really a case of what goes around comes around.

So when I see a client starting to launch into a dishonest fantasy or fiction about what happened, I generally try to show them as a matter of common sense, not to do this. I generally don't use a moral perspective or lecture to them about why this is "wrong." Rather, I just explain why their idea of lying won't fly. I tell them how hard it is to sustain a lie in the heat of negotiation.

In some cases, he simply pointed out why a client's suggested approach wouldn't work legally. As he noted:

If I feel a client is wrong I generally tell them: "The law doesn't support your position here. If you want to go forward with it, you're not likely to prevail." Or if their proposed approach is too unrealistic, I tell them: "I can't present this complaint to the other side, because no one is going to pay any attention to it, and I'll just look like an idiot."

And in one case, when a client wouldn't back down, Bill pulled out, because, as he explained:

I wasn't willing to support him in not honoring his contract or filing a frivolous lawsuit which I didn't think had merit. I wouldn't do anything if I would appear foolish, because if you make an unreasonable claim, they won't take you seriously about anything else in the future—so you have to take into consideration ongoing relationships with colleagues in the field, too.

Also, for Bill it made a difference whether the client proposing something unethical or illegal was new or a client he had worked with before. If the cleint was new, Bill was more likely to back out entirely; if a previous client, he was more likely to try to persuade the client to do the "right" thing. But even with regular clients, there was a point beyond which Bill wouldn't go. If he strongly didn't believe in the merits of a client's proposed claim, he wouldn't support it, even if it meant losing a client.

Getting into Non-Professional Relationships with Clients

Finally, one other common problem in relationships with clients is developing a personal relationship, which is often explicitly discouraged or prohibited in professional codes, because the relationship can compromise the ability to provide professional services or hurt the client. Besides the problem with business ties previously discussed, a key source of ethical conflict is the romantic involvement. While the usual concern is whether this relationship can harm the client, because the professional has the power, such a relationship can backfire on the practitioner, too. That's what Bill the lawyer found out after he grappled with his own ethical dilemma involving an attractive client. As he described what happened:

> One time when I was much younger and had been practicing law for only a year, I was attracted to a woman client, and my personal interest led me to lose sight of the fact that she was completely in the wrong in what I was defending her against. I overlooked signs of corruption and criminal activity I never would have missed otherwise.
>
> It all started when she came to my office and told me she had a two-year contract with a labor organization to publish their newsletter and was fired after three months without a reason. When she showed me the contract with her name on it, I should have been suspicious, because the amount on it was about four times what someone with her experience would have been paid to publish a newsletter. But she seemed so innocent and bewildered about what had happened that I felt this powerful macho desire to come to the rescue of this damsel in distress. So I overlooked what was really going on—that she had been hired as a front by this organization, which was using the newsletter as a front to shake down general contractors who had contracts with the union. The way it worked is some union representatives would call these contractors and ask them to put up several thousand dollars for advertising for a newsletter that was

never actually published.

She claimed to know nothing about all of this, which came out later after the FBI got involved doing a labor racketeering investigation. And she really didn't. The union just wanted to show they paid someone to run the newsletter. So they didn't tell her anything about this or what should go in the newsletter. The money was to keep her quiet as they raked in huge sums of money. But she got fired because she and her partner went outside the union and its contacts and started taking ads for this newsletter from doctors and dentists who truly expected to see advertising. Then as FBI began its investigation, she referred the FBI and other investigators to me.

I remained involved for about a month because I was attracted to her, but finally pulled back and stopped representing her because I don't handle criminal cases. That's when I realized I had let myself be taken for a ride, after she came to my office wearing a very short skirt and batting her eyes, because if I had listened to my initial suspicions I would never have done any of this. I would have been suspicious that she was paid far more than a newsletter was worth. Then, once I showed I wasn't interested in helping her with the case, she stopped pretending she was interested in a personal relationship with me.

So I was a fool, because I blinded myself to the truth. If she wasn't so attractive and if I had done the right ethical thing which is not to get involved with current clients, I would have been able to see what was going on in the first place and I wouldn't have gotten involved as I did.

ENGAGING IN BUSINESS NEGOTIATIONS AND SALES

For those in certain fields where negotiations and transactions are an everyday part of business, such as manufacturing and sales, ethical dilemmas can be especially intense. The very nature of the relationship and importance of the profit motive encourages self-interest and pragmatic considerations, rather than moral or altruistic impulses. The competitive dog-eat-dog approach reflects this highly self-oriented pragmatic approach, as does the concern with maximizing the bottom line. As a result, it can be difficult to follow altruistic, other-oriented values, though some do, in choosing the products or causes they will work with or being willing to earn less. But others find the competitive pressures too intense and ethically threatening and drop out entirely.

That's what happened to Ben, the writer, leading him to abandon a business career. He found that most of the people he worked with in the advertising business adopted a law of the jungle style of operating, and for awhile, he did, too, to achieve success. But after he was burned too many times and felt embittered by the many people who had lied to and cheated him, he left the field. He found their hard-nosed approach was too cut-throat for him and he felt he had to get out of this "den of thieves," as he described it, after a series of struggles left him burned out. As Ben commented:

> I spent about fifteen years in the advertising business. Most of those years I was in business for myself and I dealt with many clients whose ethics were often questionable, because money brings up some of the biggest ethical questions and dilemmas in our society.
>
> I started off working on the basis of trust in buying material from other people and buying media time. Initially, I was idealistic and was trained to be ethical, such as being honest with people. So I naively tried to deal with people on the basis of trust, assuming that if I was trustworthy, they would be trustworthy back.
>
> But I soon found I was in error, because virtually all of my clients eventually took me for large amounts of money—a few thousand dollars here, a few thousand dollars there, which added up, and was much more money then. They did this by promising things and not following through; taking money for work they didn't do; and not paying me money they owed me for months or not at all.
>
> Eventually, this situation created an ethical dilemma for me. Since I was screwed so much, I didn't have enough money to pay the vendors whose services and products I had bought myself. So the problem for me was how do I pay the vendors when I didn't have any more money? And the way I resolved that ethical dilemma is I skipped town.
>
> I didn't like doing it, but the amount of money was enough that I wanted to get out of advertising permanently.

Thus, it was losing rather than the lack of morality of the people he dealt with that bothered Ben the most. As he explained:

I got taken for about $40,000-50,000. I was placing successful help-wanted and classified ads for my clients, but I was working with thieves. It didn't bother me that they were stealing from other people, because until the end, they were paying me regularly, as I mounted a larger and larger effort for them.

But one day they stopped paying me, and I was responsible for all these ads I had placed. They stopped paying because they owed me so much money. It wasn't even personal. In fact, one man called me up and said: 'Look, that's the way business is. I have these partners and we need the money.' He even advised me to skip town.

It was like a bomb dropped in the middle of my life when he told me they wouldn't pay. So I went to the newspapers and explained the situation, and about half accepted my explanation that I was acting as the agent for these customers who ripped me off and they wrote of the debt. But the other ones came after me, and I started getting these threatening collection phone calls. So finally, I decided "To hell with it, I'm going," and decided to leave and put all this behind me.

Then, after he skipped, eventually relocating in California, Ben found himself on the losing end of other business deals. Finally, he decided it was time to "fold" in the game, and he walked away, becoming a writer instead.

By contrast, Andy, the salesman, currently in the telecommunications field, found a way to work with only products and companies he could feel good about, and he was able to bring a spirit of openness and integrity to his field. He sought to do this so his work would be consistent with his largely other-oriented, moral, rule-breaker approach to ethical issues. This way, he felt, he avoided the ethical compromises experienced by many people in the field. He also found the approach worked for him financially in the long run, since he could build long-term relationships with customers based on trust. As he explained:

What I look for in the products I sell is one that really supports the individuals or companies that use it. If it's got integrity, I'll sell it, and if it doesn't, I won't. It's got to give some value and be interesting to me; I only like to promote those kinds of products. Then, too, the product not only has to work well, but be

cost effective; the claims about service have to be true. It has to
be a healthy product, a fun product. And I have to feel good
about the company. Otherwise, I won't work with it.

Due to this philosophy, Andy sometimes risked losing his job when
he came up against more bottom-line, short-term profit-oriented
people in his company. But often he was able to prevail. If not, he
frequently walked away—and in his field, he could fairly easily do
this and find another position where he could apply his more idealistic approach to selling. As Andy explained:

> I've always tried to hang onto my ideals, even if it meant put-
> ting my job on the line or walking away. This is what happened
> when I was a broker in the data processing field. My job was to
> get suppliers or subcontractors to provide the work. And some
> would agree up front for a fixed price at so many dollars per
> hour. But shortly before the project was over, they would hold a
> gun to the company saying, "If you don't give me more money,
> I won't complete the project." I think it's wrong if somebody
> agrees to do the work and then asks for more when you're com-
> pletely vulnerable, because you need the work completed. As a
> broker, I won't support this.
>
> I might let it slide once if a guy previously did a good job
> and showed integrity. But in one case, a guy tried to hold us up
> twice. So I urged my company to let him go. It would cost us a
> little more to complete the job by bringing in someone new.
> But I felt what was morally good for us was to work with the
> customer, explain what happened, let our guy go, and absorb
> the extra costs ourselves. The company managers supported me
> in this decision, and that's what we did.

Andy took a similar stand when a telecommunications company he
worked for wanted to sell a device which was defective and over-
priced. Though Andy subsequently lost his job because he took an
unpopular stand, he never regretted doing it. The principle of integrity was too important to him. As Andy explained:

> About ten years ago, I was working in sales for a company in
> which two divisions engaged in a political deal. One division
> had some extra money in its budget and swapped it with the

sales division, in exchange for the product manager promising to sell a particular product.

As it turned out this product was defective, priced too high, and didn't give the customers what they wanted. Making matters worse, there was virtually no commission for the sales person, and the product was a hard sell, since it took three weeks to deliver, whereas as the product it replaced was available the next day.

Still, the sales people were told to sell it. But after I analyzed the situation, I told the other sales people the next day why I thought selling the product was a lousy idea. I told them: "It's not good for the customer. It's not good for us. It was poorly thought out. The pricing is wrong. Everything is wrong. There's no reason anyone would want this new product."

Since we were supposed to sell it, my sales manager was pretty perturbed when I said what he did. He believed you should do everything your manager asks you to do, and his manager had asked him to make us sell the product. But I felt it was bad for everyone involved, and so I stood up for what I believed.

Not too long afterwards, the company let me go. But I felt fine about that. I feel like there is an ethical ground you are walking on, and integrity is part of this ground. If you have to change your values to work for a company, it is good to know as soon as possible, so you can leave if you feel uncomfortable.

WORKING WITH A PARTNER

With partners, two key areas where ethical dilemmas arise are over issues of trust and what to do when one's partner doesn't perform. These dilemmas occur because a partnership is based on a mutual agreement about what the partners will do. But if one partner doesn't carry through for some reason, that presents various dilemmas for the other partner. Should he or she act to keep the partnership going? End the partnership and how? How serious does a breach of trust or failure to perform have to be to justify ending the partnership?

For Connie, the art director, who was very other-oriented and concerned with doing the right thing, the big issue was over trust after she realized her long-term partner couldn't be trusted. At first she tried to overlook the warning signs, since she strongly wanted to believe things would work out. But eventually she felt she had to break things off, and became more cautious in the future. As Connie described it:

> I was involved in founding a cultural arts center, and our partnership was based on trust. We had a shared vision and developed a community that was very much like a family. I put a lot of my personal money into this project and about ten years of time, until this shattered about six years ago.
>
> To make a long story short, my partner kept putting me off when I wanted to sign a contract, saying he felt uncomfortable about putting anything in writing, since it was unnecessary and showed distrust. But after all our work together, he basically dissolved the company. He had verbally promised me a tremendous amount for what I did, but I got nothing and had nothing in paper, nothing in writing. So I had no basis for any legal action.
>
> Afterwards, my bubble popped in terms of trusting people and thinking their word is their bond. I realized that's not how it really works for many people with a different ethical code than my own. They don't have any qualms about breaking their word. Also, I realized I let myself give up my own power, because I was too concerned with trying to see something from the other person's perspective, rather than considering my own needs and concerns. So I wouldn't give up my power again. And now in other business relationships, I need that level of security and assurance to feel comfortable, because I feel so ripped off by what happened six years ago.

Thus, the experience led Connie, who previously prided herself on being a very ethical person, who put moral concerns and the interests of others first, into being more pragmatic and self-interested. She changed in order to protect herself from being taken advantage of again by trusting someone too much.

For Joyce, the government researcher, the problem was what to do about another researcher she was working with on a project, when it appeared he couldn't perform, putting the project in jeopardy. As Joyce explained:

I really wanted this other researcher, Mel, to do the project with me, partly because I didn't think I could do it myself. I thought of Mel as the expert. So I invited him to participate, when I applied for a grant.

After the project was approved, I gave him a time-line of what had to be done when. Though he said his schedule might be a little tight, he assured me he could do it. But when it came time to start on the project, he frequently postponed or cancelled meetings, saying he was busy teaching at school. So eventually I developed the interview materials for the project, and I started doing the interviews myself.

As I did, I started having qualms about the arrangement. I began asking myself if I really wanted to keep working with this person. Also, I wondered about my obligation to Mel, since he still thought we were working together. So I felt more and more torn, though I kept hoping things would work out as planned, since I was still unsure I had the skills to do the project myself.

For Joyce, this state of ethical uncertainty continued for about two weeks, as she carried out her part of the project—about half the interviews. But she didn't share her deeper concerns with Mel, though she called him a few times with reminders about when things needed to be done.

But I don't think he really understood, because he seemed to believe our deadline could be postponed, though I said it couldn't. Finally, when he did start to do his interviews a few days before he left town for a week, two weeks before our deadline, the first two interviews he turned in were no good. So even if he could do the remaining interviews before he left town, I wasn't sure he could do them properly, and I now questioned his expertise for the project.

So I agonized over what to do. Though I initially felt I couldn't do the project myself and felt I needed his help, now after doing half the research on my own, I felt knew more about the subject and felt I could do the project myself after all. Also, I now felt a sense of ownership over the project, and no longer wanted him to share in it after all I had done, because I felt he had repeatedly let me down.

On the other hand, I wondered what kind of obligation I

owed to him, since he expected to be participating in the project.
Also he had conducted a few interviews and had several others
scheduled before his trip. So I kept weighing these considerations back and forth, wanting to do the right thing, though I
didn't want to be stupid in bending over backwards to give him
every chance, when I felt he had let me down so many times.

Thus, ultimately, Joyce decided to give Mel one last chance, since
she found it hard to tell him directly that his work wasn't acceptable. As Joyce explained:

> After I thought about it overnight, I called him in the morning
> and asked him to do one more interview tape I could hear be-
> fore he did anymore, so I could be sure they were all right,
> before he spent time doing additional interviews.
>
> He seemed angry that I now wanted to hear and evaluate an
> interview before he did anymore, and at first he refused, but
> then agreed. But after a week, he left a message on my tape
> saying he didn't have time to do the interviews after all. So
> finally I felt I was off the hook. Meanwhile, to make the dead-
> line, I kept doing additional interviews to complete the project.
>
> In the end, I felt I did the right thing. I felt I had given Mel
> every chance to show he could do something—but then he
> couldn't, and he had created his own blocks to doing the project.
> He didn't have the time to do it or get fully informed to do it
> properly. So I felt good about cutting him loose. I don't feel I
> pushed him out of the project—I feel he did that to himself. If
> anything, I feel I was too concerned about his feelings and car-
> ried him along further than I should.

These stories about problems in partnership arrangements highlight the need for a balance in one's ethical approach, especially to
protect oneself, if the other person is more self- and pragmatically-
oriented. In Connie's case, by not standing up for herself soon
enough, she was caught up in a disastrous, one-sided partnership
and lost everything, when it broke up. By contrast, by catching a
similar situation early enough, Joyce ended the partnership and took
back the project and her power, when her partner was unable to do
what he said he would do.

THE ART OF COMPROMISE:
BEING POLITICAL IN POLITICS

While companies and organizations have their own organizational cultures and ethical styles that affect the types of issues that come up, how people deal with them, and the type of people attracted to the field, so do institutions. A good example is politics, whether one is running for office or is part of a political campaign. Here the art of the compromise is particularly favored whether one uses a rational or intuitive style. Compromise involves a "give a little, get a little" approach that in many ways reflects a middle way or a mixture of ethical approaches on the Ethical Choices Map. For example, while one may seek gains for oneself, one must show a concern for others, too. One must temper self-interest with the pull of loyalty and being a team player. Also, one must be willing to go along with the rules, though some may be innovators and rule breakers at times. And while being pragmatic helps, a moral pull towards a particular position is common.

The interviewees involved in politics described how they had to frequently turn to compromising in various situations.

For example, Tom, the physicist running for local political office, frequently had to make compromises and temper his promises to maintain continuing support from others. As Tom explained:

> In politics you have to learn how to make compromises to maintain your leadership position, since you're drawing together the interests of disparate groups of people. Initially, when you start running, you can claim to be very ethical and take the higher moral ground in talking about what you're going to do and in how you run your campaign. But what happens to politicians, especially when they hold office, is they get co-opted by various interest groups whose support they need. In trying to serve their constituents, they find themselves first agreeing with group A and saying they will help group A. But then, group B comes along with a different agenda, and they want to help that group, too. So they end up with conflicts in what they can do for these two groups that can't be resolved except by shorting one group or the other.

As a result, they end up having to tell a little bit of a lie to one of these groups, and can get into serious trouble, if they take contributions and there's a quid pro quo or bribe they will do something in return. But an implied promise can create problems, too, if you can't keep it or if an opponent thinks you made it. I haven't run into those kinds of problems yet, because I'm still new to the game and haven't gotten into a position of power. But I'm aware that's the way things work.

Still, Tom did have to deal with the issue of making potentially conflicting promises for future possibilities, and he took the evasive "let things slide and hope they go away" approach, which was his usual way of handling ethical issues. As Tom described it:

Occasionally, I had people come to me and say: "You know if you get a certain number of votes in the primary election, you will be entitled to appoint people to the state central committee of the party." And others have directly said: "I'd like to be appointed." As a result, I had a problem with making promises I couldn't fill.

That happened one time after I promised to appoint a woman who got into trouble with the law in her community, due to a very public divorce with her husband. So for political reasons, people didn't want her appointed, which by association would hurt the party.

As a result, I had to withdraw my promise to appoint her, and a further dilemma was whether I should call to tell her I would do this or let the matter slide. Eventually, I decided to let things slide, because she was a very emotional person, who could easily be upset. Then, I didn't get enough votes in the election to make any appointments anyway, so that was definitely the right decision, not to bring it up.

Eventually with time and experience, Tom learned to be more careful in making promises, concluding that the wisest course was not to make firm promises in the first place. Then, one didn't have to break them—a basic truth he had learned about politics. Or as he put it:

I think the clever politicians—who are often the most honest, too—have a way of responding to requests with the word "maybe" or some kind of qualifier, so they never make a blanket or explicit promise unless they intend to carry it out.

In my opinion that's good politics in the long run. In the short run, you may think it's advantageous to say "yes" to everybody that comes to your office. They then leave thinking you will help them. But later when you can't accede to all the various requests, some people will be disappointed. And that disappointment will be a lot stronger than if you were honest with them—and less certain—up front. So that's what I'm trying to do now—tell it just like it is.

These ethical issues around positions, promises, and making compromises also affect those who are active in supporting candidates, not running for anything. For example, Pam, the nurse, a member of several grass roots organizations, sometimes went along with groups though she disagreed with some of their positions, because she wanted to remain a good team player. And like Tom, the physicist running for office, she felt comfortable compromising, because, she, too, had a pragmatic "do what works" ethical style. As she described her situation:

One of the groups I belong to is a lot more right wing on many issues than I am, since it's a group interested in justice, so there are a lot of law and order types. Many times I have different opinions on the issues than some of their candidates, such as their strong support for the death penalty, which I don't like. But I go along with them, because I'm involved in the group. I feel funny about doing so, but I rationalize it on the grounds that I'm active with the group because I believe strongly in certain other things that they're doing.

At the same time, I belong to a local nurse's union, and they have a totally different philosophy on many issues than this group, because they support worker's rights and women's rights, which this group doesn't. So sometimes I'm torn as to who I should work for and vote for in an election.

The way I balance the two perspectives is I set priorities and see what's more important in the situation. It's like being able to maintain a split consciousness, so I'm one way with one group and another way with the other group, and generally I fall somewhere in the middle of both. I'll vote the way I believe privately, but outwardly I try to fit in. For example, if I'm at a group meeting, I'll play along with the group and act agreeable. I'll dress like others do. I may not be really gung-ho about supporting something that everyone else does, but I will pretend I am if that seems appropriate when I'm there.

In sum, the political arena has its own code of ethics, and those who are actively involved—whether as candidates, campaign workers, or volunteers—take those guidelines into consideration, along with their own ethical ideals, in resolving ethical dilemmas, such as in making promises or in choosing to be a team player though one may personally disagree.

SUMMING UP

In sum, ethical issues are shaped by the organizational context and the customary rules and practices in that environment. Each arena has its common patterns or ethical culture for dealing with those issues, which intersect with the individual's own approach to dealing with dilemmas. In turn, to some extent individuals are drawn to certain work and organizational environments based on their own ethical approach. This is because the individual needs to feel a certain fit to be comfortable with the group or organization, or the individual may feel frustrated and leave.

For example, a person who goes into politics has to feel comfortable with the spirit of compromise, while someone who enters a business environment, like the ad game, has to feel up to participating in the competitive way of doing business to make it. Alternatively, in other fields, one might have more opportunity to be more altruistic if desired, such as in health care, although even here there may be organizational pressures to follow the bottom line.

In short, in the workplace and business setting, everyday ethical decision making is subject to many different influences—from the organization, the situation, and the individual's own approach.

CHAPTER 23

•

DEALING WITH COMMUNITY AND PUBLIC DILEMMAS

Beyond the zone of work and professional associations is the community and general public. Though any member of this category can be drawn into one of the closer zones of relationship, until they do, they are part of this larger zone.

THE LACK OF AWARENESS OF EVERYDAY ETHICAL ISSUES

Generally, because of a lack of personal closeness, everyday hassles and conflicts with members of the community or general public don't involve the emotional intensity raised by problems with those in closer relationships. In fact, many people do not think of many of these daily conflicts as ethical issues. Rather, they see them more as issues of showing consideration for others, following the rules, or going along with prevailing local customs. Thus, few interviewees mentioned any ethical dilemmas in this area.

Yet many everyday conflicts do have an ethical component. Take the common problem of who gets the parking space—the person who has been patiently waiting for another car to pull out to back into the space, or the opportunistic driver who zips in just as the car pulls out. Taking the space is really something of an ethical dilemma for the person who pulls in, since it involves considering the other person's desires or doing something to benefit oneself (the other-self dimension), deciding whether to follow the customary rule of deferring to the driver there first or break that rule (the follower-innovator dimension), and choosing whether to do the right thing (driving on) or doing what may appear the most pragmatic alternative (taking the space). Then, too, the rational-intuitive dimension comes into play as the person assesses the situation rationally (i.e., "Oh, it's just an older woman waiting, she won't fight back.") or intuitively (i.e., "Oh, go for it. You can make it!").

Other common everyday situations that might raise ethical questions include:

- The customer in line when the clerk makes a mistake in his or her favor;
- the person considering whether to cut ahead in line to get a ticket;
- the individual deciding whether to make up an excuse to take something back to recover his cost after breaking it;
- the person wondering whether to keep the money he or she found or report it;
- and other minor breaches of everyday rules and customs.

Such issues come up frequently, but are often considered so minor that they barely register on the ethical map; they don't challenge one's essence as an ethical person, whereas issues closer to oneself do. In fact, we often make everyday decisions quickly, not really thinking of our choice in ethical terms, although it is.

Thus, few interviewees thought of everyday issues in ethical terms. But those who did noted a few areas of conflict. These are:

- temptations as a consumer or citizen;
- problems over the use of public spaces;
- disputes with neighbors over property and privacy issues;
- personality conflicts in a public group;
- and requests to support others in the community.

TEMPTATIONS AS A CONSUMER OR CITIZEN

These temptations come up when one has an unexpected opportunity to take an advantage of a situation, typically because someone has made a mistake (like the clerk who incorrectly rings up a sale and charges too little). Another time they occur is when one has made a mistake and encounters an authority figure (such as the woman who makes an improper left turn and is stopped by a cop). Here the temptation is to find a way to escape the negative consequences if possible.

The ethical dilemma in these situations is whether to be truthful and risk losing the opportunity or being blamed for the mistake; or should one be deceptive and lie. In turn, one's response reflects a mixture of influences due to the circumstances (i.e., is this a small store where the clerk will pay for any losses himself or a large store which can afford any losses?) and one's general approach (i.e., usually to do what's right versus usually to do what's personally beneficial).

The pragmatic self-interested approach is common, however, in these minor consumer or citizen matters, because the relationship is impersonal, and often the victim is an institution or organization, like a company or city, rather than a person. As a result, there is little sense of hurting anyone; one feels one is primarily protecting or benefitting oneself.

For example, June the tax accountant, did what she could to evade traffic tickets and broke the occasional traffic rule to get where she was going faster, even though in personal ethical dilemmas she tended to do what she felt was morally right and placed a high value on the needs of others. As she described her approach on the road:

> When it comes to traffic laws, I don't run red lights, speed, or openly flout the law. But I will sneak ahead of a bunch of slow drivers in the slow lane by getting into the curb lane if I can. Or I'll wait at the red light and try to rush ahead of a guy who's slow to go when its green, which I know is illegal. But I try to be careful, so I don't get a ticket.
>
> For me, evading some traffic rules is like getting ahead when I'm standing in line. I mostly try to follow the rule of standing in line because I think it's rude or I don't like it when people do it to me. But if I think I can get ahead of someone and I'm not hurting anyone, I'm going to do it.

Similarly, Sam, the writer and part-time comedian, felt no qualms about playing the switching game as a customer to get extra benefits from the phone company enticing him to switch. As he explained:

> I frequently get phone calls from AT&T and MCI asking me to switch to their long distance service. Essentially, they offer a bribe each time, and I say, 'Okay, I'll switch,' because the bribe makes it worth the trouble. It seems a little unethical to me, in that I keep switching back and forth, when they are supposedly giving me a bribe for my loyalty—maybe as much as $50 in frequent flyer miles or cash.
>
> I feel if I am taking their money, I should be loyal to them. But if the other company comes up with another offer, I take that too. I've switched back and forth several times so far. I do feel a little uneasy about it, but any feelings of guilt are minimal, because they're big corporations and I don't think I'm depriving anyone of any money. And I appreciate the extra money myself.

Likewise, Sandi, the entrepreneur, was quick to take advantage of unexpected opportunities in stores, unless it was a small proprietor-owned store. As she described it:

> For me when the store clerk makes a mistake in my favor, it's like getting a gift. Of course, if the mistake is to my disadvantage I'm quick to point that out. But if it's to my benefit, in the big chain and warehouse stores where I usually go, I won't say anything. I let them charge me less or give me more than they should. I feel if it's a big store, they can afford it more than me; and if the clerk made the mistake, it's his responsibility to be correct. I wouldn't do this in a small store where the clerk is the owner, because I would feel I was hurting him personally, so I would say something. But in the big stores no.
>
> This happened one time when I was buying a new fax machine. I had selected a less expensive model with fewer features, but at the cash register, they brought me the more expensive model from the stock. I started to say something, but when I saw that it was priced incorrectly at the lower price, I shut up, and so I got the more expensive top of the line model for about $100 less. I felt good about getting this extra savings. I wouldn't have changed the prices myself, since this is illegal and I would

be afraid of getting caught. But I didn't do anything to mislead the clerk myself. So there was nothing to fear about getting caught.

PROBLEMS OVER THE USE OF PUBLIC SPACES

Using public space for activities that might be disturbing or offensive to others can also become an ethical issue. It raises questions of whose rights are being invaded and to what extent the person using the space should consider the rights of others, such as the case of smoking.

Connie the art director, for example, felt that people who smoked around others who didn't like smoking were being unethical in not considering the rights of others to be free of smoke. As she put it:

> Smoking cigarettes is an ethical issue for me, because people who smoke cigarettes should be conscious about how others feel. Then, if they realize someone is bothered by their smoking, the ethical question is whether they are considerate and go outside themselves or whether they try to impose their smoke on others.
>
> Alternately, I think nonsmokers need to treat smokers with respect, and as one myself, the ethical issue for me is how do you treat people who do something you hate in a way that is polite and proper? I feel I have become a little unethical in that area, because I really abuse smokers. I'm rude to them. I don't value them. I don't have any tolerance or sensitivity to their addiction or their problem. I simply don't want to have anything to do with them. So if it's their environment and they choose to smoke, I would remove myself. Or if its in my environment or a public place, I think they shouldn't smoke.

DISPUTES WITH NEIGHBORS OVER THE USE OF PROPERTY AND PRIVACY ISSUES

In the case of neighbors, the potential for ethical dilemmas can occur when neighbors become intrusive or engage in typical neighborhood disputes, like too much noise and overhanging trees. The ethical component occurs when such disputes escalate, raising questions about what's neighborly when neighbors go too far, and how to respond appropriately when a neighbor becomes intrusive or abusive.

Lars, the academic studying philosophy, experienced a series of such problems, because his differences in lifestyle led suburban neighbors to become concerned about his activities. He found their interest an invasion of his privacy and eventually felt justified in responding with some hostility, as a result of his self-oriented, pragmatic, make-your-own rules approach to life. As Lars described the situation:

> I personally feel that the right to privacy should be unconditional. But I had neighbors who were nosy and saw that as being neighborly and sociable. But I was very busy pursuing my graduate degree in school.
>
> I started off by introducing myself and being polite. But soon my neighbors wanted to drop in and gossip. And for several weekends in a row, two or three people came by to persuade me to go to church.
>
> But I have a different religious belief. So my choice came down to being nice or being truthful; being well liked or expressing what I feel. And I decided on the latter. After my repeated refusals to attend church didn't work and they still urged me to go, I eventually became rude in telling them to leave me alone. I didn't like doing this, but I felt I had to act in this more abrasive way, so they would leave me alone. And finally they did, though it created an uneasy truce, and eventually I also put up a fence to keep them from prying.

PERSONALITY CONFLICTS IN A PUBLIC GROUP

Another kind of ethical conflict occurs when differences between individuals in a public group go beyond an ordinary dispute involving personalities or differences in opinion. In this case, when the problem escalates, it can raise questions about what kind of response is right or wrong, and when a response goes too far and becomes "unethical."

That's what happened in a group to which Sam the writer belonged. One member had become disturbingly aggressive, interrupting people, talking too much, and Sam, like others in the group, decided to shut her out. Sam considered it an ethical dilemma, because it went against his usual nice guy way of relating to people. As he described it:

> I belong to a group of people that meet to discuss the issues of the day and current events. One woman was disruptive and no one knew what to do about her. She dominated the group and wanted more structure than anybody else wanted. When somebody was talking, she would interrupt. She would go off on long tangents. Or after the group had agreed on a topic, she would try to change it or suggest a different format. Everyone else liked having a loose, informal format, but she kept trying to impose her more formal structure.
>
> So we discussed in her absence what to do about it. At first we considered not telling her where the next meeting was, but we figured she might call someone and find out. Then we decided that someone in the group should tell her as diplomatically as possible that her style is so different from the group's that she might consider not coming. But then no one wanted to call her. Finally we decided that if she called anyone about the meeting, that person should tell her to call the woman who had originally invited her, who would tell her how the group felt and try to persuade her not to come.
>
> It was the only way, we felt, that we could keep the group going. But afterwards, each of us felt bad about trying to keep her out, because we have all been in a situation where we were excluded for some reason. We didn't like doing this to somebody else. Yet we felt this woman was destroying the cohesion of the group.

Thus, for pragmatic reasons, the group collectively decided to exclude the woman and have one member explain why to protect the group. However the continuing ethical dilemma for everyone was the difficulty of rejecting her and directly telling her why. Fortunately, though, no one had to confront this problem, perhaps because the woman got the hint without anyone telling her directly, and she never called anyone for the meeting location.

REQUESTS TO SUPPORT OTHERS IN THE COMMUNITY

Another public versus individual dilemma is the request to support others in the community when one doesn't want to or feels ambivalent about doing so. Often this is more a matter of individual choice than an ethical dilemma, as when someone asks you for a financial contribution for a good cause or asks you to sign a petition. What can turn this into an ethical dilemma is when the request taps into deeper feelings, so one feels external or internal pressures to provide support coupled with a desire not to do so.

Francine the public relations freelancer, experienced this conflict when some gay friends asked her to show support for the group by contributing an essay to a gay publication. On the one hand, she supported their cause and felt warmly towards the man who asked for her contribution. But on the other hand, she felt uncomfortable, since she didn't want to be so closely associated with the gay movement. Yet she didn't want to seem intolerant in rejecting the offer either. Thus, she agonized for several days over what to do, weighing her altruistic and self-protective impulses. As Francine explained her inner turmoil:

> I have gay friends, and my attitude is live and let live. But what created a real dilemma for me is a gay friend asked me to contribute to a gay publication. On one level, I want to participate, because I was asked by a good friend who is gay, and I feel that gays should have the same rights as everyone else. But I resist the idea, too, because I don't want to be associated with being a gay advocate. Also, I feel some conflict because I'm not sure if gays can't choose because they are gay from birth, or could choose a regular straight life if they wanted. But then I think, "Who am I to judge what should be a matter of free choice?"
>
> So there's a lot of conflict, because while I support what the group is doing, I don't want to be seen publicly as aligned with the group as a gay supporter or as gay myself. I worry about what other people are going to say.

However, if she didn't contribute, she experienced a further conflict over what to tell her friend, since she didn't feel comfortable directly telling him of her concerns.

> I really feel uncomfortable expressing my reservations to my friend. He's not really a close friend, but he's very influential in my field. I don't like playing political games, but I feel some pressure to contribute, because refusing him would not be a good strategic move in my field. And telling him why I don't want to participate would not be a good move either, because it would seem like I'm anti-gay, when I'm not. Unfortunately, contributing under another name isn't a choice either, because part of their reason for asking me is to include my name to show support for their publication.

And so Francine tossed the issue back and forth, not certain what was the right or strategic thing to do, since she felt caught between two communities with different ethical views of what was right. One was a more conservative straight community that would frown on her support of the gay community; the other a gay community that might feel affronted by her turndown. In the end, she decided to contribute, but it was an uneasy choice. While she felt contributing was the right thing to do, since it expressed her sympathies for free choice and tolerance for others, and reflected her usual other-oriented and moral approach, she still worried about the potential negative fallout from her decision.

SUMMING UP

In sum, some ordinary choices and disputes in the public/community arena can become ethical dilemmas when they trigger more deeply felt concerns or involve considerations about whether one's actions are ethical or not. We often don't think of everyday matters, like sneaking into line or giving a made-up excuse to a policeman to get out of a ticket, as ethical choices or dilemmas, since they are so casual and fleeting, sometimes involving a choice of action made in seconds. But they are ethical choices, because they involve choosing between competing ethical values (i.e., considering others versus

benefitting the self, doing the right thing versus choosing an immediate pragmatic benefit, and following the customary rules versus
breaking them for one's advantage). As in other situations, the ulti-
mate decision depends on the circumstances in that situation and
one's ethical framework and priorities.

CHAPTER 24

•

ETHICAL DILEMMAS AND SOCIETY

The most distant zone from the self is society as a whole. While the ethical issues in this zone include views about the big social questions, like abortion, cloning, and capital punishment, many people don't feel a personal connection with ethical issues at this level until they face one of these situations themselves or they become politically active around these issues.

Thus, leaving aside the big social issues that could be the topic of a book themselves, the focus here is on the more everyday social issues the interviewees faced. These major areas of ethical conflict for the interviewees included: conflicts between the principles of "political correctness" and saying what one really thinks; weighing the interests of a disadvantaged group versus the interests of the majority; and choosing between the moral teachings of religion versus personal choice. Following are some examples of the varied ways they dealt with these issues.

DEALING WITH MINORITIES AND THE DISADVANTAGED

As a society, we have established various laws and guidelines for what's acceptable in dealing with disadvantaged and minority groups to protect them. But sometimes these approaches are described mockingly as "political correctness" by others who feel these guidelines are too protective or restrictive and resent them. These two views represent a clash of ethical perspectives, between those emphasizing protection from an altruistic perspective and those with a more self-oriented pragmatic perspective, based on notions of free markets and free speech. In turn, these conflicting visions of what's right can create an ethical dilemma for those caught in the middle in deciding what to say or do.

Sam the writer and part-time comedian experienced this dilemma in his nightclub comedy acts, as did other comedians who commented on the members of minority or disadvantaged groups. What could they say or not say about them? Eventually, Sam resolved this problem by avoiding the topic, and he felt others who made jokes about members of disadvantaged groups were "unethical" because they weren't sensitive to them. As Sam observed:

> I don't do that kind of material, because I don't like making fun of certain groups of people. Many other comedians consciously avoid doing this, too. But many others do this kind of humor. I think they should feel an ethical conflict in doing what I consider offensive humor, though they don't. And many seem unaware that it's an ethical question. I've seen some comedians say they are doing what they are doing all in fun, and that makes it all right for them. But I don't agree, because they are subjecting many people to ridicule, and I think that's wrong.

SUPPORTING THE INTERESTS OF THE "PEOPLE" VERSUS THE CORPORATIONS AND THE ESTABLISHMENT

While some view many social and class issues as largely economic matters, others with a liberal political perspective see these issues in ethical terms. From their perspective, helping disadvantaged or low income people is the ethical thing to do, since it reflects an altruistic, moral choice to support the largest number of people. By contrast, they view individuals or corporations guided by the profit motive as unethical, since they are making self-interested, pragmatic choices. In other words, they see the liberal-conservative approach to social issues in ethical terms.

Andy, the sales manager, who prided himself on his integrity in a profit-oriented field, expressed this point of view when he observed:

Right now many companies are going through mergers and changes, and the acquiring companies at first claim they are going to keep everybody. But that's a lie and soon they let many people go. They say one thing for public consumption in memos and public announcements, and then they go ahead and fire people. They want to keep their workers working and happy to the end, and the managers are not supposed to tell their employees they are being laid off for this reason.

I think that's unethical, and if I were a manager in a situation like that, I would tell my employees. I would want them to know right away. I think ethics and straight-dealing with people is important.

Similarly, Lori, the teacher, with a strongly liberal perspective, viewed the current environmental situation in polar ethical terms. She regarded her concern for the "people" and the people's concern for the environment on the altruistic-moral side of the equation, while she put wealthy members of the establishment on the other side, since they focused on self-interest and bottom line gains. As she commented:

For me, the years since Reagan have been unethical, because the rich have gotten richer and the poor have gotten poorer, and with all the deregulation, we're in a lot more danger from toxins in the environment. If I became one of the rich, I would be largest philanthropist I could possibly be...But I see few rich people doing this. I can't understand why the rich people don't want to contribute to feel good about themselves. The way I see it, the class in power has taken advantage of being in power. They have not thought about the needs of the poor, of the people generally. Mostly it's been corporate greed, and I think that's wrong.

SUPPORTING TRADITIONAL MORALITY VERSUS PERSONAL CHOICE

Conversely, those with a more conservative bent claim an ethical ground, too, when they apply the other-oriented and moral dimensions to individual choice and responsibility issues. In doing so, they see those who take the opposite view as unethical.

Thus, both use key factors on the Ethical Choices Map to define their point of view as ethical, while considering those opposing them as unethical in their position. What's different is the terrain on which they wage the battle. While liberals have used economics and environmental issues to define what's ethical, conservatives have focused on religious and crime issues.

Trudy the social worker who became a born again Christian described her political fight to right key social wrongs thus:

> What's gotten me into politics is my concern for integrity in government and society, because I see so much dishonesty everywhere. There's so much hype, concealed agendas. Politicians are just trying to do what's best for themselves; not what's best for the American people; so they're not being straight with everyone.
>
> For example, if you look at the proposal for gun control, it's misleading to say you're going to stop crime by banning assault weapons, since they account for only 1% of the crime. So what's the real agenda? Politicians try to package their proposals to sell them, because they know if they're honest, the proposal won't be accepted. They try selling the public with simple slogans, like 'It's gonna stop crime,' so if people hear something enough they start to be believe it, though it's not true.
>
> What I'm trying to do is talk about those issues and what we should really do to ban crime and how gun control really goes against our second amendment. For me, that's what's ethical—being honest about the way things really are.

Similarly, Trudy faulted the media and society for the popularity of "the ends justify the means" thinking, reflected in the celebrity of immoral individuals who were reaping financial rewards for their amorality. It was another sign of the growing lack of integrity in society as a whole and a need to revive traditional moral thinking. As Trudy commented:

> I think we're in so much trouble as a society today, because people are being caught up in the kind of thinking that says the end justifies the means, and they are setting the traditional ideals of what's right and wrong aside. For example, many of our

current heroes or media stars are people who hurt or kill people. And they end up going to the bank and working for the next book contract.

The media is a big part of the problem, because the people in the media believe the ends justifies the means. So that contributes to these values pervading society. People have lost touch with traditional ideas about trust and decency. They think just of themselves and what's the most expedient way to do something. But, that way of looking at things is destroying the community as a whole.

Thus, ironically, those from very different political perspectives may see themselves taking the moral high ground in their diagnosis of what's wrong with society and what should be done. They both feel this way, since they are both adopting an other-oriented moralistic perspective rather than a self-centered pragmatic one. But what's different is their focus on what they consider a problem and how to resolve it. Whereas liberals identify big business and the profit motive as undermining society, conservatives believe the key destructive factors are the self-interest and lack of responsibility of people in major institutions. They also point to the greed of individuals engaging in crime and harming others to benefit themselves.

Then, when it comes to the role of government in resolving what they perceive as the major moral flaws in society, liberals and conservatives assess its role differently. For liberals, the government can be a moral protector, that helps tame corporate and individual greed through laws, regulations, and social programs. By contrast, conservatives see the solution in less government and more personal responsibility and more local community involvement. As Trudy put it:

> We have to get more active, because so much of this crime and other problems occurs because we have had a decline in morality, not because we have too many guns. People can kill each other without guns, and that's happening increasingly, too. Meanwhile, the government has been able to use all these problems as an excuse to take our freedom away, with the government controlling more and more of everything, although there

is so much dishonesty in government, too.

I don't think we should be giving the government all that power. It's creating oppression. For example, in the guise of helping us and providing better schooling, the government is trying to keep parents from teaching their own kids the way they want.

So I think it's time for people to get more involved and stand up for a more moral ethical society because that's what they want. We shouldn't let the government try to create this for us, because that leads to oppression and totalitarian control.

The paradox is that both conservatives like Trudy and Tom and liberals like Andy, Jeff, and Lori believe they are taking the ethical or moral view in the way they analyze what's wrong with society and what should be done. In fact, in claiming they are being ethical, they are both embracing those categories on the Map associated with traditional moral teachings as a basis for political action—concern for others and placing moral concerns over pragmatic ones. But then they are using these principles to address different problems and come up with different solutions.

In turn, this contrasting view of what's moral or ethical contributes to making it difficult for people from different perspectives to get along. That's because in seeing their own point of view as ethical, they consider others with a different view as not being ethical.

Thus, a step towards better understanding is recognizing where people from different perspectives fall on the Ethical Choices Map, rather than judging those who are different as unethical, since people with different perspectives have differing views of what's ethical.

In fact, in many ways, our ethical perspectives are affected by our social and class positions—in that those with a more secure economic and social position can often be more other-oriented and moral in perspective. That's because their security gives them a greater ability to think of others, whether they have a more liberal or conservative view in how to do this. By contrast, many who lack this security may need to be more self-oriented and pragmatic to survive. As Don the radio talk show host put it:

Certain groups have ethical standards and values driven by religion, upbringing, or education. But in order to support those standards and values, you need to be at a certain level of society. Otherwise, if survival is at stake, you have to put first things first. You have to think about yourself and do what you have to survive; so you worry about moral and ethical issues later.

We all—or at least most of us—like to think of ourselves as moral, ethical people—like moral actors on the stage. But to get on that stage and perform, you need to have some basic props. You need to be in the theater. You need to have a costume to perform. Then, with those basics, you can be ethical. You can be concerned about others; about your community; about what the traditional religious systems teach about the right way to behave.

But if you're out there struggling, you're not in the theater; you're not in the play. So all of this talk about higher ethics and morality don't make much sense at this lower level. You just want to live, and you'll do what you'll need to do that. And in that case, the ideal of being ethical can wait.

CHAPTER 25

•

DEALING WITH OTHERS WHO
ARE "UNETHICAL"

Given our different ethical perspectives, it may seem difficult to determine when someone else is being "unethical," since he or she may think that behavior is ethical from his or her own perspective. Still, we all have ideas about what we consider "unethical", when someone has crossed the line beyond what we consider acceptable.

In terms of the Ethical Choices Map, this is when someone has not acted in keeping with the traditional core ethical principles when we think they should. They have, for whatever reasons, broken the rules we expect them to follow, acted too much out of self-interest, or acted too crassly for pragmatic reason, or a combination of factors. Certainly, as discussed, people do act acceptably in any of these ways—changing rules, pursuing self-interest, or acting pragmatically. But such actions appear "unethical" at times when taken to extremes, such as violating certain strongly held rules or taboos or behaving very selfishly. Or at other times, a person's actions may be considered unethical, when other behavior is expected that is more in keeping with the traditional "ethical" response—such as going along with the group's customary practices or showing altruism to someone having serious difficulties.

For example, a person who tells a lie about his personal background to get ahead in a career may be applauded for his creativity and determination if he subsequently succeeds, because his lie ultimately benefits his employer as well as himself. But if he eventually fails and the lie is exposed, he will be criticized or worse, if the results of the lie are sufficiently harmful. As another example, a man who lies about his personal history, such as falsely saying he is unmarried, to get a woman to see him, may be considered a cad if found out. That's because in acting pragmatically for his own benefit, he has hurt not only this woman but the wife he cheated.

In turn, we have differing ways of reacting to a person we think has behaved unethically, depending on how seriously he has breached our expectations, the importance of the situation, how "ethically" we think that person has acted in the past, and our own "ethical" compass in judging others: how tolerant or judgmental we are. Then, too, we may be influenced by our own "ethical" behavior in that situation and our relationship to this person's perceived "unethical" act. Such influences include whether this is a work-related or personal matter, whether we are a participant or observer, our power relationship to that person (i.e., as a boss, underling, or coworker), and whether we have lost, gained, or been unaffected by that person's act.

Additionally, we might be influenced by our Ethical Choices Map relative to that of the other person's. For example, if we tend to be more other-oriented and moral in our approach than that person, we may be more likely to react negatively if he or she has acted for personal gain, than if we often act that way, too.

In short, each of us have our own Ethical Choices Map for responding to a situation. At times, our separate Maps are in harmony, at other times they collide. When they do, people may think someone else is behaving unethically and react accordingly, while the other person feels he or she has behaved ethically from his or her own point of view.

This range of reactions to perceived unethical behavior includes the following: quietly looking the other way, trying to avoid the person, adopting a self-protective cover around that person, and angrily confronting him or her. These responses reflect the five gen-

---

[1]Gini Graham Scott, *Resolving Conflict*, Oakland, California: New Harbinger, 1990.

eral reactions to responding to a conflict of any sort, as I described in a previous book: *Resolving Conflict*[1]:

- taking a competitive or forceful approach (confronting),
- walking away from the problem (avoiding),
- giving in to the other person (accommodating),
- working out a give and take arrangement (compromising),
- trying to seriously discuss and deal with the problem (collaborating).

These ethical dilemmas in responding to others' unethical behavior have been touched on briefly in other chapters. Here I want to focus on them. What happens when people observe or discover someone doing something unethical? How do they react? The following examples show the range of responses—from showing tolerance for a different point of view to expressing mild disapproval, to confronting, to finally severing all ties with a person, because his lack of "ethics" are considered too serious to continue the relationship.

THE DON'T DO IT RESPONSE: TRYING TO TALKING SOMEONE OUT OF DOING IT

One way people deal with actions they consider unethical is to persuade the other person not to do something, such as when a friend or associate tries to convince someone not to do something wrong or stupid.

This is what Andy, the sales manager, did when some friends tried to get him to participate in a pyramid money-making scheme. As he described the situation:

> I know a lot of people who sometimes get involved in these multilevel marketing programs that are not really selling a product. It's just an excuse to make money. These are zero sum games which they call different things, like the Circle of Gold, the Airplane, and the Friends Network. For every dollar somebody wins, there's a dollar somebody loses. There are no goods or services produced. The whole program is based on greed, and

the people at the beginning always win and the people at the end always lose.

As a result, when anybody approaches me with one of these programs, I usually explain all this and try to talk them out of it. In fact, in some cases, I talked people out of it who were big dealers in these games. In one case, this woman was the pilot of a ship and she was trying to persuade me to join. But I was able to explain why this was wrong clearly enough that she took herself out of a game, because she could see she would be setting herself up for a lot of negative karmic consequences.

In Andy's view, these "karmic" consequences were what made such games ethically wrong. As he commented:

These games always have negative consequences, because they are inherently unethical. In the first phase, someone's excited to get into the game because they think they are going to make money. Next, they experience fear and worry: "I don't know if I can get my money back?" Then they face the moral dilemma of what to do now. They have to bring somebody else into the game to get their money back. But if they bring someone in, that means they are knowingly going to screw their buddies, because whoever holds the hot potato as the game collapses gets burned.

That's what I try to point out to people when they approach me about joining these games. Another thing I tell them is "Do you want to live with the consequences of someone losing hundreds or thousands of dollars or with the way you got them into it?" And generally, I've been able to make people understand the consequences of their unethical acts, so they don't join in the first place or they stop playing and drop out.

THE PLAYING ALONG RESPONSE—AND REJECTING UNETHICAL PEOPLE LATER

An approach some people use at times is playing along with the people they feel are behaving unethically, because they want to avoid creating a scene or confrontation now. But later, when they can, they seek to distance themselves from or turn against whoever behaved "unethically."

That's what Trudy the social worker did when a group of people tried to gain her support for their program in what she considered an underhanded, deceptive, and hence unethical way. She found their misleading approach especially disturbing, since the program itself countered her deeply held conservative beliefs, so she felt their approach doubly unethical—both in form and in content. As she explained:

> I went to what I thought was a breast cancer society fundraiser to raise money for a community counseling program for women with breast cancer. I thought that was a good, positive program. But when I got to the meeting, the organization turned out to be a front for a group of gay women, who were using the support of minority groups to help them get a federal grant for their center.
>
> When they ran a video tape, the movie showed that their real agenda was to promote the ability of homosexuals to adopt children, a view that counters my own Christian beliefs. When I looked around the room after that, I realized that my husband and I were among the few heterosexual couples in the room. Another woman sitting at the table with us said she was also upset.
>
> In fact, when I was went into the ladies room shortly after the video, I heard two organizers of the event talking about the group's real agenda, when one commented: "I hope we can do this event next year without the breast cancer." So this statement helped to confirm my realization that this group had pulled us together to promote a very different agenda than we thought and use our support to help them do this.

Yet, while Trudy was deeply disturbed about what she considered unethical double-dealing, she, like the other people who felt similarly deceived, stayed at the meeting. Why? Because Trudy felt it made better strategic sense to be diplomatic about her feelings of upset and anger, rather than storming out or getting into an argument with someone at the event about her true feelings. Then, she could pull away more comfortably later. As Trudy noted:

> It's true I get very mad when I see people trying to use minorities to forward their own agendas. And it's very upsetting to be

drawn into one of these shows.

But I also believe in picking my battles. I think timing is everything. At the right time I will say something; I will stand up for what I believe. And that's why I decided to stay at this meeting and not storm out or say anything. It was almost the end of the meeting by the time I realized what was going on, and I felt it wouldn't have served any purpose to create a scene. So I just played along, like the other minority group members at my table did. Then later, I felt, we could do something that would be effective to counter this kind of duplicity.

THE GRADUAL PARTING OF THE WAYS RESPONSE

Another way people respond to perceive unethical behavior is to let a relationship fade away. They become unavailable or busy when asked to participate in future activities; or they give assorted reasons why they can't get together later. Rather than questioning the other person's different ethical view and risking a confrontation, they prefer to let the relationship quietly die.

That's what Jerry the lawyer did when he was disturbed by a long-time friend's "lack of ethics" with women. He let the friendship end without letting his friend know he decided to do this. He explained:

> Though we were friends for a couple of years, I began to see the way he treats women in a new light. It disturbed me to see his lack of openness with them and his lies to them. I think he's wrong in what he's doing. I see it has created poor relationships for him which end badly. And I feel he's unwilling to face his own dysfunctional behavior.
>
> However, I haven't wanted to confront him about this. I don't want to sound preachy; and I don't know how to educate him by sharing my own experience and realizations, because someone else's experience usually doesn't mean very much. So pretty much our friendship has terminated. I haven't called him to suggest doing anything, or I've been busy when he's called.

Lori the teacher similarly pulled away from a long-term friend who she felt had adopted an unacceptable way of living. She felt some recriminations about dropping a long-term relationship. But wanting to end it, she felt it was easier to quietly let go. As Lori explained:

> I have a long-term female friend who's a computer expert bio-chemist. But a few months ago she moved in with a man I feel is way beneath her and has been living a lifestyle I think is wrong. He puts up scaffolding for a living, drinks heavily and drives when he drinks, and is divorced and pays child support.
>
> I didn't say anything to my friend, because I learned long ago that she doesn't take anyone's advice. She just blindly goes along with him, and because of this, I don't want to spend time with her anymore. I haven't seen her for a long time. When she calls me, I'll talk to her on the telephone. But I don't call her back, as I do with other people.
>
> I suppose there's a bit of an ethical question, because whenever I disconnect from a female friendship, I feel I should write that person a letter explaining why I'm no longer friends with them in a way that won't hurt them. Because we have spent a great deal of time together, I feel I owe them that. But I didn't in this case. I decided not to say anything, because it was easier to forget about these people and move on.

THE OUTRAGED CUT IT OFF IMMEDIATELY RESPONSE

While drifting away is a popular low-risk response, sometimes a person's actions seem so unethical that one reacts with outrage. Then, one is more likely to cut off the relationship immediately, sometimes without an explanation—though sometimes one might first try to explain or angrily confront the other person. Often people like the sudden break, since it's cleaner, with less risk of arguments, emotional turmoil, or reprisals.

That's what June the tax accountant did after she went to a cabaret with friends and was appalled by what a long-time friend did. As June described what happened:

> An old out-of-town friend George and his girlfriend Julie were here from New Orleans, and at George's invitation, my partner and I joined them. The four of us went to a cabaret lounge. George was supposed to be the host, and we had a great time and ran up a $120 bill. When it came time to pay it, the waiter asked George, "Are you registered in the hotel?" and he said,

"Yes, I am," though he really wasn't. Then, George signed a phony name and a hotel number, and we walked out.

I, my lover and Julie didn't say anything at the time, because were so surprised and shocked by what had happened. But we were appalled. Soon after, when Julie and I went into the ladies room in the hotel lobby, we talked about how horrified we were. When we came out, she confronted George and told him he was a real jerk for doing what he did. But he just laughed it off, saying we were ridiculous to get upset.

We went home after this, but the incident soured our relationship. My lover and I saw George in a new light and saw how bad he was. Before we had thought of him as a creative, innovative, successful entrepreneur who made a lot of money selling swampland in Florida. But now we saw what he did as a scam. So we wanted to break off the relationship as soon as possible.

The next day, I called the hotel, because I felt bad about what happened. I explained I was with the party who had walked out and I was horrified at what he did, and was calling because I was concerned the hotel would take the money out of the waiter's paycheck. But the manager assured me the hotel wouldn't do this. So I felt better about that.

Then, my lover and I cut off any further contact with George, even though he had been a friend for a couple of years. We said good-bye after he and my lover returned from an errand in town, and that was it. We knew we never wanted to speak to him again, and fortunately, he didn't call, maybe because he realized how we felt, since we were very cool and reserved when we said good-bye.

THE AVOIDING THE PERSON RESPONSE

While one can readily ease out of or cut off a relationship with the person considered unethical in social situations, in work situations that may not be possible—unless one quits or one is the boss and can fire that person. In response, one strategy some adopt is avoiding such a person as much as possible.

That's what Ari, the public health nurse, did when she discovered that a fellow employee was engaging in underhanded activities. As she explained:

I tried to stay away from Bob, because he was a real tattletale. He would often go back to the supervisors and tell on people. I thought he was a disgraceful and immoral person on that basis, so I despised him.

Then, one day, I saw him watching me. He was walking close behind me in the hall, looking over my shoulder, which he had done before from time to time. Usually, he went to the patients' records, and looked for different types of mistakes, like a nurse charting the wrong medication for a patient. I thought he was being nosy doing this, but it wasn't prohibited and it didn't affect me directly, so I tried to ignore him doing this.

But this time, all this anger built up and I couldn't stand seeing him right behind me anymore. I turned around, stopped, and yelled at him: 'F*** off, Bob!" Then I got suddenly frightened, thinking: 'Oh, God. Now I'll really be in trouble with the authorities for cursing or yelling in the hallway or telling this guy off.'

But as it turned out, nothing happened. Bob didn't not say anything to the powers that be, and I did not get in any trouble. In fact, he stopped bugging me, and I pretty much was able to stay out of his way after that.

THE DISASSOCIATE ONESELF FROM THAT PERSON'S RESPONSE

Another reaction, if one can't avoid being around a person, is to disassociate oneself from being connected with that person in the minds of others.

That's what Don the talk show host did, when he was on a station that added the conservative commentator Rush Limbaugh to its lineup, since he was a firm believer in liberal and humanitarian causes. As Don described it:

> When my station added Rush Limbaugh to the lineup, the idea of being associated with him bothered me. I was very uncomfortable being the guy on the other side of the political fence responding to Limbaugh, since I don't like his program.
>
> So I wanted to make it clear I didn't feel as he did, and I was perhaps a little reckless in being so open about where I stood. For example, one time when I invited Limbaugh on my program, I let him know I thought he was a sexist, racist one-sided

demagogue.

It was hard to tell him these things, since he's this big national star, and he's not used to be interviewed and responding, instead of leading, so I had to keep interrupting to get him to respond. He also joked about it when I said some of the things he did were racist. But I felt I had to confront him and make it clear that I didn't support his right wing views. I wanted to make my own position clear and tried to do so by facing him directly on my show.

THE DAMAGE CONTROL RESPONSE

Besides avoiding or disassociating oneself from a person one considers unethical, another approach, sometimes combined with the foregoing, is using damage control to patch up anything that person has already done. If that person has spread rumors, one might try to stop them. Or if he or she is seeking or spreading information, one might try to seal the leak.

Kelly, the speaker and public relations consultant, used this stop the damage approach when she discovered that a man in her field was trying to obtain information she had developed for free and use it to develop his own material. As she explained:

> When I met Brad, everything at first seemed fine. He said he wanted to hire me to be a speaker and wanted me to help him develop some audiotapes in my area of expertise, in which I was writing a book. I thought him very reputable, because he has advanced degrees and is the head of a large organization.
>
> But then he couldn't get funding and had to cancel the speaking gig, as well as another contract he had with me, though he said he'd try to do it in a couple of months.
>
> In the meantime, he told me: 'I'd really like to see your manuscript of your book.' Though, I told him he couldn't, because it was now owned by a major publishing company and I didn't tell him my editor's name, he found out and wrote to my editor anyway, saying he had been talking to me and wanted to see the chapter. In addition, after telling my editor he wouldn't use anything without permission, he asked her not to charge him for what he did use, since he worked for a non-profit association.

When I heard that, I got really upset, because I felt he was finding a way to get the information I wrote for free. Then he could change it, so he could use it without giving me any credit or paying me anything. I was afraid he might do that because of the way he canceled several contracts with me and contacted my editor behind my back.

So I wrote to my editor and told her: "Please don't send out any pre-publication material without my permission, and don't talk to anybody about it without discussing with me first." That seemed to work, because a few days ago, Brad called me, saying, "I really want to work with you because I like your ideas."

So now I have to deal with him myself, and I plan to tell him if he wants to work with me, he has to pay me, and then I'll consult with him. But otherwise, I won't show him anything or talk to him about anything, because I don't trust him. I can't call him a liar or unethical, because he is quite powerful and well-known in his field. Still, I have to do what I can to protect myself from his using my material without my getting any compensation.

THE COMPLAIN TO SOMEONE ELSE RESPONSE

Another reaction to an action regarded as unethical is to complain to someone else, particularly in a work or consumer situation, where the person acting unethically has a supervisor or manager who might take action. Sometimes a person who feels wronged does complain to get the other party to change their objectionable behavior. But other times, one does so after the relationship is over to feel better about what happened. Then complaining can be a way to release bad feelings or let others know, so they might take some action against the unethical person themselves.

For example, Andy the sales manager complained after a salesman disappointed him to feel better about the incident. As he described it:

> This guy Walter was supposed to come over a do a home demonstration of a water system. I was very rushed, and to convince me to participate, he said he would give me a certificate for a couple of nights of free lodging at Lake Tahoe.

But when the time for the demonstration came, another man from the company called to say "Walter's running late, but he'll be there," so I waited and waited, until finally I had to leave. Well, Walter never showed, and nobody else called after that.

So I was really annoyed, and I called the company the following week, and told the salesman who answered: "I've been waiting for some sort of communication and I've got none, and I want to complain, because I set aside my time for the demonstration. But the salesman didn't show. So I want you to send me that coupon for those two Lake Tahoe nights anyway."

Though the salesman argued that I shouldn't get the coupons since I didn't see the demonstration, I argued back: "I made my time available and I was there." I was even ready to call the Better Business Bureau. When the salesman refused, I asked to speak to the manager, and when I explained the situation, he finally agreed and sent my certificate. I felt it was a matter of principle, based on having integrity in a communication. I made an agreement, and I was there. Then the guy didn't show.

As it turned out, I didn't go to Lake Tahoe. But for me, just complaining and getting those certificates felt good. It was the principle. It was what was necessary to make the transaction right.

THE UNSUCCESSFUL CONFRONTATION AND MAKE THE BREAK RESPONSE

Another response some people make is confronting the offender with a "shape up and we'll continue the relationship" response. But if that approach doesn't work, they make the break.

That's what happened with Iris, the therapist, when she felt someone she was both friends with and worked with wasn't being honest. As she described it:

A few years ago, I was working with this facilitator Larry, and we were friends, too. Then, one time he lied about something I said to another good friend Dave, who got angry at me based on this lie. Afterwards, when Dave and I discussed what happened, we realized Larry was being a troublemaker, and we recalled a few past situations where Larry had gotten Dave or other people to do things he wanted by making himself look good at the expense of others.

After that I confronted Larry, but he denied he had said what Dave said he did. So he would never own up to what he did and shrugged off what happened. He even seemed annoyed that I would confront him about the matter.

As a result, I decided "I'm not going to have anything to do with this man again," and I no longer facilitated anymore programs with him. I felt he was completely unethical after what happened, and realized he would do anything it took to get what he wanted, including lying and making others look bad.

It was hard to make the break, because Larry and I had been doing things socially, and he was also a client who brought in money for me when he got jobs and brought me in to work with him on them. But this was the second time I had confronted him unsuccessfully. He denied he did anything wrong each time. I didn't feel there was much to gain by trying to confront him again. So I broke off any further relationship at this point.

THE LEARN TO LIVE WITH IT BUT DON'T LIKE IT RESPONSE

While people may feel freer to respond as they wish to perceived unethical behavior in social or public situations, such as with a confrontation or by cutting off the relationship, at work people may not feel as free to respond. This is particularly so if they are an employee or in a low power position relative to the person they consider unethical. Then, due to work considerations, say to keep a job or get a promotion, they may quietly play office politics, learning to live with a situation they don't like, although some leave in the end.

That's what happened when Dick, the architect, worked on a project where he was assigned to help a widow keep an office going after her husband died. As Dick explained:

> I worked for a number of years in the office of a man who died of cancer, and I had been gone for about a year when he died. Then, the widow asked me to come back to hold things together, while she tried to sell the office to someone.
>
> After I returned, I realized that a man who worked there was

very unproductive. He was also dishonest in reporting the time he spent on projects, thereby inflating what he should be paid. So I saw my role as trying to keep him from stealing the bank and protecting the widow's interests. Meanwhile, he seemed to think he could take over the office, without having to buy it, and keep it going as his. So he went around trying to convince the clients to be loyal to him, and he tried to poison them against me, since he saw me as a threat to his plans.

It was a difficult position, because I had just come into this situation and he had been around for a long time. So it was hard to convince the widow that he was damaging the business and setting himself up to leave with the clients if he was pushed out.

Though I tried to tell her what was going on, she didn't understand how the office functioned or who really accomplished things. So she wasn't clear on who to trust or follow. As a result, this guy was able to convince her that he was doing a good job.

Thus, eventually, when I saw there wasn't much I could do, I did the best I could, tying things up and trying to find a buyer for her. So I resigned myself to live with this uncomfortable, stressful situation for about six months until I managed to find her a buyer and she sold the office.

THE ATTACK RESPONSE

One last major response is to retaliate or attack in advance of an anticipated unethical act. It's a "this is war" reaction which is fairly extreme and rare, though if a conflict escalates, it could become more likely.

For example, Henry, the supervisor, who tended to be high strung, sometimes responded in this way. As he explained:

My philosophy of responding is I don't want to hurt anybody. My ethics are if you leave me alone, I'll leave you alone. But if anybody tries to seriously hurt me or anyone involved in my life, I have no hesitation to retaliating in kind.

As I learned when I was in the military in Vietnam years ago, you have to get up to the level of the person who acting to hurt you and react to them on their level or on a higher level. It's not that anybody wants to do this. But you have to be prepared, or people can take advantage of and hurt you.

Henry gave some examples of how he applied this philosophy at work and in personal relationships.

> I had one situation at work where people didn't treat me fairly. Some people falsely accused me of harassment. They put things in reports that were wrong. They lied about me. They deliberately withheld giving me credit for things I had done by taking my ideas and putting them forth as their own.
>
> After that happened a couple of times, I showed the people who did this to me that they couldn't get away with it by responding in kind. For example, I heard one guy at work was spreading tales about me; so I started spreading even juicier ones about him, such as suggesting he had harassed a few of the women, and he really got called on the carpet about that. In another case, when a salesman told some stories about me that made me look bad, I made sure he didn't get some important messages.

Thus, in effect, Henry became a bureaucratic street-fighter, applying the lessons of the jungle and war to internal bureaucratic politics. Although few people might see everyday office political infighting in such stark terms, Henry felt it necessary to use such tactics to survive in a highly combative workplace environment. For him, life was like a "scratch and fight world" in which he believed that "all is fair in love and war." As he put it:

> The minute anyone makes a move against me, everything, including their reputations, their jobs, their lives, is open to my attack.

He carried the same approach over into the singles dating game, as well. Thus, when one man tried to attract a woman he was dating away from him, Henry spread stories about his rival, until he backed off.

In short, Henry used a fight fire with fire or reverse Golden Rule approach in responding to perceived unethical behavior. His way was to fight back aggressively or do unto others as they did unto him to hurt them more. Or as he described it:

If someone breaches what I think is right and ethical and does something to hurt me badly, I feel it fair to fight back on their level. And I have found this approach worked. When people have tried to hurt me or take something from me, whether it involves work or a personal relationship, they have soon backed off.

I feel I'm a good human being, but I've learned to be tough. So if people do bad hurtful things to me, I'll fight back. And they'll wish they didn't do it. But if people are ethical to me, I'll be quite ethical to them. So what I do depends on the situation, on who people are, and where they are coming from.

THE RANGE OF RESPONSES

As these accounts illustrate, when people feel they have been treated unethically by someone, their response may range from ignoring the situation to trying to discuss the matter to attacking back in kind. Their particular response depends on numerous factors, including the situation, the importance of the matter, how strongly they feel about what happened, the relative power of the person who they feel acted unethically, and their overall ethical approach.

To sum up, these responses include the following:

1. Don't do it response: trying to talk someone out of it (Andy)
2. Playing along response: and rejecting unethical people later (Trudy)
3. Gradual parting of the ways response (Jerry and Lori)
4. Outraged cut it off immediately response (June)
5. Avoiding the person response (Ari)
6. Disassociate oneself from that person response (Don)
7. Damage control response (Kelly)
8. Complain to someone response (Andy)
9. Unsuccessful confrontation and make the break response (Iris)
10. Learn to live with it but don't like it response (Dick)
11. Attack back response (Henry)

These varied responses to perceived unethical actions are much like the range of responses used to resolve conflicts. Accordingly, these two types of responses can be compared using a conflict resolution grid, which is based on the degree to which one attempts to satisfy one's own concerns (how assertive or unassertive one is) or the other person's concerns (how cooperative or uncooperative one is). It's a grid originally developed by Kenneth W. Thomas and Ralph H. Kilmann in 1972.

These efforts to satisfy one's concerns or another's concerns are equivalent to the self-other dimension on the Ethical Choices Map. When the two models are combined together, they create the matrix on the following page, which shows how the different responses to unethical behavior can be viewed like different styles of handling conflict.

RELATIONSHIP BETWEEN ONE'S ETHICAL APPROACH AND ONE'S RESPONSE TO OTHERS' UNETHICAL BEHAVIOR

The responses of the interviewees suggest a relationship between one's ethical approach and one's response to the other person's perceived unethical behavior. This is suggested if one looks at the interviewees' profiles on the Ethical Choices Map and at their response to this behavior on the Conflict handling Styles Matrix. As illustrated, on the next page, this matrix provides for five styles of response conflict—the Competing, Collaborating, Avoiding, Accommodating, and Compromising styles.

The following examples show how the grid can be used. For instance, the one person who adopted the Competing Style of attacking back was Henry the supervisor, who was strongly self-oriented and pragmatic, as well as something of a loner. By contrast, those who adopted the more Collaborating "Let's talk about it" style were Andy the sales manager, and Iris the therapist, who were both highly concerned about communicating with others and balanced in the self-other dimension. Those adopting the Avoiding Style—Ari the nurse, June the tax accountant, and Don the broadcaster—were other-oriented and had a strong moral orientation; while Trudy the social worker/politician, who was Accommodating and then

Avoiding, had these characteristics, too. Dick the architect, who used the Accommodating Style of "live with it but don't like it" tended to be balanced in the self-other and moral-pragmatic dimensions. Finally, those adopting the Compromising Style, Jerry the lawyer, Kelly the speaker, and Andy the sales manager, in another situation, reflected a mix of approaches.

THE RESPONSE TO UNETHICAL BEHAVIOR AND THE CONFLICT HANDLING STYLES MATRIX

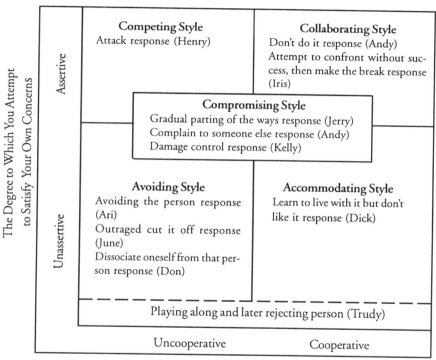

As this small sampling suggests, people may respond in a certain way based on their overall ethical perspective, when they encounter someone they consider unethical. At the same time, the circumstances may have an influence, in that one may be more likely to seek ways to compromise, collaborate, and accommodate in work, professional, and political situations, where one has to continue working or associating with someone. By contrast, in personal situations one may be better able to cut off contact or fight back aggressively, in that one may feel freer to respond based on personal feelings. As Jerry, the lawyer, who made this distinction in his own life, observed:

> How I react when I'm trying to be ethical and the person I'm relating to isn't ethical depends on the relationship. If it's a question of compromising my own ethics, I'd probably walk away from a personal relationship, unless it's a long-term relationship such as with a family member. Then. I'll take more time to try to find a way where I don't have to compromise my ethics and still remain in that relationship.
>
> But if it's a work situation, I often compromise more. For example, in the entertainment business where I practice law, a lot of people are not ethical. It's very common, say, for people to talk big and have nothing to back it up. Also, many people engage in a great deal of behind the scenes backstabbing. Though I may prefer not to have relationships with such people, sometimes I do have to continue to deal with these people, since they are in the business—many of them much longer than me. If I do work with them, then I know I need to take steps to protect myself and my clients from being hurt by them.
>
> Thus, when I'm confronted by someone who acts unethically, it's a question of deciding the best thing to do in a particular situation—avoiding them in some cases, working out compromises in others, going along with them at other times, fighting back if necessary. It all depends, whereas in my personal life, I feel much freer to cut off a relationship or let it die, if I feel the person isn't being straight and open with me.

CHAPTER 26

•

ETHICAL SYSTEMS, OTHER CULTURES, OTHER PERSONALITY SYSTEMS, AND UNDERLYING MOTIVATORS

In this book I have illustrated how everyday practical ethics are shaped by one's background, professional and social connections, current circumstances, and personal approach. As such, they may differ from more philosophical and academic notions about what ethics are or should be, or from the ideals of a particular religious or spiritual tradition.

To some extent, people are formed in their early training by traditional ethical ideas, passed on their parents' teachings about right and wrong, what works and doesn't, and what the rules and customs are. In the United States, these rules of conduct and beliefs are largely drawn from the Judeo-Christian tradition, with recent borrowing in some areas of the country from Eastern and "New Age" ideas.

Then, drawing on these foundations, people create their personalized ethical systems, based on a variety of influences of greater or lesser importance to them, depending on the source of these ideas, background influences, and other factors. These notions of what is ethical are always changing over time, as people move, change locations and occupations, make new friends, join new organizations, gain new information from the news media and entertainment industries, and otherwise change their life. Moreover, people often use different ethical approaches in different situations, much like they may adopt new social roles, personalities, and ways of relating to others, who themselves differ from setting to setting.

I have used the Ethical Choices Map and the zones around the self to illustrate how these choices vary under different conditions. In addition, these ethical choices are related to the personality factors which shape us; to psychological motivators; and to cultural patterns in different countries. Here I want to briefly describe these relationships—although each could be the basis for future research and future books.

THE RELATIONSHIP BETWEEN MAKING ETHICAL CHOICES AND PERSONALITY SYSTEMS

Just as our personality influences our choices, so our ethical outlook is affected by our personal traits and differences between individuals. These qualities have been categorized in various ways, including personality style, patterns of leadership, style of thinking or learning, and personality groupings.

Carl G. Jung, for example, distinguished between people who were thinkers and feelers, sensors and intuitives, and this distinction was further developed by the widely used Myers-Briggs Types Indicator system (MPTI), which divides people into four polar categories. Besides the thinkers, feelers, sensors, and intuitives, there are extroverts and introverts, and perceivers and judges. When these categories are charted together, it results in a 16-fold breakdown, much like that of the Ethical Choices Map, so that people can characterize themselves broadly as having one of 16 personality types. According to the Myers-Briggs system, these types are measured on four scales, which are described by initials for short:

- *Extroverts or Introverts* (measured on a scale of Extroversion or Introversion, based on whether they relate more to the external or internal world;
- *Sensors or iNtuitives* (measured on a scale of Sensing or intuition, based on how people prefer to take in or perceive information);
- *Thinkers or Feelers* (measured on a scale of Thinking or Feeling, based on how people prefer to make choices and decisions);

- *Judgers or Perceivers* (measured on a scale of Judging or Perceiving, based on whether people tend to be more organized, controlled, and evaluating in the way they live or more spontaneous, open, and receptive).

To illustrate, someone who tends to be open in relating to others rather than withdrawing (E), intuitive in making decisions rather than concerned with details (N), logical and unemotional (T), and more likely to judge and evaluate information than be receptive to perceptions (J), would be characterized as an ENTJ. Conversely, someone who tends to be introverted, fact-oriented, emotional, and perceptive would be described as an ISFP.

Given the strong influence of personality on ethics, one might expect a connection between certain personality characteristics and one's approach to making ethical choices. If so, there would a relationship between one's personality type and one's ethical approach on these two different systems—the MBTI and the Ethical Choices Map. For example:

- the *thinking* person (T) might be more likely to use a *rational* than an intuitive style in making ethical choices; while the *intuitive* person (N) might be more likely to be influenced by underlying *moral* principles than trying to look at the detailed facts to weigh and consider things pragmatically;
- the *extrovert* (E) might be more prone to be *other* oriented than self-oriented because relating to others is so important; while the *introvert* (N) might be more self-oriented, because he or she is more focused internally;
- the *judger* (J) might be more likely to *follow* the rules rather than be a rule-breaker, since he or she tends to be concerned with structure; while the *perceiver* (P) might be more apt to be an innovator when it comes to rules, since he or she tends to respond to immediate perceptions and reactions to the situation.

Similarly, there might be some relationship with another personality typing system which has gained increased popularity, the system of Enneagrams, developed originally by Helen Palmer. This system posits that individuals can be categorized in terms of nine major personality groupings or "enneagrams", which are organized around a circle. A series of lines connect personality types which are next to or across from each other on the circle, so that each person has a primary personality type, and under certain circumstances is more likely to express an adjacent personality type. In fact, two authors, Renee Baron and Elizabeth Wagele, have already done a study comparing people with different enneagram types and MBTI personality types, and they have identified certain patterns which are most or least common for different types, as described in *The Enneagram Made Easy.*[1] It would be interesting to see how one's Ethical Choices Profile fits with these two systems.

THE RELATIONSHIP BETWEEN THE ETHICAL CHOICES MAP AND THE ENNEAGRAM SYSTEM

One might expect certain types of overlap between the Ethical Choices Map and the Enneagram System, based on how some of the groups in this system are popularly described. These might be summarized and matched up with the Ethical Choices Map as follows:

- The "1s" or "Perfectionists" in the Enneagram system are concerned with living life the right way, prefer a predictable structure and rules, and are often self-critical. So they might tend to be very moral in making ethical choices, as well as likely to follow the rules.
- The "2s" or "Helpers" or "Givers", are outwardly focused, concerned with being loved and valued by others, and enjoy helping others. So they might tend to be other-oriented in their ethical approach.
- The "3s" or "Achievers" or "Performers" are characterized by their desire to be productive, gain success, create a good

---

[1]Renee Baron and Elizabeth Wagele, *The Enneagram Made Easy*, San Francisco: Harper Collins, 1994.

image, and avoid failure. So they might tend to be rule-followers and pragmatic.

- The "4s" or "Romantics" are typically very much in touch with their feelings, self-absorbed, interested in being understood, and want to be considered unique. So they might tend to be especially self-interested.

- The "5s" or "Observers" tend to seek out knowledge and are commonly very private, self-reliant, detached, and analytical in their outlook. So they might be likely to use a rational style in making ethical choices.

- The "6s" or "Questioners" or "Devil Advocates" are commonly concerned with security and are suspicious of authority. So they might be apt to be rule-breakers.

- The "7s" or "Adventurers" or "Epicures" are characterized by being friendly, warm, playful, and optimistic; seek to being happy, comfortable, and free from pain; want a sense of space or independence from others; and are concerned about their image and security. So they might tend to be other-oriented and combine a mix of both following and breaking the rules, as it suits their pleasure.

- The "8s" or "Asserters" or "Bosses" are especially concerned about feeling in control, being self-reliant and strong, and want to punish wrongdoers. So they might be drawn to a self-interested, pragmatic, rule-breaking style, beleiving they should set the standards for others;

- The "9s" or the "Peacemakers" or Mediators" like to resolve things peaceably, have difficulty saying no, show strong support for the others, and like to work in harmony with people. So they might tend to be very other-oriented in their approach.

In short, one might expect some connections between the personality groups identified in the Enneagrams system and one's mode of making choices. Research may show there are.

THE RELATIONSHIP BETWEEN THE ETHICAL CHOICES MAP AND OTHER SYSTEMS

There also might be connections with other systems for understanding the individual.

One of these is the BTSA or Benziger Thinking Styles Assessment model, initially developed by Katherine Benziger, which is based on looking at one's predominant thinking style through brain wave testing.[2] In this system, the individual's style is mapped on four variables, which are related to brain activity in the front, rear, right, and left brain lobes. These four variables are scientific and strategic, theatrical, practical, and technical ways of looking at life. It seems likely that people with different ways of thinking may have different ethical approaches, too.

Another model used by many organizations is based on classifying the different kinds of leadership styles people demonstrate. In one system, called the "Heroes at Work" model, individuals are placed into ten basic categories related to traditional archetypes. These are:

- the Innocent (who wants security and reassurance);
- the Orphan (who wants to be cared for and seeks job security);
- the Seeker (who wants to be left alone to solve problems in his or her own way);
- the Jester (who seeks a sense of fun, challenge, and zest);
- the Caregiver (who wants appreciation, care, warmth, and harmony);
- the Warrior (who seeks challenge, action, and a chance to compete and achieve);
- the Magician (who wants to be as creative and authentic as possible);
- the Ruler (who is drawn to prestige, power, and a stable, orderly environment);

---

[2]I. Katherine Benziger and Anne Sohn, *The Art of Using Your Whole Brain*, Rockwall, Texas: KBA Publishing, 1993.

- the Lover (who seeks commitment to and passion for a shared task);
- the Sage (who likes to reflect on, try out, experiment with, and teach ideas).[3]

It would be interesting to look at the relationships between different personality and thinking types in different systems and compare how they make ethical choices. It seems likely that they will tend to make ethical decisions in different ways related to personality and other traits. Further exploration could show how these patterns are related.

THE RELATIONSHIP BETWEEN ETHICAL CHOICES AND OTHER CULTURES

Since culture and upbringing are also important influences in the way we make ethical choices, one can expect people in different cultures to vary greatly in their approach to ethics, too. Since the people I interviewed for this book shared a similar cultural background as mostly middle-class urban Americans, despite wide variations in religion, political affiliation, occupation, and other factors, one might expect to see common patterns associated with mainstream American culture. And this is the case: a strong influence of individualism, independence, and materialism was reflected in the profiles of many interviewees, who were drawn to the self-interest, rule-breaking, pragmatic approach to making ethical choices.

By contrast, people from other cultures with different values would be likely to show different patterns due to their own cultural influences, tempered by their personality traits, personal experiences, and the current situation. For example, people from more group oriented, like the Chinese, Japanese, and Hispanics, who place a strong emphasis on the family and tradition, might have a greater proportion of people who show a higher level of concern for others,

---

[3]The categories are from a handout based on *Heroes at Work: A Workbook* by Carol S. Pearson and Sharon V. Seivert.

and are more likely to follow the rules and adhere to traditional moral teachings.

Moreover, the rules about what is considered ethical can differ from culture to culture. For example, Bill the lawyer talked about the confusion several American business friends felt when they tried to do business with the Japanese, because their ethics were so different. From our perspective, some of the actions of the Japanese businessmen might seem unethical, because we consider them deceptive, such as when they don't say "no," although they don't want to go ahead on a project. They may act like they are interested when they aren't or don't know, because they want to save face, keep the relationship harmonious, or leave the matter undecided, to see if the relationship develops well, before making a decision, rather than clearly stating what they want to do or don't or saying they are unsure. As Bill noted:

> We may think of them (Japanese businessmen) as being dishonest, but they have a different system of ethics. For example, they sit there at a business meeting and tell you something is true. "Yes, we will do this," they say. But they have no intention of doing it. We think of that as a terrible breach of ethics, since it seems to be a lie, because we say: "We'll do this and you'll do that," and they seemingly agree.
>
> But from the Japanese perspective, saying "Yes, we will do this" is not inconsistent with their later saying: "I do not choose to do that anymore." From their perspective, face to face communication is very important, and they want to show acceptance and approval of you. Also they want to save their own face if there is a ceremony in which an expression of agreement and good faith between the parties at that moment is very important. But their expression of agreement now has little bearing on what will happen in the future.
>
> For them, "yes" is an ongoing process. For us, "yes" is whether they signed the contract or did not sign it. For us, if you sign it, then all future time is determined by this instant. In their sense of reality, that agreement is true for this moment, but what is true for the future can change. So they do not see saying "Yes" now and "No" later as deceitful, while we do.

CHANGES IN ETHICAL CHOICES OVER TIME

Ideas about what is ethical or not also change over time, as cultures evolve and new technologies create new opportunities and possibilities. For example, when most people lived in small stable communities where people knew each other, rules and expectations about behavior were naturally stricter. In such a society, where people depended more closely on each other, notions of altruism, loyalty, and commitment to the group were much stronger, too.

But as cities have developed and grown larger, accompanied by increased anonymity and mobility, the concern with the self and pragmatism have grown. And now as society has moved into a global world linked together through technology, the potential for anonymity and mobility is even greater, causing a rising force of self-interest and pragmatism that threatens to undermine the bonds that unite society. At the same time, as traditional religious values have been undermined by current social developments (such as a greater acceptance of adultery and homosexuality, countering traditional taboos), this change has provoked a reaction from fundamentalists, trying to return to traditional teachings. But the pull of new social developments is powerful, leading views about what is ethical to change and adapt in keeping with changing social conditions.

APPLYING THE ETHICAL CHOICES MAP TO CULTURAL AND SOCIAL PATTERNS

The Ethical Choices Map cannot only be applied to characterizing individuals, but can provide a portrait of a culture itself—based on the tendency for individuals in a culture to behave in a certain ways creating an overall pattern of ethical choices for that culture. Additionally, a series of Maps can profile different cultures at different times in their history.

Then too, these Maps can show how these patterns differ for people from different groups in society in different cultures and over time. For example, certain ethical patterns may be more common for people from different social classes, religious, and ethnic groups. People in the upper classes, for instance, may have the luxury of being more altruistic, other-oriented, and more moral in their perspective because they are already secure financially. By contrast, the ethics of the street are more self-oriented and pragmatic for survival sake. It is hard to pursue a more "moral" or "ethical" approach to life when one is struggling to survive.

Thus, while each person will have his or her own Ethical Choices Profile, that profile will be heavily influenced by that person's culture and current social context. And that culture or context can have its own profile, based on an overall look at the ethical patterns of individuals in that culture or context. In short, Ethical Profiles can differ by social environment or demographics, however one wants to categorize different groups or populations. It's an area that future research might explore.

THE ETHICAL CHOICES WE MAKE AND THE MOTIVATORS THAT INFLUENCE US

The different ethical choices we make are affected by different underlying motivators that influence us. Since we may be motivated by either positive or negative forces—by reward or punishment, by the carrot or the stick, each motivator has a positive or rewarding *reinforcer* or a negative or punishing *enforcer*. In other words, if we respond in a way we consider ethical, based on our pattern of making choices, we will feel good when pulled by the positive reward, or be relieved when we aren't hurt by the negative punishment for not acting ethically.

The motivators for each dimension on the Ethical Choices Map are indicated on the chart on the following page. In any given situation we may be influenced by a number of motivators, depending on the different factors or dimensions that influence our choice. The strength of these motivators varies based on the influence of each ethical dimension in a given situation and the relative power of these motivators in shaping our behavior generally.

We are affected in varying degrees by both positive and negative motivators. As an example, take the person who behaves well at the family gathering he doesn't want to attend. A positive motivator is he knows he is pleasing his parents by being there; a negative motivator is he doesn't want to experience the disapproval that will occur if he doesn't go. By understanding the influence of these motivators, we can better understand how and why we make the choices we do. We can also better understand why others react differently than we do, which can help us improve our relationships with others.

The chart on The Underlying Motivators for the Four Ethical Dimensions below illustrates how people with different approaches on each of the dimensions are motivated differently. These motivators can be explained as follows.

THE UNDERLYING MOTIVATORS FOR THE FOUR ETHICAL DIMENSIONS

CATEGORY

PHILOSOPHY   RULES

	Moralist	Pragmatist	Follower	Innovator
+	Self-Fulfillment Self-Actualization	Results	Approval Acceptance	Effectiveness
−	Guilt	Consequences Punishment	Criticism	Rebellion

STYLE   ORIENTATION

	Intuitive	Rationalist	Other-Oriented	Self-Oriented
+	Feels Right	Reasonable Cost Effective	Contribution to Society	Personal Gain Achievement
−	Feels Wrong	Unreasonable Not Cost Effective	Being Selfish	Failure

MOTIVATOR

To begin with the Philosophy category, someone who falls high in the Moralist perspective—someone who wants to do the right thing—is motivated positively by the desire for Self-Actualization or Self-Affirmation based on having the core moral sense reaffirmed. Alternatively, the negative motivator in this situation is Guilt, feelings of having let down the moral self (the superego or externalized parent, as some psychologists might say). By contrast, the person who is more of a Pragmatist, one who wants to do what works most effectively, is motivated positively by the Results, making something work, while the negative motivator is the unfavorable Consequences or Punishment, if the effort doesn't work.

To take the Rules category, the person who is more of a Follower is strongly motivated on the positive side by gaining Approval or Acceptance from others for following the rules; he or she has a strong need to belong, to be one of the crowd. Accordingly, the negative motivator is receiving Disapproval or Criticism, which is a form of rejection for breaking the rules. Conversely, the motivators for the person who is more of an Innovator or rules-maker or breaker are whether the change is for the best. As a result, on the positive side he or she is concerned with Effectiveness, cutting through red tape, streamlining the process, and using creativity to go after what he or she wants in the most efficient way. On the other hand, the negative motivator is Rebellion, or resistance to authority. It's negative because this motivator is defined by what the person is against, rather than what he or she is for; and this spirit of rebellion can sometimes can lead one to breaking rules just for the sake of breaking them.

In the case of Style, the positive motivator for the person who is highly Intuitive is doing what Feels Right—there's a felt sense of satisfaction. Alternatively, while the negative motivator is doing something wrong which Feels Wrong, resulting in a sense of unpleasant tension or upset. For the person who is more of a Rationalist, the positive motivator is that the choice seems to be the most Reasonable or Cost-Effective alternative; while the negative motivator is that not acting would be Unreasonable or Not Cost-Effective. So a bottom-line motivation influences choice.

Lastly, to take Orientation, the person motivated positively towards the Other-Orientation is pulled by a desire to make a Contribution to Society, while the negative motivator is wanting to avoid the Appearance of Being Selfish. By contrast, the person high in Self-Orientation is motivated positively by the desire for Personal Fulfillment or Achievement, while the negative motivator is Failure.

Certainly, all of these motivators influence our behavior at one time or another. But when we are making ethical decisions in general or in particular situations, certain motivators come to the fore, having more of an influence on us at that time.

Recognizing these differences in the motivators influencing our choices can help us understand how people view and experience things in very different ways. At times, it may seem incomprehensible to us that someone could have done or not done something , which we would do or not do in that situation. However, this behavior is only incomprehensible to us, because we are seeing this person's behavior from our own moral point of view. We are thinking about how we would be motivated and behave in that situation, not how and why he or she is influenced to act.

Take the case of a serial murderer who seems outwardly like a normal, ordinary person—like Ted Bundy, for example. If we view his acts from a traditional ethical perspective, in which we expect someone to behave intuitively as a moral person, who follows the rules and thinks of others, we cannot imagine how that person could do such a thing and not feel guilty. If we committed such a heinous crime, we would certainly react that way, because a traditionally moral person would feel and show total revulsion at such an act. It would go against his identity as a "moral" person, so he or she would feel very guilty and experience the strong disapproval of others, making it hard to present a cool outer demeanor.

But a person from a totally different moral perspective might feel no such inner turmoil, guilt, or remorse. Instead, if he is strongly Pragmatic, very Self-Oriented, and ready to change the rules for his own advantage, he might feel satisfied with what he did since his actions served his purpose at the time (getting money, sex, or control over someone else), and he could readily lie and deceive to get away with the crime. He would only be concerned about the consequences of being accused and convicted, and feel no guilt over what he did. Then, if successful in convincing others he is innocent by his actions and getting away with the crime, he feels he is home free and goes calmly on with his life.

Psychologists and sociologists sometimes call such a person a psychopath or sociopath, because he or she has no conscience, which is instilled through our early moral training in all traditional religious and spiritual systems. At the extremes, such behavior becomes pathological, and many serious and violent criminals fit this profile.

A major issue for us to confront as a society is the way this pattern has become more pervasive through society generally. This is reflected in the growing ease with which many people act in antisocial ways in their own interest without remorse. More and more people do so when they aren't held back by the pragmatic or rational considerations that otherwise restrain people from acting when the rules and moral codes of right and wrong no longer influence them.

This general decline of traditional morality and civility is of major concern, because without the restraint of morality and civility, the law of the jungle and predator, the law of survival of the fittest, prevails. That's what happened in William Golding's classic *Lord of the Flies,* about a group of English boys who end up on a small island after a ship accident. They turn into savages, creating a new code of morality based on strength and power, before an English ship arrives to rescue them, bringing back the traditional codes of morality to restrain and civilize them once again.

APPLYING THE ETHICAL CHOICES MODEL IN YOUR OWN LIFE

Thus, in dealings with others, recognize that there are varying points of view and different motivators, which influence the way people act and react. While some people are more influenced by the motivators from traditional morality, others are influenced by other forces to a greater or lesser degree.

This awareness can, in turn, help you better understand others and the forces affecting them. Then you can decide with whom to relate, how to best relate to them, and who to best avoid. The Ethical Choices model described in this book is designed to help you in making better ethical choices and better resolving any ethical dilemmas you face.

APPENDIX

ETHICAL CHOICES MAPPING INSTRUMENT

Select one of the following approaches which you are more likely to use:

PERSONAL ETHICS

1. A. When I have to make a tough decision, I usually figure out what to do by weighing the pros and cons, thinking about the alternatives, and decide based on what makes the most sense. (R)
   B. When I have a major decision to make, I usually know what to do when the time is right, or I have a gut feeling about the best approach to take. (N)

2. A. I generally go by a strong set of principles I follow about what's right and wrong; some of these are ideals I learned as a child or from my parents and role models. (M)
   B. I generally decide what to do based on what seems to make the most sense in that particular situation; I consider such things as the means and the ends and the benefits to me and others. (P)

3. A. I usually prefer to follow the rules or go along with what others are doing in a particular situation. (F)
   B. I tend to follow the rules if it makes sense to do so; but I believe in breaking rules or making new ones if the old ones aren't working, and I often do that. (I)

4. A. I tend to put the interests of other people first, or to do what is in the best interests of the most people. (O)
   B. I tend to think about how something will benefit me first; I prefer to do what's best for me most of the time. (S)

5. A. When I chose the work I'm doing now, I spent some time thinking about I wanted to do, such as my skills, interests, financial considerations, my family's interests, and other factors. (R)
   B. When I chose the work I'm doing now, I felt this was something I was called to do—or it just happened, because I drifted into it. (N)

6. If I was working in a job and I had agreed to stay there for 2 or 3 years in return for getting hired and trained to do the job, I would:
   A. Keep my agreement even if I had a better job offer during this time. (M/O)
   B. Take the better job offer if it was better for me to take it. (P/S)

7. If I was in a situation where I had to choose between helping my family handle some financial or personal problems or take an opportunity I've always wanted for a career, move, or relationship, I would:
   A. Help my family overcome its problems first and then go after the career, move, or relationship I wanted. (O)
   B. Choose to go after the career, move, or relationship I want first, and then help my family. (S)

8. A. When I was growing up, I was generally well-behaved at home or was one of the gang with my friends. (F)
   B. When I was growing up, I was often the one who came up with new ideas or was something of a troublemaker or the one to rock the boat. (I)

FAMILY ETHICS

9. When one is a child, I think in general:
   A. One should follow the guidelines and principles provided by one's parents or teachers. (F/M)
   B. One should regard one's childhood as a period of self-discovery and learning; one should follow the guidelines and principles that seem sensible, but otherwise feel free to make one's own choices. (I/P/S)

10. If I was a teenager who got into trouble for committing a petty crime, like joyriding or shoplifting, I would:
    A. Confess, tell my parents I was sorry, take my punishment, and promise not to do it again (F/0)
    B. Do what I can to avoid getting punished by the authorities or my parents, and be more careful in the future (I/S/P)

11. When one is a parent, I think in general:
    A. One should put the needs of one's kids first in making choices, lsuch as deciding where to move or whether to stay together with a mate for the sake of the child. (0)
    B. One should set a good example for the kids and expect them to behave properly. (M)

12. As a parent with a teenager who misbehaves or gets into trouble, I would:
    A. Talk about the importance of behaving properly or decide on an appropriate punishment if the problem continues or is serious enough. (M/F)
    B. Try to understand why the teenager is having problems from his or her point of view and show my support to help him or her overcome the problem (P/I/O)

13. As a parent, I think in general:
    A. There are certain codes of behavior every child should know and follow, such as don't lie, cheat, or steal. (M/F)
    B. Each child is an individual, and it is important to help the child develop to his fullest potential. (I/P)

ETHICS WITH FRIENDS, DATES, AND DISTANT RELATIVES

14. A. In choosing my friends, it's important that a friend shares certain core values or beliefs with me; otherwise, it would be difficult for me to consider that person a friend. (M)
    B. In choosing my friends, what's most important is that we share certain common interests, enjoy each other's company, and get along well. (P/S)

15. If I think a friend has done something wrong, I will generally:
    A. Tell the other person what I think, since I tend to be very honest and frank, and it might help the person correct his own behavior, even if it means the end of the relationship. (M/O)
    B. Decide whether to tell or not depending on what the person has done, how I think the person will react, how valuable continuing the relationship is to me, and other factors. (P/S)

16. If a friend going through hard times comes to me for help, I would be likely to:
    A. Give what I can, feeling I want to help, even if I'm not sure the person can pay me back, because I feel a strong sense of altruism or compassion. (O)
    B. Give what I can to help, but work out an agreement that the person will pay me back, or advise the person on ways he can help himself, because I want to be practical and encourage personal responsibility. (P)

17. If I was in a dating relationship that was getting serious, and I had some personal information in my background that would put me in a bad light and might damage the relationship, I would:

   A. Tell the person, because he or she should know, and I want a relationship built on honesty and openness, whatever the consequences. (M/O)

   B. Not tell the person, because I think this is private information that happened in the past; also, I think the relationship should be based on what's happening now and don't want to damage it. (S)

18. If I was in a serious dating relationship, and family members and friends advised me not to continue seeing this person, because he or she didn't have a good enough background (i.e.: from the wrong ethnic group, lower social class, etc.) I would:

   A. Pay attention to their warnings and probably break up with the person, because the attitudes of my family and social group are important to me, and I wouldn't want to lose my relationship with them. (F/R)

   B. Listen to my heart and continue the relationship, hoping my friends and family members would finally come around, even if I was risking some of these relationships. (I/N)

ETHICS IN WORK, BUSINESS, AND PROFESSIONAL RELATIONSHIPS

19. If I found that the company I was working for or an associate was involved in activities I consider wrong or unethical, I would:

   A. Report that company or person, urge them to change their policies, and/or quit, regardless of the career risks, because I can't condone such actions. (M/I)

   B. Continue to work with that company or individual as long as necessary to avoid risking my career, while trying to leave as soon as I can. (P/F)

20. Generally, when I am part of an organization or work with one, I tend to:

    A. Go along with the current practices or corporate culture, because I think that's the best way to get along. (F/P/S)
    B. Think of myself more as a leader, idea person, change maker, or rulebreaker, because I feel that's the way to make improvements to help everyone. (I/O)

21. If I was in a profession that had a formal code of ethics, and I found that others in my local peer group were participating in practices that breach these ethics, such as sharing confidential information or engaging in informal personal relationships with clients, I would:

    A. Adhere to the formal code of ethics, because I think that's right and in the best interests of clients. (M/O)
    B. Do what seems to work best for myself in the current situation to get along with my peers, advance my career, and share information or engage in personal relationships if I can do so in a beneficial way, since I think the formal code of ethics is overly restrictive. (I/P/S)

22. I would prefer to work in a company or in a field where:

    A. I can earn a good income based doing a good job. (S/F)
    B. I can contribute to helping others, even if I earn less. (M/O)

ETHICS IN LOCAL COMMUNITY AND PUBLIC ISSUES

23. If a clerk in a store made a mistake, such as giving me too much money back as change or charging me too little for a purchase, I would:

    A. Keep the extra money or not say anything about being charged too little, since the error was the clerk's mistake, and I would consider this additional money like a gift I can use. (S/P)
    B. Tell the clerk about the mistake, since I would be concerned the clerk might be charged, and I would feel I was taking advantage of the situation. (O/M)

24. If I didn't like someone who was a member of a group I belonged to, I would:
    A. Keep my feelings to myself, and hope that others might feel the same way and do something to get this person to leave the group. (F)
    B. Take the lead in talking to others who might feel the same way, show them how this person is hurting the group, or perhaps suggest ways to get this person out. (I)

25. If I saw my neighbors involved in some kind of illegal activity, though it wasn't a threat to me personally or a danger to the neighborhood, I would be likely to:
    A. Look the other way and not complain about it, because I don't want to have trouble with the neighbors and consider what they do their private business. (P)
    B. Report them to the authorities, since they were doing something wrong, but I wouldn't use my name to avoid problems that might occur if the neighbors know I complained. (M)

26. If I was asked to lend my name to an unpopular cause which I believe in, such as by a group putting out literature or advertising about its cause, I would:
    A. Let the group use my name, because I believe in the cause and want to help. (O)
    B. Not let the group use my name, because I would be concerned if my public support for this cause might damage me, though I might help privately (S).

ETHICS IN SOCIETY AS A WHOLE

27. A. I believe there are some fundamental moral principles that are true for all societies at all times. (M)
    B. I believe that moral principles vary from society to society and over history in response to changing times and cultures. (P)

28. A. I believe that one should do what helps the most people, because it is most important to be of service to others, be unselfish, and contribute to others. (O)
    B. While I believe one shouldn't hurt others, one also has consider oneself first, because most other people consider themselves first and can take advantage of you if you aren't careful. (S)

29. A. I believe one should help low income or disadvantaged people as one can do so, because this is the ethical or moral thing to do. (M/O)
    B. I believe that low income or disadvantaged people should be helped to find jobs or get training if possible; but each of us is personally responsible for himself or herself. (P/S)

30. In deciding what to do about some of the recent technological developments creating ethical challenges for us (like new developments in medicine, fertility, life-extension, reproduction, and cloning), I think we should generally:
    A. Follow time-tested moral principles. (F)
    B. Change our traditional moral principles to adapt to the times. (I)

And I think we can determine what these moral principles should be about new situations and changing technologies because:
    A. We have a deep sense of knowing about what is right and wrong. (N)
    B. We choose the moral principles we do, because they are what make the most sense for us as a society; they help to make society work. (R)

SCORING THE ETHICAL CHOICES MAPPING INSTRUMENT

Circle the letters below which you circled on each item of the questionnaire.

	Style of Choosing		Orientation		Philosophy		Attitude to Rules	
	Intuitive (N)	Rational (R)	Other (O)	Self (S)	Moralist (M)	Pragmatist (P)	Follower (F)	Innovator (I)
1.	B	A						
2.					A	B		
3.					A	B	A	B
4.					A	B		
5.	B	A						
6.			A	B	A	B		
7.			A	B				
8.							A	B
9.				B	A	B	A	B
10.			A	B		B	A	B
11.			A	B	B		A	B
12.			B		A	B	A	B
13.					A	B	A	B
14.				B	A	B		
15.			A	B	A	B		

	Intuitive	Rational	Other	Self	Moralist	Pragmatist	Follower	Innovator
16.			A					
17.			A	B	A	B		
18.	B	A					A	B
19.							B	A
20.			B	A	A	B	A	B
21.			A	B	A	A		B
22.			B	A	B	B	A	
23.			B	A	B	A		
24.							A	B
25.					B	A		
26.			A	B				
27.				B	A	B		
28.			A	B				
29.			A	B	A	B		
30.	A	B					A	B

Total in each column:

	Intuitive	Rational	Other	Self	Moralist	Pragmatist	Follower	Innovator
% of Total	___ (4)	___ (4)	___ (16)	___ (16)	___ (16)	___ (16)	___ (12)	___ (12)